THE DAY
AMERICA CRASHED

THE DAY AMERICA CRASHED

by

Tom Shachtman

G.P. Putnam's • New York

Library of Congress Cataloging in Publishing Data

Shachtman, Tom, 1942–
    The day America crashed.
    Includes index.
    1. Depressions—1929—United States. I. Title
HB3717 1929 S53 338.5′4′0973 78-12963
ISBN 0-399-11613-3

973.917
S 524d JM

201027

for my parents, Leon
and Lucile Shachtman

Contents

THE DAY
AMERICA CRASHED

INTRODUCTION

A single instant, a single place has often come to be the focal point of major historical upheaval: on a plain in Hastings or Yorktown or Thermopylae; in a castle in St. Petersburg or in the Pope's chambers; at the edge of a guillotine in Paris or a chair in Ford's Theater. Here, an emperor burns all history books at the moment a wall to end all walls is finished building, both to hold back the barbarians; there an adventurer steps on a salty beach, that Europe's power may have somewhere to release other than inward on itself. In each instance only a relatively few people are privy to the event, yet word of it spreads until, in time, the revolution each event presaged has engulfed great segments of the world's population. The large mass of people, at the moment of change, do not know that a particular time or place is at the center of the world; in time, they recognize that it was.

Of all the places and moments at which the world takes a turn, none seems so preposterous or unworthy as the trading floor of the New York Stock Exchange's building on Wall Street on October 24, 1929. Here there are no kings, no lone assassins to dispatch the great man, no armies to emerge victorious. It is a sad day, a foolish day, a day of absurdities and wantonness, a day of humanity's disarray. Above all, though, it is a day of the mind, of the permutations and bedevilments the imagination can play on itself, a day of substituting one shattering illusion for another.

In Greek drama, at the end of a *strophe*, or section, there was a sound: a handclap, a ringing gong, a sigh. It signified the end of one action and the beginning of another. In the drama that is America's twentieth-century history, the Crash is such a sound, a watershed event which forever separates in our minds two rosily distorted abstractions: the first, of a flapper-encrusted, prosperity-dizzied era called the twenties; the second, of a depressing doldrum decade, the thirties.

As with all generalizations, this is both truth and a simplification. Nevertheless the Crash was a seminal happening. Few people experienced the event and remained untouched. For this reason, if for no other, the Crash needs to be reexamined.

October 24, 1929, was the day of the stock market's first large crash. There were larger crashes, notably that of the following Tuesday, October 29; some people call the Crash the entire three weeks from October 24 to November 13, 1929; and, of course, bottom was not reached until some years later. But October 24 was the first big shock.

I study the day because, as a first shock, it took so many people unawares, and because of the many incredible, circuitous, vexatious, self-contradictory events within its borders. My goal was to find and define America at "that particular point in time," and also to study the minutiae of a disaster. October 24 was a real humdinger of a day, full of public and private balderdash, delusions both self-induced and mass-produced, funny, and achingly bitter. Cupidity throbs through the day. So does a current of pain.

Pain is a curious warning signal in human behavior; we ignore it at our peril. It is also interesting in that our bodies have a mechanism for blanking out the specific memory of what occurs in moments of pain. Somehow, we know it is better for us not to remember too precisely the shocks we are enduring. As a country, as a people, we have forgotten now most of the pain of the Crash. The event seems a cartoon, the rich being fleeced at last. Not so. Ordinary people suffered the most, as in all other disasters. During the course of research on this book, I have been fortunate enough to correspond with several hundred older people throughout the country whose lives were wrenched by the

Crash and what followed. You will find their stories salted through the book, some by name, others by abbreviations, still more—the vast majority—by inference and absorption into the spirit and body of the material here presented. They are the soul of this book.

An important idea runs through their letters: that the forgetting of the pain of those days is a bad thing. They wonder what sort of people will be left when those who lived through the actual pain are gone. Will we still understand that aspect of our past well enough to reap lessons from it? Will we blithely feel that our sort of modern prosperity can go on forever, unchallenged? Is an entire country going to equate freedom with wealth, and view both as rights rather than as privileges? These are some of the concerns of people who went through the Crash and found their lives vastly changed.

I can't answer those questions. The future will do that. For the present, the task seems to me to provide a clear view of a seminal event which affected a great many people. Of the 125 million in the United States in 1929, it is estimated that the Crash touched directly between 15 million and 25 million people who consisted of stockholders and their families. The Crash hurt not only those 600,000 people who had margin accounts: there were, for instance, over one million factory workers who owned stock in companies that were deeply affected by the Crash. The Crash served as trigger to the Depression: within weeks, hundreds of thousands were unemployed; in the four years that followed the Crash, each Friday saw an average of another hundred thousand more getting pink slips, until 20 million were unemployed and the country submerged in the Depression.

Despite the Crash's enormous impact, we know in general little about the event. It is virtually ignored in our schools, reduced to a formula in college, passed over as a non-event in many histories. Senator Carter Glass and bank president Charles Mitchell, their battle long over, have both sunk to oblivion, deserved or not.

That our education system has ignored the Crash does not mean the event was insignificant; more likely, it tells us that it has been misunderstood. Explained in simplistic terms. Dismissed as an aberration. Yet it was an event so splendidly American that some understanding of it seems to me essential for anyone who seeks to comprehend the American character. In an age of bland politicians, invisible bankers, and forgivable villains, the protean actors of the Crash era give pause for thought.

Many events are not easily subsumed under our usual rubric: crashes, wars, assassinations, riots, eruptions which disturb the quiescent fabric of our society. Today we must increasingly view such events as demanding study; we need to fit them into our complicated mind-picture of human behavior. The Crash is not an aberration, but a manifestation of the best and worst of human behavior in a time of crisis.

We could say we're not like that anymore. Fifty years is so vastly long ago that the *Congressional Record* of the day shows worried discussions about pensions for Civil War veterans and what to do about excessive horse manure on the Washington streets. But it is such a short time ago that the same pages reflect worries about farm price supports, the balance of trade, and the difficulty of censoring movies.

Every mirror, however dark, shows us ourselves.

Chapter One

IN THE COUNTRY
5:00 A.M.

At 5 A.M. on the still, dark morning of October 24, 1929, a mill whistle began to blow in Gaston County, North Carolina. High, piercing, unmistakable, the whistle from the first mill was joined by that of another, then a third, until soon over the entire country, from end to end, the whistles of a hundred cotton mills were heard echoing over the red clay, the tobacco farms, the two million spindles, the twenty-five thousand workers. The whistles were inescapable: those who worked for the mills, and those who did not, all heard them and awoke. In the mill towns, in the mill villages, on the subsistence farms, in the paperboard shacks with walls you could pierce with your little finger, people of mountain heritage who no longer could make do as croppers opened their eyes and began to prepare for the day's work. Breakfast was readied under the naked light bulb or two which served to ease the morning's darkness. Men and boys put on overalls or three-dollar pairs of trousers; the women and girls dressed in gingham or cotton. Anyone over fourteen could work for the mills, and usually did. By thirty-five, workers were considered over the hill. All had cotton lint from the previous day's work still clinging to their hair. It was impossible to get out.

At 5:30, with the dawn's light still an hour away, the whistles blew throughout the country once again. Local chambers of commerce boasted of "a mill a mile" all over the Piedmont:

from Lynchburg to Danville, Greenboro, High Point, Salisbury, through Charlotte, Gastonia, Daffney, Spartansburg, Greenville, and Gainesville, the whistles blew for three hundred thousand mill hands, at 5:00, at 5:30, at 5:45. By 5:55 they must all be at work at the spinning departments, the weave shops, the spools, the slasher rooms, the warps, the doffers, the bobbins, to start their twelve-hour days.

The morning wore on. At dawn in Melrose, Massachusetts, Ernest and Marjorie Leger ate breakfast together. Their small child slept. Marjorie had been a secretary for a company making oils, greases, and chemicals for the tanning industry; Ernest was a carpenter for a construction firm. They discussed the fact that work on some of the big new homes in the suburbs of Boston would have to be finished before the winter set in.

Out of his tenement window in Chicago, trolley motorman Frank E. saw the snow and ice, and he groaned. It was early in the year, but the Midwest had had a bad storm, and he knew what bad storms meant. The cold days were the worst: he and the conductor on the streetcar would be working all day long with the doors open. The icy gusts that swept through the car would turn their hands blue and chill them to the bone. No matter how bad it was, it still beat being on welfare for him and the kids at home, teen-ager Marie and the little ones left when his wife passed on. Frank was glad to have his job.

In Paterson, New Jersey, Marty Ducceschi got up to go to work at the throwing mill down on Gray Street. Out the window he could hear the gentle clop-clop of the milkman's horse-drawn wagon going down the quiet street. Marty had lied about his age in order to get the job. For a moment, as he lay in bed, he thought about the beautiful 160-acre farm they used to have in the lush Monongahela Valley, out in Pennsylvania, but these thoughts were too bitter, and he pushed them out of his mind and started to get dressed.

On a bench in the New York Curb Exchange's locker room, Mike Kelley and a few of the other young clerks were getting ready for a quick shower, to dispel the effects of a night visiting some of the speakeasies in Hoboken, before putting on their green uniforms and headsets for the day's work. Wall Street was the most exciting place in the world for a young gent of twenty-one to be, Mike thought. He and his gang seemed never to stop going; if it wasn't work, it was partying. There was hardly ever time to sleep, just some short naps once in a while. There were weeks when he was never home but to change clothes.

In America in October of 1929, the time you got up in the morning indicated your station in life. There was a chasm, a great divide that determined in large measure what a person's life was like. If you stood on one side of that divide, your life would be of a certain sort; if on the other, of a different sort. In "Middletown," a medium-sized city in the Midwest, where R.S. Lynd and his wife had just finished studying the habits of ordinary Americans, the chasm determined not only what time one arose and had breakfast, but:

> what one does all day long throughout one's life; whom one marries . . . whether one belongs to the Holy Roller or Presbyterian church; or drives a Ford or a Buick; whether or not one's daughter makes the desirable high school Violet Club . . . or one's wife meets with the Sew We Do Club or with the Art Students' League; whether one belongs to the Odd Fellows or the Masonite Shrine; whether one sits about evenings with one's necktie off; and so on indefinitely throughout the daily comings and goings of a Middletown man, woman, or child.[1]

The chasm that divided the Working Class from the Business Class was made of money. With money, certain things were possible. Without money, much was impossible. It was almost impossible to cross the chasm, but a folk legend, common throughout the land, said that it could sometimes be done.

The legend held that a boy from the Working Class, by hard effort, persistence, intelligence, innovation, and luck, with the aid of a woman who was willing to peel the potatoes a bit thinner and turn the hems so as not to spend for new when old would do, could cross the chasm into the Business Class one day and ensure that his children, and his children's children, would be henceforth blessed with money.

The Horatio Alger story was not a myth. Everyone knew someone like Horatio Alger: small-town boys, farm boys, boys from the tenements of the great cities. Samuel Insull had gone to work as a secretary to Thomas Alva Edison many years ago. Now, as Edison and some friends were celebrating the fiftieth

anniversary of the perfection of the very first light bulb, Insull
was the head of a vast electric utilities empire that ruled Chicago and the Midwest more surely than did the iron hand of Alphonse Capone. John J. Raskob, who had grown up in a cold-
water walk-up in lower Manhattan, got a job as private secretary
to Pierre S. Du Pont. Today he was many times a millionaire,
the head of the Democratic party's National Committee, fingers
in a dozen important pies, involved in financing what was going
to be the world's tallest edifice, the Empire State Building. Just a
month or so ago, Raskob had announced in the pages of the *Ladies' Home Journal* that "Everybody Ought to Be Rich." He
wanted to let the working men and women in on the tremendous profits being made in American business. He proposed a
new entity, Equities Security Company, to buy common stocks
of approved industries and turn over the profits to the shareholders. Clerks, factory workers, housewives would buy shares as
they did everything else, on the installment plan:

> The corporation I am thinking of would be different than
> the ordinary investment trust. It would have a board of di-
> rectors in whom the public had explicit trust. It would only
> operate in common stock of proven worth. Its holdings
> would be listed publicly, and there would be nothing secret
> about its transactions. It would meet the requirements of
> the New York Stock Exchange, and it would not deal in
> speculative stocks.[2]

Raskob urged everyone to save just $15 a month. By letting divi-
dends and rights accumulate, within twenty years the prudent
person would have $80,000. Saving $15 a month would undoubtedly be difficult for the average American, whose salary was less
than $25 a week but it could be done. To those who thought this
smacked of socialism, or, worse, communism, Raskob de-
murred, and countered that the rewards would extend far
beyond the individual in more important ways:

> Given wide-spread prosperity, the need for charity will di-
> minish. A growing population largely without financial
> worries will raise ambitious, contented children. A great
> affliction is . . . want, if not actual poverty in old age. I be-
> lieve that condition can be alleviated, if not abolished.[3]

Some may have disagreed with the particulars of Raskob's scheme, but few, if any, would argue with the basic tenet: everybody ought to be rich. It was agreed upon. Everybody would be rich, eventually. The legend said so.

The legend further held—admittedly in exceptional cases, but definitely in some actual cases—that a boy from an ordinary background could go so far in this country of unlimited opportunity that he could become President of the United States. In fact, people would tell you, one boy had just done that about a year ago. His name was Herbert Hoover.

In the early morning of October 24, 1929, President Hoover was aboard a train that had left Louisville, Kentucky, late the previous night. He was returning to Washington and the White House after his longest trip away from the official residence thus far in his seven-and-a-half months as President, at the height of his powers and of the traditional President's honeymoon with the public. Last week he concluded a memorable set of talks with British Prime Minister Ramsay MacDonald. He and Mac had sat on a log at Rapidan, dangled their feet, smoked pipes, and, as the newspapers characterized it and every cartoonist in the country drew it, talked casually of disarmament and the destiny of the free world. J . L Garvin, writing in the London *Observer*, said he wouldn't be surprised if Hoover turned out to be "the greatest President and statesman that America has produced since Lincoln." In various foreign chancelleries there was an abiding faith that the Hoover administration was going to rectify the long-felt need for America to take a more definite share in the governance of world affairs.

On October 21, Hoover had participated in Henry Ford's celebration for Edison, marking the fiftieth anniversary of the making of the light bulb that had revolutionized the world. A current myth, almost equivalent to that of Washington hurling a coin across the Delaware, apotheosized Edison as a young "news butcher" on a train, performing chemical experiments in the baggage car. When Edison's experiments set the car aflame, so the legend went, the trainman boxed his ears (causing his deafness) and put him off the train, whereupon he entered a lifetime of invention. Fifty years later, on an antique train provided by Ford for the occasion, Edison obligingly hawked a peach to the President and Mrs. Hoover as they took a short run from Detroit out to Greenfield Village. Harvey Firestone, Charles Schwab of U. S. Steel, Will Rogers, and Madame Curie, among others, awaited the man of myth. He had not invented the light bulb, but only perfected it; no matter, he was the genius. To the small village Ford had painstakingly and at great expense transported Edison's old workshop, restored to its original state. Ford had even shipped to Dearborn seven carloads of Menlo Park clay that the dirt underfoot might be authentic. When, the day before, Ford had brought Edison in to see the handiwork, the eighty-two-year-old man had fallen silent for ten minutes, looking about in awe and memory. None present dared to say a word. He sat there,

> his arms folded, an indescribably lonely figure, lonely in the loneliness of genius, of one who, somehow, has passed the others, who no longer has equals to share his world, his thoughts, his feelings.[4]

On October 22, in the elegant time capsule, in the history machine of the man who said history was bunk, history was re-created: the now-venerable Francis Jehl did the work as Edison supervised, Hoover and Ford watched, and Graham McNamee broadcast the whole works. The room was only dimly lit with gaslight. Edison spoke, and the replica of the first incandescent electric lamp glowed through the blackness. It was a magic moment.

Later a wireless blazed forth, in crackling, intermittent German, a three-minute congratulatory message coming from Berlin, from the world's most illustrious theoretical scientist, the renowned Dr. Albert Einstein. No one could understand a word of it, but the crowd was respectfully silent.

Then there was a parade in Detroit, and it rained. The President walked in it and got drenched.

He got soaked again in Cincinnati as he waited to dedicate a nine-foot granite marker to the completion of "the dream of half a century,"[5] the deepening of the Ohio River from Pittsburgh all the way down to Cairo, Illinois, where it joined the Mississippi. As he was waiting, he met with young Martin Egan, an emissary from Thomas W. Lamont, senior partner of the J. P. Morgan banking house on Wall Street. Egan hand-delivered to him a long letter from Lamont, which Hoover's emissary to New York, Harry Robinson, had asked for a month ago, on the state of the stock market. The President told Egan that two matters were causing him great concern, and that he had given more thought to these than to many another problem of his administration. One was the high cost of money, the other, the size and extent of stock market operations. He feared, he told the young man, that both of these might finally affect the general business prosperity of the country. The high cost of money was already, he noted, being reflected in certain lines of industry. Hoover noted with satisfaction the declines in stocks that had started last week and asked Egan if the market would continue downward. Egan gracefully disdained any knowledge, but said he thought the market might react upward in a day or so. Hoover nodded and said he had been dubious about doing anything for fear that more harm that good might result. Egan urged the memo from Lamont on him again, and Hoover actually started to read it, but the Ohio governor was insistent that they get going on the speech. As he went to face the crowd, he turned to Egan and said, "I dread these shows, but I do not have many of them."[6]

A big man with an overcoat, with his left hand rattling the keys in his left trouser pocket, his right shoulder working up and down, Hoover stood out in the rain and spoke with precision and detail. By the time he was through, and so sodden that his private physician was worried lest he catch cold from the prolonged exposure to the rain, the applause was thunderous. Brushing aside the doctor's concerns, Hoover boarded the light tender *Greenbrier* for a ride down the Ohio to test the new system. A flotilla of fifteen assorted craft followed after, the press grumbling that they'd gotten the worst scow of them all. Speaker Longworth and other dignitaries, along with dozens of Secret Service men, attended. It was a wild ride. Swollen by rain and unseasonal flooding, the river was on a rampage, snarling and bumping the President and his party along at a more exotic pace than they had all bargained for. Hoover could only see one new lock; the others were covered thoroughly by water and the whole mini-navy sailed right over them. Only his own boat reached the overnight anchorage in Madison, Indiana; the others had to find shelter where they could.

Next morning, during Hoover's speech in Madison, an honor

guard of National Guardsmen, firing a salute to the Executive, experienced an explosion. Gunpowder killed young Robert Earls and injured three others, but the President was not immediately informed. The other craft caught up, and they all went on towards Louisville, huge waves rolling the boats. The rains continued unabated.

In Louisville, in contrast to 150,000 people and the "intense enthusiasm" of Cincinnati, Hoover found only "pronounced apathy" as he delivered a major address. He had a dream, the Great Engineer's greatest engineering project, one which, he hoped, would be remembered in fifty years as tremendously important. Hoover was going to grid America with usable waterways, till the maps would reveal a New World Venice on a magnificent scale, nine thousand miles of the Mississippi River system navigable from end to end.

Already 2,200 miles had been "modernized" to nine feet. Another 1,400 drew six feet. But 5,000 other miles needed work. He'd deepen all 9,000 miles within five years, at a trifling cost even though the amount of construction would be three to four times that of the Panama Canal! The Mississippi, the Ohio, the Missouri, the Cumberland, the Tennessee, the Arkansas, the Illinois, the Ouachita! Another thousand miles of intracoastal canals! Better flood control for the lower Mississippi! The completion of the St. Lawrence Seaway making all the Great Lakes cities international ports! All would be done. In five years Hoover envisioned

> a great North and South trunk waterway entirely across our country from the Gulf to the Northern boundaries, and a great East and West route halfway across the United States.

This would not, Hoover admitted, bring back the "romantic steamboatin' days of Mark Twain," but what the river lost in romance it would gain in tonnage, in business, in revenue, in the lifting of towns that lay alongside the river from what a newspaper of the day termed the "continuous and melancholy decay" that had characterized them for a half century. Already the government was spending $85 million yearly on such work. The improvements Hoover was suggesting would cost a mere $20 million a year additional, for five short years. That was, he pointed out, half the cost of one battleship per year. He'd save the money to do the job at the forthcoming Naval Disarmament Conference in London, on which he'd just concluded his important talks with Ramsay MacDonald. "Nothing," he concluded, "could be a finer or more vivid conversion of swords to plowshares."[7]

The audience cheered and said amen.

On the morning of the 24th, then, sometime between the 6:45 *Tower Health Exercises* on NBC's Red Network (WEAF) and the tunes "Parting the Clouds with Sunshine" and "Wait for the Happy Ending" that were part of the morning's *Rise and Shine* broadcast at 7:30 over the Blue Network (WJZ),[8] President Hoover and his wife Lou awoke aboard the Presidential Special bound for Washington from Louisville. The train would not arrive in Washington until the late afternoon.

An early riser, when in the White House Hoover exercised and tossed around a heavy medicine ball before breakfast, with friends who included a Supreme Court justice and a favored reporter. No "medicine ball cabinet" today, but despite three bouts of standing in the rain, the Chief Executive had not a trace of a cold, according to his doctor. Sometime in the morning Hoover was told of a curious incident that had delayed his train about eighteen minutes the night before. Two black men had put on the track, in the path of Hoover's oncoming train, an old sedan which one of them had bought but could not finish paying for. They hoped to collect the insurance when the sedan was totaled by the speeding train, but it didn't happen that way. Alert Enoch Keller of rural Indiana saw the jalopy, called ahead to caution the train, and the car was towed off before impact. The two culprits were shortly thereafter taken into custody. Rumors of a "plot to get the President"[9] having thus been disproved, the journey continued without further delay. At breakfast Hoover was informed of the accident to the National Guardsmen the day before in Madison. He and Lou were quite upset over this, and Hoover dictated telegrams to one of his secretaries (there were five bright young men in all) that went to the parents of young Robert Earls and to Madison's Mayor Marcus A. Selzer, expressing sympathy. Another telegram of the morning went to Carlos Ibañez del Campo, president of Chile, congratulating a fellow head of state on his escape from a recent attempted assassination by a young anarchist, which had failed when the anarchist's firearm had malfunctioned.

Curiously, at this same hour faraway in the main square in Brussels, the heir to the Italian throne, Prince Umberto, was escaping assassination as well. Would-be assassin Fernando de Rosa of Turin slipped on a cobblestone, his shots went wild, and he was instantly captured, while Umberto coolly continued placing a wreath on the Tomb of the Unknown Soldier, in the company of his fiancée, Marie-Jose, daughter of Belgium's King Albert.

At this hour many of the several hundred guests at the West Baden Springs Hotel, a few miles northwest of Louisville, in Indiana, were waking for the day. Many of these wealthy people had worked hard to put Hoover in office; a few of them had journeyed to Louisville the night before to see the Chief Executive, then had returned to their vacations.

The hotel was known far and wide as the Eighth Wonder of the World, a spa for the wealthy and mighty in an era of splendor and opulence. A hotel had existed here for many years, centered on the mineral springs. It burned in 1901, and Colonel Lee Sinclair rebuilt on a majestic scale. The grandiose Pompeian Court, the building's center, was an architectural marvel, an enormous circular room over three hundred feet in diameter, topped by a glass-and-steel dome one hundred and fifty feet high. Forty thousand square feet of Italian marble covered the floor. Many guests said that it put the Capitol Building in Washington to shame. The golf course, the enclosed double-decker bicycle and pony track, the trolley which took guests to gamble at a casino nearby, the productions in the Opera House (which sometimes included acts from the Hagenback-Wallace Circus which wintered nearby), all gave to West Baden the air of the very best money could buy. The spa's mineral waters were said to cure cancer, sterility, rheumatism, asthma, and alcoholism. Guests had included the governors of neighboring states, Mayor "Big Bill" Thompson of Chicago, Alphonse Capone of the same metropolis, and others. A half-dozen of the nation's major league baseball teams had at various times held spring training in the enclosed bicycle and pony track area.

The stock exchange room, where visitors could keep up with Chicago and New York exchanges while on vacation, had become most popular. A quote board, tickers, banks of operators and telephones—no expense had been spared because it was important that the many newly wealthy people who had made money on stocks in order to come here, be able to keep in touch with their source. During the wonderful, ever-changing fall foliage season the hotel was crowded; during trading hours the stock exchange room was jammed as well.

On this cold, drizzly morning, the opening of the New York Stock Exchange was still several hours away, as the President sped towards Washington and the hotel's guests began to rouse themselves. Many were already up and "taking the cure" in one way or another. West Baden suggested guests start the day drinking two glasses of "hot No. 7x" (from the seventh spring), which was supposed to be soothing to both stomach and intestines, followed by a chaser of concentrated No. 7. As the glasses should be downed at twenty-minute intervals, the hotel advised that the time in between be spent walking over the spongy, wooded sawdust paths about the place, or in some other form of mild exercise. Following this ritual, the guests straggled into the dining area. This day they read about Hoover's speech, clucked to themselves at the extensive damage done to the Chicago waterfront by raging waters which had drowned crews and sunk several boats. The first meal of the day could be chosen from a half-dozen courses listing over fifty separate entries from Calf's Brains and Scrambled Eggs to Finnan Haddie Delmonico. The new owner, Ed Ballard, who had recently sold the Hagenback-Wallace Circus to John Ringling, obtained supplies daily from farms in the area. The food at the hotel, guests from big cities were fond of remarking, was that wonderful thing almost unheard-of in these days of supermarkets, canned goods, and heavily advertised and packaged products—it was farm-fresh.

Outside a small town on the Illinois-Iowa border, ten-year-old Werner Willke was walking towards the one-room schoolhouse with his brother, in the early morning rain under dark clouds. He thought, not about the rain, but of the weekend when he would spend all of his time at his grandfather's farm, a small one of eighty acres. It was a wonderful place. Werner pulled his coat tighter against the cold winds. In a month they'd have to be wearing not only long underwear but also several pairs of buckle overshoes, which they'd leave in boxes at the school to dry out next to the wood-and-coal stove during the school day.

On the farm, Werner had many chores that centered on the three-story barn. To feed the horses, he needed a bushel basket with enough ear corn to provide four ears each, and a scoop of oats. While they were munching he'd fix their stalls with timothy hay from a chute. The calves got a small bucket of half-ground oats and some whole oats, and their stalls got clover, not timothy. The cows got ear corn, oats, and a half-scoop of bran. When they were all tethered to their stanchions, he could get on to the chickens, feeding them and collecting the eggs from their individual nests. At certain times he had the job of training some of the calves to drink milk from a bucket by using one or two fingers submerged in the milk as tasting-trainers, until they got used to the idea.

In the milk house the cream was separated by a De Laval separator. Some of the skim went to the chickens, some went into the slops for the hogs, and some went over the back fence. After feeding all the animals, he had to wash out the barrels and milk cans and prepare them for the next day. There were four horses, twelve cows, six calves, forty hogs, two hundred chickens—but what they produced was a stupendous quantity of food. Friday nights the cream would be churned into butter—it took about an hour and a half of turning the crank—and the butter would be slightly salted and put into porcelain crocks of from one to ten pounds each. Some of the skim went into cottage cheese. Buttermilk was in gallon syrup pails. Eggs were packed in twelve-dozen, twenty-four dozen, or thirty-dozen crates, sorted for grade.

On Saturday mornings Werner's grandfather would load the open Democrat buggy with dairy products, hitch up two horses, deliver the week's largesse. It kept plenty of families in food. Five acres of Mississippi mud furnished maple, ash, oak, and hickory enough for a year for the family. Two hogs and a calf would see them through the winter. A half-acre garden and a several-acre orchard provided four kinds of apples, peaches, pears, red and black raspberries, radishes, onions, cabbage, kohlrabi, cauliflower, peas, beans, potatoes, carrots, green kale, turnips, sweet corn, pumpkin, watermelon, and squash enough for the year.

At ten, Werner knew how to use the horses and some machines, to plant, to harvest, to do many chores. In his spare time he'd trap the gophers which bothered many of the farmers, getting five cents from the farmer and ten cents from the county for each.

Grandpa had given him a fifty-dollar bill for his birthday in February. He'd made some money from gophers and chores. With all this he'd bought a bed and a first long-pants suit and had still managed to save ninety dollars, which he'd put in the Lyons Savings Bank. When he grew up, Werner didn't know whether he wanted to have a farm like his grandpa, or work on the railroad as his father did.

Dad was a section hand on the Chicago and Northwestern Midland Railroad. In the mornings he went up from Andover to Lyons, Iowa—six miles—checking for broken rails, bad ties and crossings, fixing and clearing them as he went; in the afternoon he'd come back down, fixing some more. Then he'd report what he'd done and what needed work. It wasn't the best job in the world, but it was less exhausting than farm work, and it was secure and regular. Dad's biggest problem 'at the moment was to figure out how to repay his brothers, who'd built a fine new house for him and his family next to their old decrepit one.

Werner, his father, and his grandfather existed in a world where they perceived many things to be relatively fixed; certainly a world whose defines were as known and understandable as the inescapable progression of the seasons, and the broad, straight-cornered grid on which towns like Lyons were laid out in the Midwest. Goods were paid for in cash; checks were used only occasionally for payment of taxes and insurance. Life was filled with an enormous amount of hard work and manual labor, but that was the way things had always been. Werner, walking to school with his six-year-old brother and a passel of other kids, hearing the familiar train whistle off in the distance, firmly expected his universe to remain constant and knowable, on into that none-too-distant future in which he would become a man. He had purchased his long-pants suit and the bed towards that eventuality.

Alfred North Whitehead had a different view. He saw the philosophical framework of the world he knew crumbling right before his eyes. The "unbroken tradition of great thinkers and of practical examples from the age of Plato" was being shattered for the first time in recorded history, he thought. Why?

The whole of this tradition is warped by the vicious assumption that each generation will live substantially amid the conditions governing the lives of its fathers and will transmit those conditions to mould with equal force the lives of its children. *We are living in the first period of human history for which this assumption is false."* [Italics added.][10]

The world was changing. Right at this moment. Werner's childhood, and his future, were in peril this day, as they would have been from an earthquake or a typhoon or a train crash—and with the same feeling of inevitability.

Trains, busy symbols of an industrious age, the hopes of a streamlined future, whistled all over the country. There were thousands of them. Twenty crack passenger liners a day plied the rails between New York and Chicago alone. More went on other routes. Twenty thousand locomotives were in constant use about the country.

A train going from Washington to New York City was at this moment leaving an interim stop, Baltimore. Tailor Max Klitenic, in his shop downtown near Hochschild Kohn's big department store, may have heard the train, but he paid it little attention; there were more important matters on his mind. The shop was doing well. Next to Maurice Jolson, cousin of the famous Jazz Singer, Max considered himself to be the best tailor in Baltimore. He had good, steady customers. The doctors, lawyers, professional men in aviation, business executives, a well-known photographer—they were all buying tailor-made suits right and left. Blue serge was a big seller. After school his children would often come in and help him refold the big bolts of cloth that he draped across his knee to show customers how the cloth would look as a suit. His daughter, Lillian, especially delighted in this exercise, for some reason he could not fathom. With the proceeds from the shop he had bought a little property. He wasn't living like a Rothschild, but it was a comfortable existence. And yet, there had been the visit from his cousin that upset him, his wife, everybody, a week ago.

The cousin had come over for dinner and had told him about how he and a Mr. Panitz and some other men had formed a building-and-loan association, and how Panitz—whom the cousin had called brilliant—was investing the proceeds in stocks that were going up. The cousin pressed Max to "scrape together every penny you can" and to become part of the action because, he promised, he would become overnight rich.

"*Nu*, Max," his wife had said. Lillian, listening with rapt attention in the corner, seemed enthralled. But Max was afraid. This annoyed his cousin.

"What! You don't trust me? Your own cousin?"

"I trust you, I trust you," said Max. "But I'm afraid of the stock market, it can't last. I'm afraid of using other people's money to gamble."

At those words the cousin had lost his temper. He shouted, "I came to make you rich, but you have no sense! I've put everything I own in . . . and I'll come out with twice as much. You'll see!" The cousin put on his coat and went towards the door. "You'll never forget this! You'll regret it! You'll be a *schlepper* all your life!"

Max turned the incident over and over in his mind as he opened the shop and got ready for business. He didn't want to be a *schlepper*, a poor dunce who would never amount to anything, but how could he put his money into this scheme? Was his cousin right? Maybe he should reconsider. The train whistle sounded far away and going still farther. Were all his dreams of success going with it?

On that train that had just left Baltimore, speeding towards New York City, was fifty-four-year-old Winston Churchill. He was, a contemporary observer wrote,

> a short man, rather plump, with hair that was once fiery red; with somewhat freckled face, keen blue eyes, and a self-satisfied smile that trembles between a grin and a pout.[11]

For the first time in many years Churchill was out of a job in British politics. Since the fall of the Baldwin government on June 7, he had been simply the ex-chancellor of the exchequer. More than that, though, his own Conservative party had been seriously about the business of putting quite a bit of daylight between themselves and the *enfant terrible*. Churchill had worked hard to earn that epithet. He took firm action to crush the general strike of 1926 that was virtually a class war between the old-line, upper-class, establishment people (whom he championed) and the underpaid lower classes who were simply demanding a bigger slice of the pie. He had taken Britain back to the Gold Standard, causing enormous havoc in the weighty corridors of international finance. He was against letting go of India. He was adamant that the Jews not get too much in Palestine. "The British people," Americans read in *The Nation*,

> are convinced that Winston Churchill is the man chiefly responsible for a series of the worst calamities of the period.
> . . . They feel towards him a kind of angry distrust such as is not aroused in them by any other public man. . . . True, Winston Churchill is the most stupid of brilliant men. His hostility to the Labor Party is childish; his fear of the Bolsheviks is grotesque. . . . If Winston Churchill at the crisis of the world had resolved to stand by his own convictions and to come out for them, he would have been Prime Minister of England years ago.[12]

Prime Minister: that was one thing Churchill wanted, and it didn't seem to be happening. It depressed him that Neville Chamberlain, not he, was emerging as Baldwin's obvious successor in the Conservative party. He wrote to his wife:

> I have made up my mind that if N. Ch. is made leader of the CP or anyone else of that kind, I clear out of politics & see if I cannot make you & the kittens a little more comfortable before I die. Only one goal still attracts me, & if that were barred I shd quit the dreary field for pastures anew.[13]

At the moment he was pursuing those new pastures with vigor. He had spent a delightful and thoughtful week exploring Civil War battlefields in preparation for a series of articles he was in the process of doing for *Collier's*. This was part of a whole aspect of his career that seemed to have taken wing recently. Of course, he had always written—he had begun his career as a battlefield correspondent—but it was just this year that his writings had started to return handsome sums. The last volume of his monumental five-volume history of the World War, *The World Crisis*, had been published in the spring to tremendous acclaim. Now he was getting started on a biography of his illustrious ancestor, the Duke of Marlborough, a project which he had talked about since the time of his first visit to America in 1900, when he was twenty-five.

This trip was a vacation of sorts, a lecture tour, visits to old friends. Accompanied by his brother Jack, his son Randolph, and his nephew Johnny, Churchill had gone across Canada from east to west, then entered the United States at Puget Sound—with his liquor stashed away in medicine bottles to avoid losing the stuff to federal agents. They came across country from west to east, staying at the homes of the mighty. From the sixth to the eighteenth of October Churchill had stayed in New York with his old friend, the market wizard Bernard Baruch, at Baruch's home at 1055 Fifth Avenue. There had been a glittering dinner in his honor at Mrs. Randolph Hearst's Riverside Drive apartment, attended by the most important figures in American publishing. While in New York, Churchill had sent, with piquant pleasure and timing, a birthday telegram to Ramsay MacDonald in Washington, just to remind the PM that Churchill was alive and in America at the same time, though he was not receiving any ticker-tape parades. Following in person his telegram to Washington, Churchill met ever so briefly with Hoover—almost like a presentation to the King, a matter of protocol—and then went to the battlefields. The brief meeting did nothing to ameliorate Churchill's avowed impression that Hoover would accelerate the pace at which the British Empire would sink into the past, finally to be obscured by an America redolent with resources and energy.

On the whole it was a satisfactory trip for Churchill. He was doing well. From new articles for which he had already contracted, he estimated he would have £40,000 before June. Tonight on his return he was to stay with industrialist Percy Rockefeller, in his "flat" at 300 Park Avenue. There was, however, to be a dinner at Baruch's, with forty people invited, mostly from the business sector. At the party he would undoubtedly, as he had a hundred times thus far on the trip, be asked about the dole being given out in England because of hard times. "I was asked continually," Churchill wrote shortly thereafter in the *Saturday Evening Post,*

"Do you think this new government will have the courage to abolish the dole and save the old country?" And then I had to explain a lot about the dole and how that word only applied to a minority of those who drew the benefits of unemployment insurance. . . . During the whole of the 20th century, British people have been building up these great insurance systems. They are unexampled in the world. There is contributory insurance on a compulsory and nation-wide basis against sickness, invalidity, accident, old age, widowhood, and unemployment. We have brought the magic of averages to the rescue of the millions. . . . A future generation will have to judge whether all this policy of national insurance—for which, next to Mr. Lloyd George, I have been more directly concerned than almost anyone else—will have made for the enduring strength and vigor of the British race.[14]

It would undoubtedly be an interesting day. If the train got in on time, Churchill wanted to visit the New York Stock Exchange, down on Wall Street in lower Manhattan.

Chapter Two

"AMERICAN MOTION"
7:00 A.M.

The bulldozer had been removed from the lobby of the Waldorf Astoria a few days ago, but in the early morning of October 24 the rest of the demolition team got going, tearing down the symbol of a gilded, gaslit past, preparing the way for the most modern and streamlined of futures. If New York City felt itself to be the center of the world, then this spot was the center of the center. Teddy Roosevelt had dined here after his election to the presidency. Chinese diplomat Li Hung-Chang had often been seen in the lobby with his yellow silk robes, reportedly smoking opium. Albert and Elizabeth of Belgium, the Prince of Wales, General Pershing, and thousands of commoners had stayed here up until a few short months ago. A grand last supper had been held on May 1, with seven hundred privileged guests drinking mineral water from crystal and silver fountains that had once spurted champagne, singing *Auld Lang Syne* to what *The New York Times* called "a center of American social, political and financial activities for two generations." In the rococo balconies with trailing arbutus and magnolia blossoms, many of the guests made plans to buy at the coming auction something with the hotel's famous monogram on it, such as a ballroom chair with the emblem hand-painted. Two-and-a-half-million-dollars' worth of souvenir ashtrays, candelabras, and a variety of other opulent furnishings were auctioned off. Requests came from all over the country, especially for beds in which couples had spent their wedding nights. Someone even wanted the door to the room in which Ruth Snyder, the notorious "pig woman," and Judd Gray had passed the night after their sensational murder of her husband in New Jersey. Now the auction was over, the guests and furnishings had been dispersed, and demolition had been started on October 1. Soon, the Waldorf Astoria would go the way of millionaire's row on upper Fifth Avenue; of the old and beautiful Stanford White Madison Square Garden down on Twenty-third, which had been replaced by New York Life's citadel of power; of a thousand other luxuries such as gaslit street lamps and hand-wrought gates on townhouses that were too entwined with the past to survive the twenties. Manhattan had been losing population to the suburbs since 1910. Queens and Brooklyn were growing at a rapid rate. The Bronx was the fourth largest city in the country, even though crime was increasing, and a local clergyman described the borough as "amorphous, awkward, adolescent, racially cosmic, boisterously immature, and noisily incomplete."[1]

And so, on this morning, seven hundred men with derricks, compressors, and torches were at work. No one had wanted any part of the ornamentation. The copper roof and steel superstructure were the only parts worth saving for scrap. The bulk of the hotel was being carted off in trucks and would go out on barges five miles past Sandy Hook, New Jersey, to be dumped in the sea. Why was the Waldorf Astoria going? Taxes. Real-estate values. Prohibition. The American obsession with closing the books on the past and making something new. Whatever the reasons, it was going, and on the $20-million, two-acre site was to be erected the most grandiose project of the new age of prosperity, the Empire State Building.

"Well," said the architect who was struggling through the umpteenth revision of Rockefeller Center to Empire State's designer William F. Lamb, "there's one thing you won't have to struggle with, to make it look tall!"[2]

The inspiration for the dramatic shape of the Empire State Building was said to be an upright pencil Lamb toyed with on his desk one day. "Form follows function," Louis Sullivan had said, and this building would express that idea completely.

It would be the tallest, the biggest, the newest, the one with the most modern equipment. Miraculous elevators. Chrome. Glass. Construction was on a rigid schedule, with foreknowledge of exactly how many bolts, bricks, and other materials were needed. Time-motion studies and assessments of the capabilities of the various materials to be used—some of them quite new—were taken into account before the schedule was issued. The construction was under the aegis of the Starrett Corporation, whose stock was daily rising in price, and the whole affair was funded by stock market wizards under the direction of the ubiquitous John J. Raskob.

> To Europeans, [writes Robert Sklar] what epitomized American life was movement. Compared to themselves—encrusted with traditions, weighted down by forms, customs, habits, procedures; measured, lugubrious, drained of life—American motion . . . possessed an enchanting, irresistible allure.[3]

"Today," French social scientist André Siegfried announced in his best seller *America Comes of Age* (in 1929 in its fourteenth printing),

> as a result of the revolutionary changes brought about by modern methods of production, [America] has again become a new world.[4]

This new world, acolytes said in 1929, was being experienced by most every person in the United States, and certainly by most everyone in the cities. Electric irons, vacuum cleaners, washing machines, and refrigerators were becoming commonplace. If you could not buy them outright, they could easily be had on the installment plan. Linoleum replaced wood on floors. Fresh fruits and vegetables were in the stores all year 'round, so you didn't have to go on winter food and later suffer spring sickness from lack of energy. Pyrex, Bakelite, cellophane, celanese, rayon, dry ice, airplane skywriting, neon signs, sound movies, air-conditioned theaters, and radio broadcasting had come onto the scene in the last ten years. The birthrate for cars exceeded the birthrate for people; one car came off the assembly line every five seconds in Ford's new Model-A plants. There were 23 million cars for 125 million Americans, and 80 percent of the newest ones were being bought on time. Industrial production had climbed 50 percent between 1920 and 1929. Our national income exceeded that of Great Britain, France, Italy, Spain, Germany, Japan, and a dozen other nations *combined*. There were 6,000 golf courses, compared with 2,000 a decade ago; 40,000 bowling teams hogged lanes where 5,000 had romped in 1920. Prosperity was here; consumption was here. Everyone was a salesman of sorts, a booster, whether he thought of himself as one or not. And what they were selling—to each other, or to foreign nations—was America. Bruce Barton, who grew up down the street from Ernest Hemingway in the good gray suburb of Oak Park, Illinois, and went on to found the great advertising agency Batten, Barton, Durstine, and Osborn (BBD&O), had written another best seller, *The Man Nobody Knows*, about Jesus Christ. Christ, said Barton, was the man who took twelve men from the lower ranks of society and forged a business organization that had changed the world. Barton had no doubt that if Christ were alive today, he'd be an account executive in an ad agency, selling goods that sold America. The Lions Club claimed Christ as the first clubman, the Lion of Judah; the Rotarians claimed the Savior was, in effect, their first president. If the followers of Woollcott or Mencken despised the Rotarians as Babbitts or members of the "booboisie," why that description applied to a great many more people than those wrongheaded snobs ever thought about. Every college boy was thought to have a copy of the *American Mercury* in one pocket, a hip flask in the other. Rabbi Abba Hillel Silver took a hard look at the daring young men and girls devoted to butterscotch sundaes and Kahlil Gibran, and said their incidental bad manners might be revolting to their elders but did not constitute an authentic revolt. Silver said there was

> no more conservative, stand-pat young man in the world than the raccoon-coated "homo sapiens" on the American campus. . . . In matters that really count . . . in questions of social justice, war and peace . . . [they are] as orthodox, as unimaginative, and as submissive as the most hidebound Babbitts of their day.[5]

Even in those who were obsessed with the idea of serious dissent, the bohemian aspect of it was triumphant over the radical side. Malcolm Cowley called those who went to Paris to escape the machine-age, products of its largesse nonetheless—free spirits engendered by a bedrock of prosperity at home. The consumption ethic, he said in *Exile's Return*, fitted in very well with the Greenwich Village sort of bohemian idea:

> Thus *self-expression* and *paganism* encouraged a demand for all sorts of products—modern furniture, beach pajamas, cosmetics, colored bathrooms with toilet paper to match. *Living for the moment* meant buying an automobile, a radio or a house, using it now and paying for it tomorrow. *Female equality* was capable of doubling the consumption of products—cigarettes, for example—that had formerly been used by men alone. . . . Everything fitted into the business picture.

The heroes of the age were the businessmen, men who made and worked in the affluent society. Those men, almost universally, had been turning to the stock market in the last several years. A European observer noted that although European stock markets reflected the economies of their countries in a steady, conservative fashion, the American stock markets had a different function—they *led* the economy of the country.

Let us imagine a middle-class businessman going to work in the midtown area of New York City, around 7:30 on the morning of October 24, 1929. A manufacturer, he has a home in the suburbs, a good income, a family with a wife who does not work, and several children who our man expects will go to college someday though he himself has not. There was still a vestige of darkness as he got off his train and came out of Grand Central Station, though the sun was up—another one of New York's typically gray days. Around him he saw signs of prosperity: three of the city's four newest skyscrapers. He walked crosstown. At the corner of Forty-second Street and Fifth Avenue he took a look at the grandly imposing New York Public Library, and remembered a story in *The New York Times* which he had underneath his arm, an editorial about the death yesterday of the library's designer, Thomas Hastings. Hastings "never took kindly to the skyscraper," the editorial notes:

He once read somewhere a prophecy that the office buildings of the future, equipped with artificial sunlight and mechanical ventilation, would require no windows at all. "Possibly," was his comment, "but who wants to be that sort of mole in a human world?"[6]

Our businessman sighed: progress was progress, skyscrapers wonderful and inevitable. Going through Times Square, he saw the magnificent Paramount Building, and, as he headed up the Great White Way of Broadway, brightly lit even in the morning hours, he saw the familiar Wrigley sign on the west side between Forty-third and Forty-fourth, the six Wrigley soldiers going through their military drill routine over and over.

What did this man know about American business and the stock market at this moment in time?

He knew that the New York Stock Exchange had become the focus of business expectations and a means of expanding income that was unparalleled in intensity throughout the world. Should his small company grow up and become bigger and more solid, he might have his stock traded at first over-the-counter, then later on the New York Curb Exchange, and finally, when it was big enough and respectable enough, on the New York Stock Exchange.

That body started in the early days of the republic, and though as late as the First World War there were only 150 companies listed on it, today there were over 550 on the Exchange, most of them America's industrial giants.[7] For half a century, consolidation and centralization had been taking place at an ever-increasing rate. For every 1,500 little guys—himself, for example—there was one giant, but the giants had been growing at a phenomenal rate which had been increasing all the time: each giant was now doing two-thirds as much business as all 1,500 little guys *combined*. The 200 largest nonbanking corporations, almost all of which were listed on the Exchange, were doing so well of late, for another instance, that they were making profits in excess of 10 percent after taxes.

In the prosperous years from 1922 to 1929, these companies had poured much money into new plants, into expanding production capacity, into becoming automated so they didn't have a lot of excess people hanging around doing jobs manually that could be better done by machine, into becoming as solid as they could from a manufacturing standpoint. Significantly, they had done this in new ways, taking their excess cash from those 10 percent profit margins and plowing it back into the business, and *not* borrowing from banks for this expansion. Many companies had built clean new factories with many safety features, had installed cafeterias, had spawned glee clubs, bowling teams; they had even sold stock to employees—a million of them by 1929. With such prosperity, the threat that labor organizers posed to their plants at the turn of the century had faded: the unions couldn't fight an employer who was being "generous," and so had lost millions of members through the decade of prosperity.

As a manufacturer himself, our businessman knew that this meant that the big companies were well geared for present and for future production, that is, for the chance to become even bigger than they were now. Bigness was American: three life insurance companies controlled the bulk of insurance; chain stores did a fifth of all retail business, with A&P alone accounting for one-tenth of all food sold at retail in the country; the big three automakers sold 83 percent of all cars; four meat-packers controlled 70 percent of packaged meat production; four tobacco companies sold 94 percent of the cigarettes. Of the 25,000 banks in the country, 250, or one percent, controlled 46 percent of the resources. Mergers had become the order of the day. In 1928 Chrysler took over Dodge; Postum married Maxwell House; Colgate united with Palmolive-Peet; and Batten, Barton, Durstine and Osborn formed their Madison Avenue barbershop quartet. Many of the companies on the Exchange's board had already grown so that they did more than manufacture goods— they were holding companies, as well. About a fifth of the listed companies had evolved so far that they were *purely* holding companies: they no longer manufactured anything, but they did hold controlling interests in other companies which did operate. Nine such holding companies, for instance, controlled three-fourths of the country's entire power resources.

Our businessman had some spare money to invest. There were many reasons to buy the stock of a listed company, among them the dividends paid on a regular basis. But dividends were not the main attraction—they were low, 3 to 5 percent a year, no better than bonds or a savings account. The main attraction was something else: the fact that the prices of most listed companies had been going up steadily, with only slight dips, for more than five years.

This meant that with great regularity he had been able to buy a stock at 100, wait until it had marched up to 120, and sell it, realizing a 20 percent profit on his investment. This would be a good return for, say, two years—but often our businessman had been able to reap it in only two months! Why, at such a rate he might make 120 percent a year! Ten percent a month was so healthy a return that it made the 3-5 percent a year one might realize out of a dividend pale by comparison.

With this in mind, our businessman had engaged in "the exchange of present money for expectation of future money," or, to put it in the parlance of the day, stock speculation. He hoped to get rich—or richer—quickly. His manufacturing business had been going all right; now he hired managers to take care of what he once worked dawn to dusk to oversee, so he could pursue broader horizons.

He had gone into business, as had so many in the postwar era, to make money and be his own boss. It was the time of the private entrepreneur, of individual enterprise in a great many fields. He had been no different from most and had achieved modest success. *But then he had seen a way to make money faster than he could do it in his own business.* As with many Americans, he believed not only the myth that everyone ought to be rich, but the more cynical middle-class tenet that it took money to make money; that big money begat really big and serious money; that without capital to start with, an immense fortune cannot be accumulated. But our man did have money to start with: the proceeds from his business. Ten percent a month! Perhaps more, if he paid intelligent attention to the ever-rising market. He tried it and did well. He tried it again: even better. He began to feel that he could make more money in the market, more quickly, than he could by steadily aggrandizing his own business. He might never make as much as the really big boys at the Knickerbocker, Metropolitan, Century, Brook, Creek, and Union Clubs, but he felt sure he'd do a heck of a lot better than the guy who had no money to invest and could never get his hands on anything more than a small savings account or a Liberty Bond.

At first he bought stocks outright. But, having made money this way, he was offered a margin account by his broker, as a matter of course. At the time, buying on margin was compared favorably with buying a house and taking on a mortgage to a bank; put another way, you and the bank owned the house. In a margin account, you and the broker owned the stock.

He had $1,000 to invest. His broker gave him 25 percent margin, which enabled him to *buy* 40 shares of Instant Marbles at 100, instead of *owning outright* 10 shares. His total investment—the total price of the "house" of IM—was actually $4,000, of which the broker had loaned him $3,000 at a modest charge. IM went to 125, his 40 shares were now worth $5,000. He sold them, gave the broker back his $3,000, and walked away with 100 percent profit on his money even though the stock went up only 25 percent.

Next time out, he decided not to sell when the price went up but to hang on. When a stock at 100 went to 125, he left in his original $1,000, and the $1,000 profit, and reinvested—with the broker's margin account, he bought $8,000 worth of stock, on a $6,000 loan—all on that first, basic, $1,000 of his own money. It happened again. And again. And again. Now he had $10,000 worth of profits, and, incredibly, his broker was still willing to work on that 25 percent margin, which meant he could utilize $10,000 plus $30,000, or $40,000!

If he was making a lot of money, he knew he also owed a lot to his broker. But he now owned, with the loan, 100 shares of Mercantile Department Stores, which was selling at 400. Should the price of that stock slip—say, 40 points, to 360—his broker would require that he bring additional money so that the *broker's own loan* was protected, or that some of the stock be sold to maintain the correct margin-to-investment ratio. But if that stock continued to go up, as it had been doing all along, this would never happen. At this moment, it hadn't happened to our businessman in several years of investing.

Let's look at it from the other side of the coin, from the point of view of a chief officer of a $20-million-a-year concern which was doing well. The plant had been mostly paid off, production capacity was high, orders were continuing to roll in, there were no union problems because the men were reasonably well satisfied with steady work and had rejected union overtures. The chief executive officer wanted to take his company from $20 million a year to double that size. They could use new salesmen, a whole new line of merchandise to complement the present line, more operating capital. How would he get it?

In the old days he would go to a bank. Now, he could float a new issue or sell shares of his concern to the public. This diluted ownership of the company but could be done in such a way that control would continue to rest in the hands of his faction, which even now had only 15 percent of the company's stock, but more than anyone else could amass. The public had shown itself eager for new issues, usually pushing up the price of a stock way beyond that at which it was initially offered. He decided to float a new issue.

Here's how it was done exactly a year before, on October 24, 1928.

Harry F. Sinclair, once of Teapot Dome scandal fame as the man who paid the bribes that went to the Cabinet member who leased the oil that shouldn't have been leased, was chairman of the board of Sinclair Consolidated Oil. To float his new issue, he went to experienced market trader Arthur W. Cutten.

A bespectacled, stiffly collared, ex-bookkeeper from Guelph, Ontario, by way of Chicago, fifty-eight-year-old Arthur Cutten had been in the New York market only a few years but was already legendary. A contemporary observer thought him a "quiet, salt-and-pepper soul, a cross between a Main Street merchant and a college professor."[8] In Chicago he had been one of the most ruthless men ever seen in the grain pits: once he had cornered the market so completely that all the wheat in Chicago belonged to him, and rivals had to resort to the courts to get wheat awaiting delivery in railroad cars, to fulfill his future orders. In New York, Cutten had become one of the biggest of bulls, a heavy investor who had pyramided $15 million into much more than that. Sinclair counted on Cutten as a big fish whom others would follow.

Cutten listened to Sinclair's proposal in early October of 1928 and agreed to a scheme. Cutten, Sinclair, and others purchased (without paying for them) from Sinclair Oil 1,130,000 new shares at $30 a share. Besides Cutten and Sinclair, the other partners were Chase Securities, a subsidiary of the Chase Bank; a small investment company owned by the president of the

Chase, Albert H. Wiggin ("the most loved banker on Wall Street"), called the Shermar Corporation for one of Wiggin's daughters and her husband; and the Blair Company. The partners put up no actual money to buy the stock at this time, as it was agreed that delivery need not take place on the stock until December of 1928.

So, on October 24, 1928, the new issue was announced with suitable fanfare. Sinclair Oil had been selling at 28. By the end of that day it was at 36. By December it was even higher. Then the partners had the option of selling what stock they held, taking a profit estimated at $2 million, and paying the company the offering price. This they chose not to do. Two million dollars was small potatoes. They were playing manipulation games, trying to make the stock go higher, using a "pool" which buys and sells up and down and up again. As they knew it would, the stock went higher. Their brokers, E. F. Hutton and Company, advanced the money to cover the offering price of the stock to the partners at that time, simultaneously borrowing the money to do so from Mr. Wiggin's accommodating Chase National Bank. By January 1, 1929, everybody was happy: Sinclair Oil had its capital in cash, and the partners were sitting pretty, with an estimated $4 million in profits waiting. The partners felt no sense of wrongdoing. Pools operated in 105 of the stocks listed on the Exchange in the banner year of 1929—they were doing no differently than other market "operators."

Sinclair Oil continued on its way up, and by April 16, 1929, not only had the original 1,130,000 shares been sold, but also an additional 700,000. The partners divested themselves of all the new stock, paid off their brokers who in turn paid off the bank, and the profits were divided. Sinclair himself was the big winner: for six months' time he made $2,632,000 from his own company's stock. Blair Company got the same. Cutten made $1,755,000; so did Chase Securities; Shermar got $877,000. Besides this, Sinclair Oil had new operating capital—and it all came about without the company or the partners in the original syndicate putting up a single dime in cash.

Let us suppose, though, that floating a new issue is not for our $20-million-a-year business. It had enough operating capital, perhaps even a surplus of cash. The operating officer may not have wanted this cash to leak out to the government in taxes; he wanted to do something with it. He had options: put it in a bank, build excess plant capacity for the future, invest in gilt-edged bonds. He could even speculate in other stocks with it, for no laws prevented him from doing so, and many of his fellow businessmen were doing just that. Even better than those options, however, was lending that excess money to other investors, at rates which were not only wonderfully high, but which were secured by collateral—stocks—and which (most miraculously of all) he could have back at any moment he saw fit to "call" the money.

The demand for money to invest in the stock market in the past few years had been insatiable. So many people had seen the opportunities there to make money that they were willing to pay high rates to borrow money, so they could be assured of having enough to buy the stocks that would return them all that they had borrowed, and more. Money used for this purpose—to buy stocks instead of the commodities which a regular bank loan to a manufacturing concern would usually purchase—was known as *call money*.

Call money could be provided by anyone who had cash to lend—banks, companies, individuals. It was money lent to a broker, who in turn lent it to his customers, often at no charge or only a minimal charge. In the past year from October 1928 to October 1929, call money had gone up from 6 and 7 percent to 12 percent, and even higher, depending on each day's demand. How could an investor afford to pay 15 percent on a loan? He could afford it because he hoped to keep the money only a few days or weeks, and to make, say, 20 percent on that money within a month; therefore he could pay the one or 1.25 percent per month (15 percent a year divided by 12) for the privilege of using borrowed money to make his own money. The market was going up so fast that for the investor, whatever he paid in call money seemed a small matter to be settled when he was in clover, and not before.

By late summer of 1929, even conservative businessmen were finding it hard to resist the lure of making call money available to brokers. During the year 1929, the average amount—not the total, but the average amount—out on call loans at any given time was: Standard Oil of New Jersey, $69 million; Electric Bond and Share, $100 million; Sinclair Consolidated, $12.5 million (now where did that come from?); Cities Service, $49 million. Bethlehem Steel was in on the bonanza, so were Anaconda and Chrysler. A mind-boggled financial observer wrote in the *Atlantic Monthly* that summer:

> The spirit of speculation has obtained such a hold upon the investment public that previously accepted standards of value and the operation of economic laws have been discarded in the blind belief that the old order has changed and old methods should be discarded.[9]

This was all too true. Among the old methods being discarded were modest dividends as a way of increasing income, and, perhaps more important than that, bank financing of business expansion in general. Where this really hurt was in the area of small and medium-sized businesses, such as those of our original modest-income manufacturer. What the impossibly advancing market meant, in the long run, was that banks were being forced to lend money to speculators. They couldn't lend it to big businesses, because those big businesses didn't need it; they could just as easily float a new issue. And they didn't wish anymore to lend it to small businessmen, because they could get better rates out of the speculators! For the small- and medium-sized businessmen, then, call money and the spirit of speculation meant stagnation, and in the American economy, stagnation has always meant a lingering death. Standing still is equivalent to being left behind.

Look at it this way. Small Company Better Weezers and Big Company Weezers compete for the weezer market in Podunk, Small's home area. Heretofore Small has always done well enough, because Podunk was home base and they have covered it well. Now Big has floated a stock issue and obtained a huge hunk of new capital, and has sent three permanent salesmen to Podunk, where all work hard to undercut Small's share of the market. Small can't do much about this because, among other reasons, it can't get money at the bank to finance its own expansion.

Put in larger terms, this meant that Montgomery Ward could open 285 new facilities in 1927 and 1928, and put approximately that number of smaller enterprises virtually out of business. Ward used expansion capital to buy up the best leases in any given town, the best salesmen, the best sources of supply. Money equaled control.

Some people grumbled that the Federal Reserve Board was supposed to prevent abuses of call money. That was why it had been set up after the 1907 panic, to insure that too much credit couldn't be pumped into the market by banks. But

> of the nearly $6 billion of brokers loans [in June of 1929], nearly $3 billion, commonly known as "bootleg loans," got into the market in the same helter-skelter manner, although not through the same channels, as loans for speculation prior to the establishment of the Federal Reserve System.[10]

By October, that $6 billion had climbed to $6.6 billion. It was a wonderful business, call money, and the banks didn't seem to mind the competition from the private lenders at all: there was enough of a pie for everyone to get a slice.

Striding down Fifth Avenue at this moment, on his way from his residence at 934 Fifth Avenue to his workplace five miles away in Wall Street, was the hero of call money, Charles E. Mitchell, chairman of the board of the National City Bank, the largest bank in the country.[11] He held to a brisk pace for a man of fifty: five miles an hour. Let us put him at the northeast corner of Seventy-ninth and Fifth Avenue, across from the Metropolitan Museum of Art. Later today, Mitchell would perhaps be aware, a bitter court battle would take place among the heirs of the late Isaac V. Brokaw, who built the four beautifully matched houses on the corner property, one for each child, in 1866. Apartment buildings had been sprouting up in the area since 1913 when Brokaw died, but these four beauties had not yet been touched by New York's building boom. Before the day was out, they would be torn asunder. A glance, and Mitchell walked on.

Charlie Mitchell had grown up in the suburbs of Boston in the eighties and nineties, had graduated from Amherst College in 1899 to take a job with the Western Electric Company in Chicago, where by 1904 he had become assistant manager. A go-getter, he decided that his real line of work was banking, and he took a job as assistant to Oakleigh Thomas, president of the Trust Company of North America, in New York. In October of 1907 there was a panic and crash on Wall Street and a run on the banks—the worst day was October 24, 1907. J. P. Morgan the elder had to be persuaded to step in and stop it, personally. Mitchell watched the panic—his bank did not close—and learned from it, working towards the country's financial rehabilitation following that debacle. In 1911, restless, he started his own investment firm, selling securities and studying banking and investments in the United States and abroad. Control of Wall Street was passing from the old pirates to a new breed. "In place of the three traditional virtues of the Industrious Apprentice, honesty, industry, and thrift," Preston W. Slosson wrote,

> current magazine fiction applauded the ability to carry through a bluff, to put up a huge front on small capital, to break out a new path, and snatch victory from defeat by daring assumptions of risk and defiance of orders—an economic romanticism superseding the economic classicism of Ben Franklin's day.[12]

At that time everyone was buying; there was a war economy, and war bonds had to be sold. They were lapped up as fast as they could be printed. It was a sign. Mitchell and others studied the banking laws and figured out that while it was illegal for a bank to sell stocks, it was not illegal for a bank to have a "security affiliate" which could sell stocks. Moreover, that security affiliate could legally do two astounding things: 1) sell the bank's own stock, and 2) not publish statements of earnings as the banks themselves must do. This way a bank could sell stocks and pay dividends on the proceeds of such sales only to the directors of the security affiliate, if it wanted to. Mitchell joined the National City Company, security affiliate of the National City Bank.

As the twenties started roaring, the enthusiasm for war bonds was translated by people like Mitchell into enthusiasm to buy stocks and bonds of different sorts. Mitchell was a salesman and an administrator of salesmen, something bankers had not been up until this time. Instead of being conservative and gray, he was active and aggressive, hiring people to go out and drum up customers and then sell them something. It was a measure of how well the affiliate was doing that in 1921 Mitchell was made president of National City Bank, as well as of the security affiliate. The eyes of George F. Baker, Sr., and his son George F. Baker, Jr., were upon him.

By 1927 bank affiliates such as the NCC—other banks having

by this time emulated the idea—were doing one-sixth as much business in selling securities as private bankers. And the tail was wagging the dog: the securities affiliates were making money hand over fist, at a faster rate than the banks could make it themselves through standard loans, or even call money. In 1928 the bank affiliates sold one-third as much as the private bankers; in 1929 four-fifths as much. Mitchell's compensation in addition to his salary, primarily from NCC business, was in the neighborhood of $1 million a year. NCC had 350 salesmen in 58 cities across the country connected to the New York office by 11,000 miles of private telephone wire, all selling stocks and bonds.[13] It was estimated that in the years 1924-1929 such security affiliates sold $40 million worth of securities to Americans. Among the most actively pushed stocks by NCC was the stock of National City Bank itself. A million shares of NCB were sold by NCC in 1929 at an average price of well over $500 a share, or about half-a-billion dollars' worth of the bank's stock. Said a former NCC salesman:

> Some of our largest banks . . . put on crews of Savings Account Exterminators who squirted stocks into every cranny of the land after the fashion of a man spraying a room full of Flit.[14]

In January of 1929 President Coolidge said he thought stocks were cheap at their current prices and boosted market optimism. Hoover's inauguration on March 4, 1929, brought even more optimism. There were rumors shortly thereafter, though, that down in Washington the Federal Reserve Board was meeting daily. About what, there was no word—in fact, reporters got only no comment from those who attended the meetings. These meetings were nonetheless taken as evidence that the Federal Reserve Board was against the speculative fever, and they caused flutters in the market. On Monday, March 25, after the Federal Reserve Board had had an unprecedented Saturday meeting, speculative favorites on the New York markets dropped 10-12 points, and banks began curtailing their loans in the call money area. As a consequence, the rate for call money jumped to a new high, 14 percent, for that time. The next day, with the Fed still meeting and still saying nothing at all either positive or negative, an astounding 8 million shares were traded (5 million was a big day), breaking all records for volume, and 20- and 30-point losses in many stocks were commonplace. And call money jumped to 20 percent. "March 26, 1929," says John Kenneth Galbraith, "could have been the end."[15]

Mitchell was angry at the Fed for what he thought to be unwarranted intervention in the activities of a free enterprise market system. Though the Fed had done and said nothing, it had pointedly not denied rumors that it was against speculation, and its silence was deafening. Secretary of the Treasury Andrew Mellon did nothing to allay Mitchell's fears, because he did nothing himself but tell the public that bonds were good buys right now—another backhanded slap at stock speculation.

On March 26 there was a quandary. The fears not allayed by word from the Fed were roiling the market, leading to price drops. A threat hung heavy over the banks' heads: that the Federal Bank of New York, a part of the Federal Reserve Board system, would not lend the banks money so they could rediscount it (or, in plainer language, re-lend it to brokers as call money). Mitchell was called on the phone by George L. Harrison, the director or governor of the Federal Reserve Bank of New York. Harrison had been governor only a few months. His predecessor, Benjamin Strong, had been a giant in financial circles, influencing policy far beyond what his position as head of one bank would have indicated.[16] Strong had died in October of 1928, talking to associates about the terrible speculation that had already completely taken hold of the country. Governor Harrison, deputy governor since 1920, listened carefully to what Charlie Mitchell, a director of the Federal Reserve Bank of New York as well as head of the largest bank in the country, had to say. And Harrison assured Mitchell that

the call money problem was now the problem of the New York money market, that is, the member banks and the private bankers, that it must be obvious that we could not suggest whether a member bank should or should not place money on call in the present circumstances, for if we did so we would put ourselves in the position of determining at what point intervention should be made and indirectly determine at what point call money should be pegged. . . . In

other words . . . in a period of great stress the Federal Reserve Bank should be in the position of freely lending
money at its going rate in order that there might not be any
charge that it had arbitrarily refused or rationed credit.[17]

With this assurance, Mitchell leaped into action and called a
press conference. There he announced that, despite what the Fed
in Washington might say or think behind its closed doors, *his*
bank stood ready to lend an immediate $25 million on the call
money market, because people should not have to bear losses
unduly. National City would lend $5 million when the rate was
16 percent, and an additional $5 million every percentage point
thereafter (on the down side), and that this money would be
backstopped by borrowings from the Federal Reserve Bank of
New York City. As Galbraith says, this statement was Mitchell's equivalent of Mayor Hague's famous manifesto: "I am the
law in Jersey City."

By the end of the trading day on the twenty-sixth, the market
had rallied, call money had gone down to 15 percent, and Charlie
Mitchell was a hero. Five days later he was elected chairman of
the board of the National City Bank. An individual banker had
gone to a showdown at the corral and had won a shoot-out, a victory for stock-market investors everywhere. Most of the criticism that followed in the wake of the shoot-out was directed at
the Federal Reserve Board for trying to stop the upward-surging
market. Only Senator Carter Glass had unkind things to say
about Mitchell, and Glass, who had helped to set up the Federal
Reserve Board, was known as a bit of a grump in financial
matters.

Chapter Three

MARKET GAMES
7:30 A.M.

Charles Mitchell, on October 24, was just back from Europe, having cut short his vacation there. In the interim between April and October the National City had grown even more, absorbing the Farmer's Loan and Trust Company for a net worth of $2.3 billion. Now another merger was about to be consummated, with the Corn Exchange Bank. Mitchell had treated employees of both organizations to a joint theater party, a get-acquainted night on a grand scale.

In the interim between April and October, as well, the amount of call money had increased dramatically. This worried conservative government officials like Howard Douglas Dozier:

> Just what would be the result if that state of the public mind which has made possible the present inflation of stock prices should receive a sudden shock? . . . Should some mishap befall the stock market, each [private corporation which had lent call money] would be so busy saving himself that he would have scant time or inclination to save others. . . . The calling of the loans made to brokers by a half-dozen or so large corporations, if the calls should be made simultaneously, would shock the stock market.[1]

And the *Atlantic*'s "Financial Counselor" Amory Thorndike, citing the inflated call money figures, warned:

In view of these figures it is needless to emphasize the danger of any proportion of these loans being called within a week, and the impossibility of finding enough investment money to absorb the pledged securities within that week . . . The alarmist school of bankers and financial men . . . are saying that, if the market should have a sensational break, a large part of their assets might be frozen.[2]

Mitchell found out, on his return October 23, that precisely what had been feared—the calling of loans by corporate lenders—had been going on all week. He walked a bit more quickly towards his office. His steps took him past the corner of Sixtieth and Fifth, where the Pierre Hotel was going up, replacing the wonderful old Gerry family mansion.

Another few blocks brought him to Fifty-seventh and an eighteen-story building wherein were located the offices of the legendary "bad bear" of Wall Street, Jesse Lauriston Livermore. There were rumors afoot that Livermore was raiding the market on the bear, or down, side. Mitchell had heard of these and read of them. He did not stop to see whether they were true.

A would-be visitor to Livermore this day would have had a hard time. The Heckscher building's tenant list said nothing of the man; the elevator attendant was paid to claim there was no penthouse that overlooked Central Park. Should one make one's way nonetheless upstairs to a frosted door, it would be found to be guarded by a "bulging Irishman" who would not let anyone in without an appointment. But Livermore was in there.

With blond, almost white hair at fifty-two, a clear, ruddy, unlined face, wearer of dark suits and owner of a half-dozen residences worldwide, a yellow Rolls-Royce and a steel yacht, Livermore was a flamboyant figure, a maker and loser of great fortunes. On his right pinky he wore a huge sapphire in a gold setting, which had once been ripped off his hand in a robbery and given back to him when his wife implored the thugs to return it. Across his chest, in two pockets of his vest, he wore a gold chain. At one end, in a pocket, a pencil; at the other, a small knife. He would not shake hands with men, abhorred physical contact with males. His propensity for women, however, was legendary: he had lovers all over the world, many of whom waited for him for years in various watering spots. His current wife, once very beautiful, had already started drinking quite heavily. Of Livermore's proclivities, his customer's man had said:

When Mr. Livermore was gambling, he was thinking of screwing; when he was screwing he was thinking of gambling.[3]

Born on a farm in Shrewsbury, Massachusetts, Livermore went to work at an early age around the State Street market in Boston. He was phenomenal with figures, could add, subtract, multiply, and divide in his head quicker than most people could do it on paper. He marked quotes on a board at Paine, Webber: white for the whole numbers, orange for fractions. After the market would close for the day, fifteen-year-old Jesse would stay, make notations for himself, and play the bucket shops. These were like casinos: you bet whether a stock would go up or down without having actually to buy the stock. He beat the house odds consistently—so consistently that he had to resort to disguises and aliases because many of the shops refused to take his bets since he was beating them too regularly.

From the bucket shops, he graduated to playing the market itself. He developed nerves of steel and gut impulses that he followed when they came to him at odd moments, such as when he was fishing or playing golf. He had a deep respect for occult forces; in later life he would trade up or down depending on whether or not a black cat owned by a friend had had a litter of kittens. By 1906 he had accumulated a sizable fortune and was on a vacation in Atlantic City. He wandered by a broker's office on the boardwalk and sold a thousand shares of Union Pacific short. When the broker questioned doing this in one of the market's leading upward-bound stocks, Livermore tripled his order. The earthquake hit San Francisco the next day, and the day after, Union Pacific started to fall. Going for the jugular, Livermore sold even more short, and in a few days covered, and made, a quarter million on the move. His pattern was set. In the panic of 1907 he did similar things; after he had made a million dollars, he got a message from J.P. Morgan to please stop selling short because the market was at his mercy and could take no more. It was at once an ultimatum and an offering of homage. Livermore graciously agreed and emerged with $3 million, a nationally known man.

Selling short has been universally maligned and misunderstood. It is not as simple as buying a stock and waiting for it to go up. It is a more complex game, requiring the active participation of a broker, a bank account or other credit source willing to let itself be used, lots of intuition, and an understanding of market psychology far beyond what most investors can usually manage. To sell short in 1929 was an art as well as a very dangerous game, and Livermore was a past master.

Here's how the game worked.

United Amalgamated was selling at 100. A knowledgeable investor believed that, although it had been creeping up steadily, it was destined to go down. So the investor called his broker and told him to sell a thousand shares of UA at 95. Did he own these shares at that moment? No, but he gave his pledge to provide a thousand shares when they were requested—and in the meantime his broker lent them to him out of his own inventory (or borrowed them from another broker's inventory). Since 95 was an attractive price for a stock selling otherwise at 100, a buyer was found quickly. That buyer took delivery of the stock and paid the broker $95,000 for it. Meanwhile, our investor sat and waited for the stock to do something.

It started down, hit 95, then slipped to 90 and hit 85. At this point the investor had a choice of waiting to see what it would do further, or of "covering." Should he believe it would not go any lower, he would tell his broker to purchase a thousand shares of UA at 85, or, in market terms, "cover" at 85. He then delivered to his broker $85,000 worth of UA, and took delivery of the $95,000 the broker had gotten for his sale of UA a few days previous—and kept the difference of $10,000 as his profit (minus sales and carrying charges deducted by the broker). He was a winner, he had made $10,000, and he owned no stock. Should he have believed the stock would go further down, he could have hung on longer, covered at a lower price, and made a larger profit from the resulting spread between the low figure and the original 95.

That was, of course, only if the investor were right. If the stock, at 100, had not gone down but up, contrary to his expectations, the investor would have been a loser—he would have had to cover at, say, 105, and, by similar calculations, would have lost $10,000.

The time the investor had, in order to cover, varied according to the nerves of his broker and the broker's knowledge of the investor's personal finances. Generally, one had about a week.

The investor was selling something he didn't own, which took confidence all around and could only happen in an atmosphere where people were taken at their word. The code said you would deliver and deliver you did, even if you took a beating—that was Wall Street.

Was selling short a reprehensible practice? Absolutely not, the bears argued. In an open market there must be buyers and sellers, both going up and going down. And both must have the opportunity to make money, optimists by saying the stock would go up, pessimists by saying the stock would go down. Without the short bettors, the pessimists said, there would not be a market, because there would not always be both askers and bidders, sellers and takers.

Jesse Livermore had made his money selling short. But the money of 1907 that he had made was all gone by 1915, and he was broke and bankrupt. When a bear makes bad bets, he takes terrific losses. Undaunted, Livermore borrowed money to speculate in steels, and by 1917 had paid off his creditors and bought Liberty Bonds to give him a secure income. These he placed in an irrevocable trust—even when he wanted to, he couldn't sell them. It was the smartest thing he ever did. In 1919 he sold steels short after having made the Liberty Bond money by selling them long—and made money. In the bad days of 1920 and 1921, he made still more by selling short again. In 1922 he played a game with the lambs in Baldwin Locomotive, Studebaker, General Electric, and U.S. Steel. Rumors flew that he and George Whelan, then head of United Cigar, had millions of shares short; though it wasn't true, people gleefully tried to ruin them by making the market for these stocks go up—and found out that Whelan and Livermore had been long in the stocks and had made more millions.

In 1923 Clarence Saunders hired Livermore to make Piggly-Wiggly look active by, on successive days, buying and selling many hundreds of thousands of shares. Livermore agreed to do this for a friend, without his usual fee. It was a trick to make the stock look like a good buy. It was also, in this instance, an attempt by Saunders to stick Livermore with worthless stock by double-crossing him. Unfortunately for Saunders, Livermore figured out the trick and managed to stick Saunders with his own worthless stock, making the man lose tens of millions of dollars. Livermore won, but added to his list of enemies. A bear has many of them.

Livermore made some bad bets. He figured the market to go down in 1924, and lost. He tried again, and lost. A third time—and he got suspicious. He discovered that his private phone lines had been tapped, that the losses were forced. Admitting this publicly, he ripped out the phones, the tickers, the whole office, let his assistants go—and got out of stocks. He lay on the beach at the Riviera, he visited women, and he dabbled in the grains and commodities markets. The world which he contemplated seemed to have gone mad—there was no need for bears, because the bulls were making money *without anyone betting on the down side*! If the investor bought at 100, then sold at 110, and his buyer then resold at 120, nobody lost and everybody won. Livermore contemplated this, and the fact that every time he went in there were letters threatening to have his house robbed and his two children kidnapped, and stayed out. But he did gamble with grains, and tangled for the first time with Arthur W. Cutten, in Chicago. "Somewhere in the long rise that sent wheat up and over the $2 top in 1924–1925," says reporter Earl Sparling,

> Cutten became aware that there was a gray-eyed stranger riding behind him as close as his shadow. When Cutten bought, his shadow bought, and when Cutten sold it was as two men selling.[4]

The two became cordial enemies. In late March of 1925, with wheat very high, both men took Florida vacations, Livermore in Palm Beach, Cutten in Miami. To escape the chatter of Miami, Cutten took an automobile trip. As he was on the road, the storm broke. Livermore sold huge amounts of wheat on the Chicago market on what was known as Black Friday, April 3, 1925. Cutten lost millions. It was rumored that Livermore had arranged for Cutten's auto trip. Livermore not only denied the rumor, but offered a $10,000 reward to anyone who could prove Cutten had been out of touch with the market at any time. No takers.

It was after this foray that Cutten had gone to New York and the stock market; it was after this that Livermore as well had gotten the urge again. But this time things were different. Cutten, using his millions to get more millions, bought stocks heavily, often in conjunction with men such as the Fisher Brothers and William Crapo Durant, who had made many millions from automobiles. By the year 1928 Cutten's wealth was said to be approaching $100 million, and all of his stocks were completely paid up. Not so Livermore. Each time the great bear would bet on the down side, the rising market would vexatiously continue on up, and Livermore would lose. Many said Cutten was trying hard to make Livermore lose, but others said it was just the great bull market that would not be denied. Many times burned, Livermore could not keep away. He had to give up his townhouse and take an apartment, but he went back into the market. By 1929 his offices with the frosted door and large guard outside were in working order. It was necessary, Livermore felt, that stocks would break:

> What has happened . . . is the inevitable result of continuous rank manipulation of many stock issues to prices many times their actual worth based upon real earnings and yield returns. . . . If anyone will take the trouble to analyze the prices of . . . stocks . . . They must look at them as selling at ridiculously high prices.[5]

The outer offices held a portrait of his yacht, a sailfish he had caught in the Gulf Stream, and an enlargement of the ticker tape from the worst moment of the panic of 1901 when J. P. Morgan was trying to keep the Northern Pacific from being seized by E. H.Harriman. Twenty employees crowded the inner offices, with telephones having unlisted numbers, a quote board, banks of files, typewriters, a system of private wires and a private telegraph operator, and a squad of statisticians. Livermore shone, he always said, because of his statistical work, which he carried on often until late at night.

In mid-October the market was going down. It had hit a high point on September 3 and had been losing steadily ever since. Cutten was on vacation in Atlantic City. Watching the ticker, he expressed confidence to reporters that stocks would soon resume their upward trend. Livermore started to sell. Immediately the market was filled with rumors about him, shot through with overtones of his long battle with Cutten. The big men said they were not fighting each other. *The New York Times* printed a long article contrasting the two men, and their styles—Livermore flamboyant and erratic, Cutten

> shy, quiet, and unassuming, he has many times sat back in the corner of a Pullman smoking room and heard casual travelers discuss his stock market feats without disclosing his identity.[6]

A year had passed since the Sinclair Oil flyer—smiling, pudgy Harry Sinclair was finally in jail, though expected out soon—and Cutten was worth a purported $150 million. Cutten left Atlantic City and returned to his 800-acre farm in Illinois, where he kept twenty work horses in pasture because he felt sorry for them and had the work done by tractor. He was about to go on a hunting trip in his native Canada.

Livermore accepted an interview invitation from *The New York Times*. He called the reporter up to his suite overlooking the park and handed him a statement, on October 21, which said:

> In connection with the various reports which have been industriously spread during the last few days to the effect that a large bear pool has been headed by myself and financed by various well-known capitalists, I wish to state that there is no truth whatsoever in such rumors, so far as I am concerned, and I know of no such combination having been formed by others. What little business I have done in the stock market has always been as an individual, and will continue to be done on such a basis.[7]

No one in the country believed him.

No one believed Livermore because investors both small- and medium-sized knew and adhered to the potent American myth of the shark and the pilot fish. Small pilot fish follow a big shark, twisting and turning as the giant does; when the shark feeds, there is something left for the smaller fish; they prosper in their leader's wake. Livermore ought to have known: he had been a pilot fish to Cutten's shark in the grain markets of Chicago, before becoming a shark himself. In America of 1929, the Livermores, Mitchells, Cuttens, Durants, Fishers, and Raskobs had been slavishly followed—when smaller investors could actually find out what it was the big boys were doing (which wasn't always what they said they were doing). It was, for example, already part of the folklore to speak of the plain fact that Raskob had made eighty executives of General Motors millionaires, by insisting that they do as he had done and invest in GM stock, which they later sold at great profits to an avid public.

The tendency to trust the market judgment, savvy, and clout of others had led to the current popularity of investment trusts. An investment trust was essentially a holding company formed by another entity, usually a stock brokerage house, whose business it was to invest in stocks of other companies. An investor, instead of buying a share of GM, would buy a share of the investment trust. The trust, on the other hand, with the accumulated buying power of many investors, would buy a wide variety of stocks in some depth, with a good amount of clout and possibly at a good or better price than the individual investor might have done. The theory was that the small investor would lessen his risk by putting his money in an investment trust, for many reasons. First, because his money would be buying, not one stock, but many, so that if Stock A chanced to go down, he would still have Stock B, Stock C, and Stock D and many others which were going up, to balance out this Stock A loss. Second, and more important, the investor would be relying on the judgment of those running the trust, who obviously knew more about the market than he did. After all, they were indeed the experts, in and out of a hundred stocks all day long, and they would know what they were doing. The small management fee the investor paid for their services was more than justified by the larger return he would get on his money for investing in the trust. The idea had come to the country in force, from Britain, around 1920. It gathered speed slowly, but by 1927 there were 160 such trusts, and another 140 were formed that year. One hundred eighty-six more were born in 1928. Two hundred and sixty-five trusts came into being in 1929, about one per business day, representing more than one-quarter of all new issues, and more than $3 billion.

The New York Stock Exchange had a rule that an investment trust could be listed on the Big Board only if that trust would post its holdings—the stocks and bonds it owned, and their market value—so that the public could see what it was they were buying. The Exchange felt this to be a quite reasonable request, in an era of very reasonable requests and little regulation. Brokerage houses which sponsored trusts felt this to be an outrageous hamstring. Secrecy, they argued, was imperative if the trust's managers were to be able to make good moves and increase the value of their holdings. The public, they argued, would have to trust to the credentials of the managers and their intentions. As a result, few trusts were listed on the Big Board. This did not deter investors, who bought them over-the-counter, or from smaller exchanges in other cities. The myth of the pilot fish worked well: many of the trusts were bought up the first day they were issued—or before.

"Sponsorship of a trust," says Galbraith, "was not without its rewards."

> The sponsoring firm normally executed a management contract with its offspring. Under the usual terms, the sponsor ran the investment trust, invested its funds, and received a fee based on a percentage of capital or earnings. Were the sponsor a stock exchange firm, it also received commissions on the purchase and sale of securities for its trust. Many of the sponsors were investment banking firms, which meant, in effect, that the firm was manufacturing securities it could then bring to market. This was an excellent way of insuring an adequate supply of business.[8]

The Goldman, Sachs brokerage firm issued a typical investment trust in December of 1928, called the Goldman, Sachs Trading Corporation. All of the stock at $100 per share was originally bought by the parent company, to the tune of $100 million, and 90 percent of that was sold to the public at 104, but control remained with the parent company by virtue of an iron-clad management contract and other devices. By February this trading corporation had sold more stock and was about to merge with another company, Financial and Industrial Securities Corporation. So great was public enthusiasm for this anticipated merger that two weeks before it occurred the Trading Corporation's stock went up to 222½ or approximately twice the current total worth of the corporation. Curiously, the Trading Corporation was buying its own stock—by March 14, over 500,000 shares for a total outlay of $57,021,936—which had the effect of boosting the corporation's stock price even higher. It then sold some to market operator William Durant, but on July 26, Goldman, Sachs Trading Corporation created (in association with Harrison Williams) the Shenandoah Corporation. (The board of directors included young lawyer John Foster Dulles.) The stock was issued at $17.50 a share, opened at 30 and went to 36 on the first day of issue, doubling in price before it was hardly dry. Shenandoah then turned around and sponsored Blue Ridge, another investment trust, *only twenty-five days later*, on August 20. Blue Ridge offered the private investor a chance to turn in his other stocks, such as AT&T, GE, SONJ, Kodak, and many others, for shares of Blue Ridge. Many people did just that. Two days later Goldman, Sachs Trading Corporation announced the acquisition of a West Coast investment trust which owned also a bank with many branches in California and had a capital of around $100 million—and issued new stock which it exchanged with that trust, to gain control. Goldman, Sachs Trading Corporation had just issued a quarter of a billion dollars in securities in less than a month.

The effect of the investment trusts was to pull many stocks off the marketplace and into the trusts' portfolios—estimates ranged from $1 to $3 billions' worth—which, by the law of supply and demand, drove up the prices of those stocks even further. And some of the trusts inevitably took the money they had been making and turned it around to lend as call money.

As with the activities of big traders and companies which floated new issues for capital, the activities of the investment trusts made most money for the insiders. Insiders and their information obsessed the Street. They were the basic topic for the speculative grist mill as they had been when James Madison wrote to Thomas Jefferson in 1792 that the domestic conversation of the townspeople of New York bore almost entirely on gambling.

The myth of the insider—the man with good connections, such as a trustee of a company, or its lawyer or accountant—was held widely, and with good reason. Insiders did have a privileged position. This was never more apparent than in the activities of the redoubtable J.P. Morgan Company, private bankers.

Twenty-three Wall Street, just across the street from the New

York Stock Exchange, was the Morgan headquarters, commonly called the Corner. There was no name on the outer part of the building, no name on the outer door, no indication of what the business of the building was; indeed, regulations, said Morgan, did not permit them to say what business they were in. No records were made of meetings that the partners held daily in their English-style boardroom. The Morgan bank was beyond question the most influential organization in Wall Street and in the financial circles of the entire country. Some fifty corporations, including the following, deposited *daily* with Morgan an average of a million dollars:

American Telephone and Telegraph
International Telephone and Telegraph
Atchison, Topeka and Santa Fe Railway
Chesapeake and Ohio Railway
Erie Lackawanna Railroad
Lehigh Valley Railroad
Pullman Car
Continental Oil of Delaware
Humble Oil
Marland Oil
Standard Oil of New Jersey
Commonwealth and Southern (utility)
Niagara Hudson Power
United Gas Improvement
Du Pont
General Motors
Johns-Manville
United States Steel
Bethlehem Steel
Kennecott Copper

And Morgan was not tightfisted with money; the bank lent it generously to people like Charles E. Mitchell ($10 million), the heads of the half-dozen other largest banks in the country, and to about 150–200 officers or directors of nonbanking corporations. "They are friends of ours," a Morgan officer said, "and we know that they are good, sound, straight fellows."[9] There was no bank examiner; there was no balance sheet provided for the public— or for depositors.

Partners of Morgan, or their associated firm Drexel and Company, held 20 directorships in 15 big banks and trusts, 12 in 10 railroads, 19 in 13 utilities, and so on, for a total of 126 directorships in 89 entities with combined assets of $20 billion. "Incomparably," says Ferdinand Pecora, "the greatest reach of power in private hands in our entire history." The list of men associated with Morgan in these directorships—537 people—and their directorships in thousands of other corporations runs to thirty-three pages of fine print. Pecora estimated that corporations on which a Morgan partner sat on the board himself, or exerted influence in one way or another, controlled one-quarter of the entire corporate wealth of the country.

J.P. Morgan the younger distributed, with quaint anonymity, some five tons of China tea to the company's friends and customers every Christmas, as his father had done before him.[10] Jack was kindly eyed, with a white moustache, black eyebrows, the bearing and demeanor of an English gentlemen. He permitted no divorces in his firm, was courageous and physically strong—back in 1915 he had overcome, in hand-to-hand combat, a would-be assassin armed with two revolvers and a stick of dynamite in the Morgan Glen Cove mansion. His motto was: "Do your work; be honest; keep your word; help when you can; be fair."[11] J.P. Morgan and Company were conservative to a fault, but by January of 1929 even they could not hold out any longer against the speculative tide and undertook formation of the United Corporation, a holding company.

The company was created when Morgan and Bonbright (another company) bought into and controlled Mohawk Hudson Power Corporation, Public Service Corporation of New Jersey, and United Gas Improvement Company. These had many subsidiaries combining these companies and a capital of $20 million from within, the United Corporation was formed. UC, whose books were kept in the Morgan office, gave the Morgan company 600,000 shares of preferred, 1,200,000 shares of common stock (which it bought at $22.50), and 1,714,200 "perpetual option rights to purchase additional common at $27.50 per share." Morgan paid for these option rights one dollar apiece. UC very soon built up and exercised working control over a vast network of utilities, from Niagara to the Atlantic, over twelve states from Michigan through New Jersey. UC controlled 38 percent of the power in those twelve states, and 20 percent of power in the

United States. The stock of UC rose to 70, and the option rights that Morgan had purchased for one dollar each were now worth $47.50 each. They sold $8 million worth of them and kept the rest.

As with two other large corporations formed by Morgan that year—Alleghany in February and Standard Brands in September—Morgan's initial underwriting was quickly taken off their hands by favored customers. A soothing letter would go out to a list of friends. Here's one, to a former Cabinet officer, about Alleghany:

> We have kept for our own investment some of the common stock at $20 a share. . . . As it is not in the class of security we wish to offer publicly, we are asking some of our close friends if they would like some of this stock at the same price that it is costing us, namely $20 a share. I believe the stock is selling in the market around $35 or $37 a share, which means very little except that people wish to speculate. . . . There are no strings to this stock, so you can sell it whenever you wish.[12]

On the list of 660 people to whom such letters went on a regular basis, were, among others:

Calvin A. Coolidge (former President)
General John Pershing (retired)
Charles A. Lindbergh (son-in-law of a Morgan partner)
Charles Francis Adams (Secretary of the Navy)*
Newton D. Baker (former Secretary of War)
Wm. Gibbs McAdoo (former Secretary of the Treasury)
John J. Raskob (needs no introduction)
John W. Davis (former Democratic presidential nominee)
Silas Strawn (U.S. Chamber of Commerce)
Charles E. Mitchell
Albert H. Wiggin
George F. Baker
Otto Kahn (head of rival firm Kuhn, Loeb)
Bernard Baruch

---

*Adams was excluded from the list while he actually held government office, as was the Morgan practice in all cases, according to senior partner Thomas W. Lamont.

Percy Rockefeller
Owen D. Young (General Electric)
Charles Dawes (of the Dawes Plan)
Myron C. Taylor (U.S. Steel)
Walter Teagle (SONJ)
Clarence Mackay (Postal Telegraph)
S. Z. Mitchell (Electric Bond and Share)
Walter Gifford (AT&T)
Sosthenes Behn (IT&T)
Frederick H. Ecker (Metropolitan Life Insurance)

Raskob was on vacation when he received his letter about Alleghany. Morgan had "reserved" 2000 shares for him; he sent his check for $40,000 and a letter hoping he could be of service to Morgan in the future. Many others did the same, and, when they had received their stock, turned around and sold it at the current market price, for a virtually guaranteed good return—in Raskob's case, for instance, about $35,000, or more than an average American made in his entire lifetime at work.

When these lists came to light four years later, there was great controversy. Lamont wrote to many people of influence trying to explain why they were used. One letter, to *New York Times* publisher Adolph Ochs—not for publication—averred that

> We never issue common stocks to the public for the obvious reason that they are too much subject to the ups and downs of business, and therefore we must find some other outlet. We naturally turned in part to individuals who had ample means and who understand the nature of common stock—men who are quite prepared to take a chance with their money. . . . It was a case where we had an equity stock which we desired to sell. We thought it unwise to offer it in our own name to the public. So we got our private customers to join in with us.[13]

Another to whom such a letter was sent was editor William Allen White, a fixture of American public life for forty years. White read the letter and wrote back that he understood that such lists were common in business, but wondered about them:

> I suppose business and business favours are more or less like love—largely a matter of taste; probably there is a

strong element of envy in the rest of us who care only inci-
dentally for money in large sums, when we see it made in
terms of millions by those who seem to give only slight social value in return for their gains. . . . [I have had] income
and capital without my paying much attention to
it. . . . Yet I confess I get a twinge of mean distaste for a
system which permits men to pile up wealth in terms of
tens of millions with the luxuries thereunto appertaining—
luxuries which passed on to the second generation are on
the whole, socially menacing in an order which should have
some sort of approximate approach to social justice. . . . I
realize [these men] were not favoured for their influence on
politics, but merely for their influence on suckers in the
great financial stream.[14]

It was eight o'clock on the morning of October 24, 1929. Our
businessman of modest means had reached Central Park South,
along which a great building boom was in progress: soon there
would be many whose offices could overlook beautiful Central
Park, as Livermore's did. Our man knew in principle, and possibly in some detail, about the wonderful lists of Morgan, as well
as about the Livermores and Cuttens, the shenanigans of the
Sinclairs, the leverages of the investment trusts. About all of
these he was not bitter, but rather envious and admiring. He
wished he himself were on the inside, able to benefit as the Morgan listees did. He hoped fervently to perhaps one day be in their
position, to be a mover and a shaker and an accumulator on a
large scale, not merely a medium-sized fish and a consumer of
their prefabricated stocks. For the moment, however, he was
content to look up at the sign above Columbus Circle with some
satisfaction. It said:

You should have $10,000 at the age of 30; $25,000 at the age
of 40; $50,000 at 50.[15]

And that, he might have added, was only for openers.

Chapter Four

THE PEOPLE NOBODY KNEW
8:00 A.M.

Down on Wall Street, at eight o'clock on the morning of October 24, the bells of Trinity Church tolled the hour. There was much construction work in the area, evidence of America's booming times. Slow progress was being made on the Eighth Avenue subway, and it was, though no one probably remembered, the anniversary of the opening of the city's subway system twenty-five years ago. At the "chimney pot" corner of Wall and Broadway, the rusty pipes sticking up from the Irving Trust Company's excavation jetted steam regularly, and at a site on Wall Street itself a sixty-five-story building which would house the Bank of Manhattan was on a twenty-four-hour-a-day construction schedule.

Young civil engineer Walter Peterson was thankful, as he stepped into the wooden construction elevator with a bunch of steelworkers, that the foundations were essentially complete and that he no longer had to attend the graveyard shift of 8 P.M. to 6 A.M. Soon the weather would be getting cold, and days were warmer than nights. The elevator, a vertically moving eggcrate, went its way up the shaftway and Walter went with it, having his habitual pangs of feeling the elevator was not quite safe. He was to assist in the work on the structural steel and masonry location for the balance of the project, now that the basic framework and outer stone walls were already done. The building's top floors afforded a wonderful, panoramic view of Manhattan.

A few skyscrapers were scattered about, mostly in the downtown area, though a few were clustered about Grand Central and the Forty-second Street transverse.

The Bank of Manhattan building was being erected on a financial concoction put together by thirty-four-year-old investment banker George L. Ohrstrom and Colonel William A. Starrett of the Starrett Brothers construction firm. Supervisor Andrew J. Eken had been ordered to smash all previous records for erecting this kind of building which, when completed, would be, for a time, the world's tallest. If Eken completed the building in less than a year, he would get a fat bonus, and he was now on schedule. Construction was expensive; the total cost would run $20 million.

After young Walter made his way to the top in the shaft's construction elevator, he could see through the morning's grayness the buildings of the great engineering school of Cooper Union, a mile away, from which he was a recent graduate. As with many of the other young engineers, he had taken a chunk of his weekly wages and bought the Starrett Company's stock, which was going up consistently. Right now, not many Wall Streeters could be seen, sixty-five stories down: their work really wouldn't get going for another hour.

Several miles uptown, in the shadow of Lenox Hill Hospital, Matty Harris parked his enormous 1926 Buick two-tone roadster and went into the small rooms he occupied for his business. His office was on the first floor, but the "works" were in the basement: this being the ninth year of Prohibition, Matty was a flourishing bootlegger. Every week or so he'd make a connection and go out to Freeport, on Long Island, with the big car. There he'd jaw with the rumrunners, pay for and load twenty cases of Scotch in a rack in the false bottom of the car, and drive back to his office. Police Sergeant Terry McM. of New York's finest had gotten him the rooms and now lived conveniently in the back. He and Terry had a good relationship, for a Polish immigrant and an Irish cop: when Matty wanted to make a difficult delivery, he'd call up the station house and ask Terry to come over and watch things for a while; conversely, when Terry found out that the heat was going to be present on a particular day or place, he'd call and tell Matty to lie low for a while. So far, everything had worked out just fine. The customers wanted so much Scotch that Matty could hardly keep up with the demand. He'd cut the Freeport hootch in the basement, three for one, and put it back into bottles—some in the original bottles, the rest in bought bottles with new labels. The customers knew it was cut and liked it anyhow. So far Matty had been arrested twenty-one times, but his lawyer had good Tammany Hall connections and knew every judge in the city worth knowing.

Once Matty had been delivering a case of his best Scotch to a private customer in an apartment house. A cop got on the elevator. The conversation went like this:

"Where you going?"

"To see a friend," Matty said. The case was on the floor next to him, but he wasn't touching it.

"What floor?"

"I forget."

"That case yours?" asked the cop.

"Naw. It was here when I got on the elevator."

"A likely story. That your car outside?"

"Yeah."

"Pick up the case and put it in your car," ordered the cop.

"If it's not mine, why should I do that? If you want it in the car, *you* pick it up and put it in the car!"

"Yer under arrest!"

The judge ruled that, indeed, Matty had not had possession of the case of liquor, and, even though caught red-handed, Matty did not go to jail. In twenty-one arrests, he'd never gone to prison. After being on his own just a short time, Matty had amassed quite a sum for a young man in his twenties. But the bootlegging business was undeniably risky, so he was easing himself out of the game, into something more solid. He had taken all of his profits so far, $42,000, and put them into the stock market.

Out in Port Jefferson, at the Packard Agency, Frank Ayers was happy. He had finally found, at a dealer's in Red Bank, New Jersey, the special 1929 Packard convertible coupe for his rich customer. The 1930 models were already in and the 1929s hard to find, he'd told the Woodys, but they insisted on this particular car, even though the price tag was over $2,500 and comparable models of Fords cost only around $1,000. Mrs. Woody wanted Packard Blue, which was very conservative, but Mr. Woody had said he'd take whatever was available as long as it was that particular coupe. Now Frank had found it, and at a very good price from the Red Bank dealer which would allow him to clear $500 profit on the sale. The Woodys could afford it. Mr. Woody, Frank knew, had a seat on the prestigious New York Stock Exchange. Frank also knew some of the less wonderful things about the family. Just after the war, a "gob" from the Navy eloped with a daughter of the family, and both were disowned for a while. But the gob had invested his mustering-out pay, on a tip from a friend who was a switchboard operator, and had made a mint within a few years. Seeing this, the Woodys had taken them both back and, in fact, made the son-in-law manager of the Wall Street brokerage house. Now, in 1929, the ex-Navy man had made millions and was famous for being seen in fast company. The Packard dealer knew he had given his wife a new Cadillac, but also owned a $15,000 Belgian Minerva car himself and had made a present to actress Gilda Gray of an Irish jumping mare whose name was Prudence, after one of his stock companies. Later in the day Frank would call the Woodys with the good news that he'd found the car they'd been looking for.

By ten after nine, Irv Wolfe was in his car at the old Poughkeepsie station, halfway between New York and Albany, ready to start out on the road. For a recent school graduate, he had a swell job: selling calendars and other advertising novelties for Brown and Bigelow, throughout the counties of Dutchess, Columbia, Rockland, Orange, Ulster, Sullivan, and Greene, in the Hudson Valley. It was a mighty big territory for a twenty-year-old. Irv nosed the used 1927 Model T, bought with a $125 loan from his parents, out into the sparse traffic of the town and headed for Pleasant Valley and Millbrook. He was the youngest salesman on the force, but he wasn't doing badly at all—he'd even had some money to invest in the stock market.

By this time in October, almost all of the calendars he had were sold and delivered, and he was pushing advertising novelties. This morning he was going to try and interest the Millbrook Creamery in some "point of purchase" signs. If he had time, he was thinking of coming back to the famous Smith Brothers Restaurant in Poughkeepsie for lunch. The place was always crowded, but the food was worth the wait. And he'd be able to check in on the brokerage office next door, to see how things were going.

Al Baxter was supervising the garage on Manning Street in the center of Philadelphia, and, as always in the morning, the cars were coming in fast. The makes were almost too numerous to remember. Among the Fords and General Motors cars were some Dusenbergs, Marmons, Jordans, Pierce-Arrows, Hupmobiles, a Peerless, a Cleveland, a Franklin, a Chandler, a McFarland. The manager of a big hotel nearby brought in his 1929 Stutz-Bearcat, which had come with a guarantee that it would go 100 miles an hour. The floor guys worked hard, and hardly stopped when the numbers boy came around to take their bets. Many of them had "dream books" which supposedly guaranteed excellent tips. A nickel could pay off $27, and a quarter, $138. Sometimes one of them made a heavy hit and wouldn't be seen for a week or so, until the money was all gone. Al's wife's birthday was coming up, and he had gone to the bank to take out some money to buy her the warm blue coat she wanted. It was lovely, but expensive, and he wouldn't have done it except that times were good and he felt he didn't have to worry about his job. The garage had been started by three ex-Marines. Recently the partners had jockeyed for control, and one, the sales manager for the local Pierce-Arrow agency, bought out the other partners. Al was in good with the man, and so he managed the garage and felt secure in doing so. With the Shubert Theater, the several banks, a catering firm, the Academy of Music, and a whole host of hotels, businesses, and doctors' offices nearby, the garage was a gold mine. The owner told Al that there had been a man who wanted to buy the entire block and do something with it, and had balked only slightly at paying $1 million for the garage.

In Leon Khalaf's battery shop in Newark, New Jersey, everything was humming. Calls were coming in for batteries to be picked up, and Leon was taking them as fast as he could. Meanwhile, the driver loaded tagged batteries onto the truck, and two other guys were tagging the ones that had just come off the recharger, where they'd been all night. It took the five-horse-power generator twelve hours to charge a radio's battery, and it ran twenty-four hours a day. Business was booming; the place was a gold mine for a hardworking immigrant in his midtwenties. Every radio had one A and two B batteries: the A had to be recharged every two weeks, for which Leon's price was a dollar and a half. With home radios, the new car radios, car and truck batteries and ignition equipment, there was quite a volume of business, and the place was hectic. Many of Leon's customers were doing all right too. There was the manager for the phone company who'd bought himself a big home and two cars on the proceeds of stock investments. The Chevrolet dealer had plowed his own stock profits into the expansion of his dealership. The man with the chain of Warner movie theaters was doing very well. And Leon himself had bought a home, a car, and had some money in building loan stocks, which were all paid up.

Another winner was Boston "road man" Earl P. At his office in the downtown section, he decided he'd let the automobile dealers in the area go hang for the day and visit them tomorrow. Today was his thirty-fifth birthday, and life was beautiful. The son of a Philadelphia physician, he'd used his native intelligence not only to become a crackerjack salesman for the auto company, but to turn $10,000 into $250,000 in just a few years' time.

The $10,000 had been part of his wife Bea's inheritance from her mother. Bea and her mother had been in a podiatry practice together for a few years before the mother had died at the early age of forty. After the funeral, the young couple decided to get married immediately. Bea ran the podiatry practice and gave Earl the $10,000 inheritance to use as he wished. He put it in the market, but never forgot where the stake had come from. He was a responsible man, and he used the money brilliantly. Now their stocks were worth $250,000. In the past few days, Earl had become concerned that the market was dropping and advised his friends to get out. They had heeded his advice before and made money, and they heeded it now—but he himself did not. He wanted to try and ride it out just a bit longer. With just a bit more money maybe Bea could retire from the practice and raise a few kids.

Retirement was on the mind of Dr. Lynn Rumbold, a few hundred miles away in Rochester, New York. All about him, doctors were retiring from medical practice at early ages, with the profits from stock speculation. Rumbold wondered if he weren't doing things the hard way, struggling with his own practice to make money, as so many other physicians seemed to have stopped seeing patients altogether. In the hospital's lounge he had difficulty using the phone for his normal calls, because many of the staff members were on the horn to their brokers,

even before the market in New York opened for the day. He himself had heard the siren call; his banker told him his credit was
good, and that he would lend the doctor the money to buy a certain surefire stock, on margin if he wanted to. As he was already
in debt to the bank for his house, office, and car, he wasn't so
sure he wanted to take the plunge, but it was tempting.

He was having a hard time getting started. After completing
postgraduate surgical training, he'd come to Rochester in 1924.
It might have been much more profitable to go to a rural area
where you had a monopoly on medical service, but he'd wanted
a medium-sized city. It was difficult to build up a practice: most
people felt the older physician was the one to consult, and young
men were left with the calls the older men didn't want—usually
those who didn't pay their fees right away, or who were otherwise difficult. Dr. Rumbold had long office hours, made many
house calls, and spent much time at the hospital. Working as an
anesthesiologist, in some homes he saw kitchen-table surgery—
tonsils and adenoids, D and Cs, and himself did an occasional
home delivery. Some of the few specialists in the city had minor
operating rooms in conjunction with their offices, with a few
overnight beds and attendant nurses, but Rumbold had a large
enough overhead as it was and couldn't swing that. There was
little money for extras, but he wasn't starving, and he knew that
eventually the system would work out so he'd get a following.
There was still that tantalizing offer from his banker to consider.
The siren call. He really ought to give the man a decision, today.

The times were heady, but signs of the impending crash had
been in the air for some time. Most people did not see them, or
chose not to see them. But if one looked, the signs were not hard
to find.

Gloria Heller had started with Western Union in 1925 when
she was not quite seventeen. They had pushed her to finish high
school at night, and, when she had done so, promoted her steadily. She had seen the Morse code go and the Simplex come in, and
now she had the responsibility of opening up the busy office at
41 East 46 Street, between Madison and Vanderbilt, near Grand
Central Station in New York and many of the Park Avenue
offices of big businesses. Near eight o'clock, she came to the
door. Even before she took her hat and coat off, she plugged in
the machine which had messages transmitted after the office

had been closed at 1:30 earlier that morning. Twenty or so messenger boys straggled in behind her. The office was growing: it serviced places like the Ritz-Carlton, where many rich and famous people often stayed, and also ran an errand service that delivered packages as well as telegrams.

Gloria put her hat and coat away, opened the safe, then turned round to look at the machine. It was clacking away a mile a minute and had already spewed out on the floor a hundred telegrams' worth of gummed tape, an enormously large volume. All the messages were "2 Stars," really important ones—and they were all the same, with only names and amounts changed from one to another. They were all margin calls, demands for money. With a sigh she directed the delivery clerks to start separating the individual messages for gumming down on the telegraph blanks, after which they could be stuck in envelopes for delivery. Telegrams continued to pour out of the machine as quickly as they could gum the messages down on the blanks. At this rate, they'd never catch up with the damned machine! It was going to be one of those terrible days, she could feel it already. At least, on her salary of fifteen dollars a week, she didn't have to worry about a margin call!

Ed Uhl, in charge of the loan department in a downtown Philadelphia bank, knew it would be a long day. Margin calls were his unpleasant business. Everyone including the bootblack in their building seemed to be in the market, getting tips from the brokers in the area, spreading the word about the possibility of a rise in this or that stock, or a split-up in another. Ed could never understand why when a stock split it seemed that the two half-shares were worth more than a full share. But these were the days of the bulls. The only bear he ever came across was in the zoo. In the meantime, shifting prices meant a tremendous load of work for his loan department, which had much money out that was secured by stocks as collateral. In many banks across the country, the unsettled market that had existed since Labor Day had caused loan officers to reconsider their margin requirements daily. High-flying stocks were discounted many points, and then margin was computed for each account. Margins were generally at 25 percent, except for these high-flying stocks. Since Labor Day cautious bankers had been pushing them up to 35 and even to 50 percent. But the situation was changing every day, and loans, as well as loan officers, had to be flexible. You didn't want to lose a customer by raising the margin too high, but at the same time you didn't want the bank to lose money if the market fell sharply, more sharply than had been anticipated. So, of late, the routine had been that after the bank and the markets had closed, Ed's people would be there until nine, ten, eleven o'clock before going home, making their notes on the loan cards. These they did with the aid of the evening newspapers with the closing prices. Each night the collateral on each card was re-priced and retotaled, the margin was computed, and, if it was inadequate, the card was set aside to be reviewed by three officers, who would decide on what kind of a letter to be sent to a borrower.

Letter number 1 was a notice that margin was impaired, please deposit additional collateral or cash. There was no time limit on these letters, but most people came the next day and put up what was needed. In case they didn't, the next day they'd be sent letter number 2, which told them to come in as soon as possible the next day. Most of the people with loans were depositors in the bank; they usually reduced the loan with their money on deposit if additional collateral was not available. All of the loans were payable on demand. If a borrower's loan of $1,000 was secured by shares worth $1,250, when the value of the stocks had dropped to, say, $1,100, the bank would request additional collateral worth $150 or its equivalent in cash. If the borrower had enough cash or collateral to keep up the loan to the required amount, after letters 1 and 2, fine. If not, he got letter number 3. Inside the bank, this was known as a "hereby do." Sent by special delivery, it stated that it was necessary to call the loan for payment at a certain hour the next day, which we "hereby do." The letter had been composed by the bank's lawyers and further said that all collateral would be sold by the bank if the demand was not met. Even though there might be an excess if everything a borrower held as collateral were sold, the bank couldn't very well sell selectively, and would possibly have been subject to a borrower's suit if they didn't protect him from a greater loss, say if the market continued to fall.

For the first time in a while there had been a fair number of "hereby do" letters in the batch sent out last night. In another three hours, those people ought to show up and pay on their loans, or Ed would have to go through the unpleasant task of selling their securities. As yesterday's market had been unsettled, this was a distinct possibility for today.

Marty Ducceschi, working at the throwing mill on Gray Street in Paterson, New Jersey, had mixed thoughts about banks, loans, and everything that had to do with the dream house of his childhood. In 1927, when he was fifteen, the house and the 160-acre farm in Donora, Pennsylvania, near the Monongahela River, had seemed paradise. They had some cows and pigs, a nice house, barrels outside to catch the rainwater which was soft and good for washing clothes. His older brother worked in a blast furnace at a nearby steel mill, and Marty thought he might do that someday as well, and possibly play soccer for the Gallatin town team, which was one of the best in an area filled with many good ones. On nice days they'd drive over to Uniontown and see some of the beautiful mansions put up by the people who owned the steel and zinc mills and the coal mines. Marty had also witnessed at Uniontown his first coal miner's strike and an explosion, neither of them pretty sights. Nearly every night, at the farm, Marty's family and his uncle's family would get together. The men were brothers. They'd play cards and drink homemade wine or beer in the front, while the women would talk and knit or darn socks in the kitchen, and the cousins would all play games. It was lots of fun. But then things changed.

Marty's uncle had, somehow, gotten inside information that the Donora bank was going to close and withdrew his money in time. Throughout the twenties, nearly a thousand banks had closed all over the country, usually small state banks in rural areas. The depression of 1920–1921, which for farmers had lengthened to include most of the decade of the twenties, had taken its toll in these small state banks which were not under federal control and had no guarantees for depositors. As the loans to farmers were defaulted, and those to the city dwellers who serviced the farmers caved in soon thereafter, whole areas were deeply affected with financial blight. In some states as many as 43 percent of the banks had closed, and no state was immune from the disease. Putting your money in a state bank was not the safest thing in world, as people were finding out to their chagrin. Here, the people of the Monongahela Valley were affected in Donora, Webster, Charleroi, Monessen, New Eagle, Gallatin, Cement City, Uniontown, Turkey Hollows, Monongahela, and Black Diamond.

For some reason, Marty's uncle hadn't told his brother of the coming closing, and it hit Marty's family hard. With many others, they joined the crowds around the bank's doors, trying to get at their life's savings, but to no avail. They lost the farm. Father was bitter at his brother for not having told him of the bank's impending close. Then—the worst thing!—Marty's uncle purchased the farm from the bank's receivers and moved his family in where Marty's had once been. This occasioned a blood feud. No one talked to a member of the opposite faction. The cousins grew apart. One night Marty's father had gone and smashed the rain barrels at the old place in a hopeless gesture of anger.

At last they all piled into the old Ford and headed for New Jersey. Marty's job at the mill helped, now: it brought ten dollars a week.

A few miles away, in Newark, nineteen-year-old Matthew Cascino got up late, as he had done for the past two months. He wasn't ordinarily a late riser, but he was out of work. During the summer he'd had a fantastic job working as a lather on homes in the Newark area, raking in eighty dollars a week including overtime. He put up lath and plaster boards, and then the masons would come and put adamant over what he'd done. All of a sudden, one Friday in August, the boss had called all the men together and had told them there would be no work as of Monday. The builders had run out of money. That was it, as quick as that. Two months later, in October, Matt was still out of work, couldn't find a job, and the row on row of houses stood uncompleted. The people who were waiting for their dream homes sure wouldn't be getting them this year.

Elizabeth Levy, a secretary in the Kensington district of Philadelphia's public schools, watched the children come in for the day's session, and worried about them. For the past six weeks since school began there had been increasing problems with attendance. Notes would come in to the effect that Johnny was out because he had no shoes, or Mary because there was no underwear for her to put on. In this mill and factory district, many of the family breadwinners were out of work. Often in the past few years mills had closed in bad times, only to open again a month or two later, when things got better. The workers had come to expect it—the prosperity of which the newspapers talked came to them only in fits and starts, here today, gone as soon as there was a slack season. Only this year the slack season seemed to have lengthened out into more than a few months. Some factories had been on half-staff since the late spring. At the school, the problems of the factory hands' children had galvanized one of the school's counselors into a project to take care of the kids. The faculty was bringing in all the clothing they could spare, and it was all arranged by Elizabeth in a big closet according to size. Some of the adults contributed money as well, which was used to buy food. You weren't really supposed to do this, but when you took a look at the poor, cold, wet, hungry kids as they came through the doors on a weekday morning, what else was there to do? Soon it would be winter, Elizabeth thought. At least as the weather got worse, attendance would actually increase, because the parents knew the youngsters would be warm and dry at school.

Charlie Anderson was finishing his leisurely breakfast at the convention in the Adirondacks, and felt glad to be out of New York City. The road up to Yanna Farms had been a riot of fall color, the leaves a thousand different shades from green to bright red, the car crowded with guys on the way to having a good time. Yanna Farms had been built by an advertising agency to entertain the likes of Edison, Ford, and Firestone, but now it was being used for conventions. It was great because, with no phones and no newspapers and no radios, it was completely out of touch with the world, which was relaxing. Also, the Farms had managed to wangle a special dispensation to make their own wine, and Champagne or Sparkling Burgundy was served at dinner. They'd all been there for two days, all the *Hearst International Cosmopolitan* men, about forty salesmen and management people from all over the country. The convention was fun, planning for more space sales in the magazine and how to obtain them. The research department had plotted out the routes the salesmen took, the calls they made, the time spent on each call—places like Bristol-Myers, Campbell Soup, BP&G. The salesmen looked at these things interestedly—they helped to reroute themselves to save time and money.

Charlie was one of the youngest men there. All of them, he thought, including himself, seemed quite successful, prosperously middle class. *Cosmopolitan* had the highest-paid editor in the country, Ray Long, and the rest of the staff, especially in sales and management, were equally well paid. And almost all were playing the market. Including Charlie, until a curious thing happened.

He had a loan from the National City office on Fifty-seventh in Manhattan, with which he had been buying stock on margin. The stocks would go up regularly, and he'd pay off the loan and keep going. Early in October the bank's manager, a tall and forbidding Scotsman with whom Charlie had never talked because he was scared of him, called the young salesman into his office. The guy had given Charlie a lecture: "You've got a cute trick going," the Scotsman had said, "but I am going to put a stop to it right now, for your own good. You have a five-thousand-dollar loan and the stock as collateral. I want you to call your broker and sell it; you have a fifteen-hundred-dollar profit, so it won't hurt you. When money begins acting as it has, it's time to clear out of the market."

Charlie had been thoroughly intimidated, had called his broker and duly sold the stock as ordered—but of course he was still in the market on other things. Even so, he brooded about what the Scotsman had said. His broker had pretty much echoed those gloomy thoughts, even saying he was going to get out himself, buy an apple orchard upstate somewhere. So, after all the guys had piled in his car and were on their way up to Yanna Farms, Charlie had stopped in Middletown, New York, made a last phone call to his broker, and told him to sell everything. That was two days ago. Now his mind was resting easier: maybe, after this morning's seminar, there'd be time for a round of golf before the afternoon's session.

It was 9:45 A.M. as Frank Howell waited on the ground floor of the office building on Broadway near Wall Street. He'd gotten in a moment too soon and had to wait for another elevator as the Box went up. The Box contained the firm's securities. It had been kept overnight in the vault of a nearby bank, and each Box—they had several, being a large firm—was so heavy that it required two men to carry it and an armed man to guard it. No one other than the guards and carriers could ride in the same elevator as the Box, so Frank had to wait for the next car.

On the eighth floor, Frank walked through the front office,

where the partners and the customer's men were located, and into the back. There, everything was in turmoil, and much of the turmoil came from the Cage.

The Cage was a wire-enclosed area that was off limits to everybody including partners, unless bonded and holding one of the special keys. Here, securities and money were physically handled. Everything that transpired in the Cage was entered by hand on the daily blotter, and trying to match the entries with the work done on the floor of the Exchange provided a living for quite a few people. Frank didn't have to start his bookkeeping until 9:45, because no actual work could be done until the Cage released the previous day's blotter at 10:00 when the Exchange opened a new day's trading.

As he walked to his desk, Frank could see the Box being unloaded into the Cage. About a dozen messengers, some young boys, others "old men" of fifty, sat on a bench facing the Cage's windows. They ran between brokerage firms, carrying securities that had been traded. Through the day, runners would come and go, shouting their firm's names as they took places on the bench. When the Cage was ready to deal with that company's business, someone inside would shout out the company's name, and its runner would come to a window.

On the other side of the back office was the Wire Room, which had telephonic connections with the front office, the Exchange floor, the Curb, and with over-the-counter firms, as well as telegraphic communication with the company's offices in other cities. The Wire Room was glass-enclosed, supposedly to keep the firm's dealings on the floor of the Exchange secret, but noise, tips, and hot stories came out of the Wire Room in an endless stream.

Frank worked halfway between the Wire Room and the Cage, operating a flatbed bookkeeping machine which contributed to the general racket. Immediately outside the door to the Cage were the stock record clerks, who recorded all physical transactions affecting securities in the Box on handwritten cards. These, and the margin clerks who worked near bookkeepers like Frank, were at high, sloping desks, mostly standing up, although high stools were available. Against the windowless back wall were the dividend clerks, foreign exchange people, and comptometer operators.

Frank and a half-dozen others made daily transaction entries in the accounts of the firm's New York customers. Most of them hoped to become margin clerks. These "supermen" had to maintain daily records of customers' margins but were well placed to get extremely important tips on the market. The head of the margin department was a middle-aged woman, a frosty, aristocratic widow of the firm's largest European customer. She didn't think much of Wall Street in general, or of back office clerks like Frank in particular. Maybe he'd never get to be a margin clerk.

At the moment he didn't care much, because he, along with every other person in the office, was speculating in the market. Of course it was against the Exchange's rules, but it was easy to find ways around that. Frank's specialty was penny stocks which sold for a dollar or less. They never made much money, but they never lost too much, either. One of the office boys had made a practice of buying ten shares of Radio—at four hundred dollars and up a share!—when he went out to lunch, and then would sell it when he came back: he had a friend with the Radio pool that was manipulating the stock earlier in the year, and he usually made more than enough to offset the infrequent losses. The money for playing the market came from salaries, which were augmented by overtime, and even by Sunday work, for which Frank could expect a ten-dollar bonus. In previous years, he knew, all of the firm's employees had also received as much as a full year's salary as a bonus at Christmastime.

Most of the people in the back office were men, except for the woman who headed the margin department, and a few other females. A couple of them were real good-lookers, but Frank had been warned that so-and-so was Partner A's girl, and another one was Partner B's girl, so he should not even try his luck. Frank's last girl had given him the gate a couple of months ago, and he was using his leisure time to study the market rather than to pursue women which was what twenty-year-olds ought to do. Those who really knew the market could do well. The firm had purchased Stock Exchange seats for several Wire Room employees recently (when the Exchange "declared a dividend," giving every seat-holder a chance to purchase an additional quarter of a seat for every one he held) because the pace of trading on the Exchange floor had become too much for the older members. Now everyone in the Wire Room and in the back office in general had taken to wearing broker's gray suits with conservative ties and sometimes even gardenias, in hopes that they would be noticed for the next available seat.

In the past two weeks trading had gotten hectic, and this meant changes in the daily routine. It also meant added overtime, which in turn meant more money with which to play the market. So Frank welcomed the high-volume days, even if the work was so overwhelming that lunch had to be sent in and he couldn't take his daily stroll down to the Battery.

The margin clerks had the additional job of calling or telegraphing customers to bring in more money or collateral when stocks went down. This they did, and the customers came in, or sent in the needed funds. The market would go down for a day or two, then recover. Nobody thought it was very serious. There was a lot of work, though. Margin clerks took to getting their prices from the tape, rather than from the evening newspapers. There was so much work that a few new margin clerks had been hired—from the outside, to the chagrin of the bookkeepers and other back-room personnel. This was the doing of the margin department head, who seemed to have her hand in everything.

For instance, she demanded that when the tape was running late—as it had been the last several days—members of the firm who were on the trading floor of the Exchange should telephone in the latest quotes, even if it meant losing a chance to earn some juicy commissions. She insisted on it, so that the margin records and the customers' accounts could be kept as up-to-date as possible. These telephoned prices were shouted loud and clear in both front and back offices.

This morning, as Frank prepared to work, the office was in pandemonium. Yesterday's volume had kept the Cage at work on the blotter up until nearly the very last minute before the Exchange opened at 10:00 A.M. And the frosty margin department head was having a battle royal with one of the senior partners, who'd ventured back here from the front office. As Frank could make it out, it was about people who'd failed to meet their margin calls. The aristocratic woman wanted to sell them out as soon as trading began on the floor. The senior partner said this was unnecessary, because the market would soon recover and they would lose disgruntled customers. She insisted it had to be done, to prevent people from losing even more. The senior partner countered that he knew other margin departments all over the Street were carrying people for a while, so why should they be different? The margin department head stood her ground, and the senior partner finally caved in: they would sell out people who had failed to answer margin calls the moment the Exchange opened for the day.

The bells at Trinity Church chimed, the clocks struck ten, and the most momentous day Wall Street had ever known, began.

Chapter Five

THE TRADING DAY BEGINS
10:00 A.M.

A stock exchange is a fiction, a piece of invention that has been agreed to by many people at once. It designates a particular arena as the space in which men will barter the future of certain business enterprises. The New York Stock Exchange proudly proclaimed in 1929 that it was

> an organized market, completely and readily open to the entire public. Its transactions are dictated by orders representing public opinion. . . . All the efforts of the Exchange must be exerted at the sufferance of supply and demand, as these are generated by public opinion.[1]

The exchange—any exchange—limits possibilities of buying and selling these particular futures, confining such activity to its own designated space, under its own rules of give and take.

In a stock exchange, those futures are divided into shares of stock. They could as well be divided into tulip bulbs, or rawhide, but in a stock exchange they are shares of stock. A share of stock is a second fiction, a piece of paper with some writing on it. Unlike a promissory note or a bond, this paper does not guarantee an obligation on anyone's part. Rather, it is a certificate of part ownership in a corporation. When you hold a stock, you hold part of a company, but also part of the future, an invention.

When we ask the question Why is a particular piece of the future called one share of Stock A worth $100? the answer usually is that that's what it can be bought (or sold) for on the exchange. Interpreting this through the mechanics of an exchange, this means that $100 is the last price at which some shares of Stock A were bought. Looking deeper, what we're saying in shorthand is that both a buyer and a seller have agreed jointly upon an idea: that a piece of the future represented by a paper with some writing on it has, in a transaction between the two, brought $100 to the seller (which can be used to purchase gold or lamb chops of known worth). This transaction has taken place in an area known as the exchange during its hours of operation. Is this idea—that the stock is worth $100—the truth? Not exactly: it is an agreed-upon fiction that serves for truth so long as buyer and seller agree.

But what if they don't agree? What if, sometime during the long hours of the night between trading sessions, there creeps in the specter of discord? Suppose the buyer at $100 thinks next morning that it is still worth $100—but a man who *chooses to believe* it is worth only $90 disagrees? Who is right? The guy at $100 or the guy at $90?

So long as he can find somebody on the floor of the exchange willing to buy Stock A from him at $100, the guy at $100 is right. But if he can't find a buyer? What does he do then?

A stock exchange is operated on the assumption that because the brokers do represent many millions of people, there will always be some who want to buy, and some who want to sell Stock A at any given moment. There are millions of people interested here, and the fact that they are so numerous and diverse makes for a *market*—a place where a trade can take place, at a price. There is no law that says that if you want to sell something at a price in a free market and a free enterprise system, that there must be a buyer at your price. But there *ordinarily* is; generally someone is willing to buy what it is you're offering at somewhere near the price you think your commodity is worth. That is the idea—people have been calling it a law—of supply and demand. It had been cited for years as the real reason behind the rising market: when supply was low (there were not enough stocks, or enough of a certain stock) the demand pushed the price up. It ought to have worked even better in reverse: if you wanted to sell your stock—your supply—at $100, and there were no buyers, there should have been many more potential buyers—demanders—at $99, $98, and $97 successively. The tenet held that the potential buying audience went up as the price dropped.

But what if that didn't happen? What if, one cloudy October morning, your extended personality (in the trappings of a broker's floor trader) stepped out on the trading floor of the New York Stock Exchange and offered your piece of paper, your one share of Stock A at $100, and there were no takers? It ought to have been simple: he dropped the price a bit, and then there will be takers. But what if he dropped the price to $99, $98, $97—$95—$90!—and there were *still* no takers?

And what if, alongside your broker, there were a thousand others? And they were all offering five hundred other stocks—B, C, D, X,Y, Z—at bargain prices, and no one wanted them, either?

The crevasse yawned, as if an earthquake had suddenly sliced the world right next to you. What had seemed a few moments before absolutely solid now was precarious. Truth was floating beyond reach. An assumption on which you had staked gold and lamb chops had been thrown into a cocked hat. Fictions to which you and others had agreed, fictions and supposed laws which were as much a part of your life as the requirements that civilized men wear clothes in public, remain monogamous, and go to church on Sundays—these ideational compacts were being rent and punctured, as you stared in disbelief. Could the center hold? Would everything fall apart? What was to be done?

You had choices. You could pull back from the gorge's lip and decide that, after all, your stock really was worth $100, and you would wait until the earthquake passed and the firmament returned to normal, and the potential buyers out there had regained their senses. In order to step back, though, you had to possess a certain equanimity of mind, and to possess that, you had to have very little at stake or pressuring you. If $100 meant nothing to you, either because it was a trifling sum, or because your life-style did not require money, then perhaps some kind of equanimity (worthy of a Buddha) was within the bounds of possibility.

But what if there was pressure? What if you had predicated a life-style on many multiples of your $100, and your broker knew it? What if you had utilized that other agreed-upon fiction called *margin* and were now being forced to sell certain stocks in order to maintain ownership of others? What if your broker had been ordered to sell out certain accounts such as yours "at the market," or at whatever price they might bring at any given moment, because if he did not, his firm might lose many thousands of dollars of its own money?

These were the conditions which faced many shareholders as the New York Stock Exchange opened for trading at 10:00 A.M. on Thursday, October 24, 1929. Short, slim William H. Crawford leaned over the gallery and tapped a mallet to a gong, and on the vast trading floor the exquisitely sensitive machinery of the New York Stock Exchange sprang into action.

To someone standing by young Mr. Crawford, the scene might have seemed surreal: thousands of scurrying pint-sized people moving about, making a huge din, flapping arms and waving things, creating, as they moved, a carpeting of scraps of paper that would grow constantly. Above the floor, hieroglyphic symbols slowly circulated, magnified images against luminous screens, numbers and letters in an endless stream. The trading floor was the heart of the Exchange. From here, a network stretched that encompassed 50,000 people in the Wall Street area who were intimately connected with the Exchange's work; from there to brokerage offices all over the city and the country in towns both big and small; from there to the estimated 5 million Americans (including one million factory workers) who owned stock; from there to the families of these stock-owners who were assumed to be between 15 million and 25 million people out of a total American population of 125 million.*

Shares were held at this moment by a larger number of people than ever before. The increase in the past year of the number of stockholders had been estimated at 65 percent, even with investment trusts buying up much of the available excess. Montgomery Ward, owned in January by 7,710 stockholders, was today owned by about 40,000; General Motors, at 71,185 in January, was today (after a split) held by over 150,000 people. Many working people had bought stock. Questions were being raised

---

*The average size of an American family at this time was 3.5 persons. The senate hearings of 1933 estimated the number of people affected by the Crash at 25 million, probably too high a figure, given the average family size.

as to whether such a marriage of capital and labor was vitiating labor's effectiveness at the bargaining table; but it was generally agreed that the more stockholders, the greater the basis for happiness in American business.

We are at the heart: someone as knowledgeable as Mr. Crawford might point out to a visitor that there was not chaos on the trading floor, but an accurately devised order. All those people down there had specific purposes.

Against the walls, behind brass rails which separated them from the floor, were some of the direct links to the outside world: telephone clerks, employed by the various brokerage houses, about a thousand of them. They received calls from those offices with buy and sell orders, which they then gave to the many floor traders, signaling them by means of call boards on the north and south ends of the great hall. A number was uncovered and covered again—winking, it seemed—when a particular trader was wanted.

The Exchange was well prepared for October 24. The events of the past week had not gone unnoticed. Usually there were about 750 traders on the floor, but because volume was expected to be heavy, almost all of the people allowed to trade on the floor were there that day, over a thousand men. In the past half-year, older members had often left the moment-to-moment transactions to younger men, but today all the older ones were here in force, because every second would count. The only man conspicuous by his absence was elderly E. H. H. Simmons, the president of the Exchange; he was on a honeymoon in Hawaii. Many of the floor traders were decked out as veritable dandies, gardenias in their pearl-gray suits, starched collars. They were peacocks of the walk; their claim to fame and riches was, in the best ones, their savvy ability to execute an order quickly. Speed was important because of the volume of sales that had to squeeze into this space and time every day. The greater the volume, the faster they had to work, and the less time for reflection on the larger ramifications of every transaction.

How did the potential seller of Stock A find a buyer for that stock in this vast jumble? It was not a hit-or-miss affair. There were conventions which enabled the process to be speeded up.

In the old days under the buttonwood tree a broker simply yelled out his stock loud enough and long enough until someone was attracted; that was now obviously outmoded, and another middleman operation had been superimposed on the first. Specialists had become mini-exchanges in themselves. Here's how that worked: the broker with a sell order proceeded to a particular spot on the trading floor where stocks of the type of Stock A were always traded. Here he found a "post," a large U-shaped affair which seated some clerks and had numerous file drawers, plugs for telephone jacks, and pegs upon which to hang hats. Here the potential seller relayed his request to the specialist, who acted as a go-between for this man and a potential buying broker. Of the Exchange's 1,354 members, 207 were specialists.

At post number 6, for example, one usually found Charley Wright, one of the most popular specialists, a man who had earned the trust of many other brokers on the floor. Charley handled the "book," or list of orders, on such stocks as ENX (Eaton Axle and Spring Co.); FO (Foundation Co.); GGPR (B.F. Goodrich Co.); IRR (Indian Refining Co.); PFD (Panhandle Producing and Refining Co.); SVE (Seagrave Corp.); and UCL (Union Oil of California).[2] There were sixteen such posts on the trading floor—number 15 had AT&T and other communications stocks, number 2 had U. S. Steel and other steel company stocks. The sixteen would shortly be consolidated into twelve. Under ordinary circumstances, a trader would look about for anyone else in the area immediately interested in his stock, and, should he find a buyer there, make the sale and report it to Charley for his book in that stock. Should he be unable to make the sale immediately, he could leave his order with Charley and the book, to be executed when some other broker came up with a reasonably matching buy order. When a transaction had taken place, it was recorded on paper and sent, by a uniformed attendant, via pneumatic tube to the center of the floor, where it was also recorded on the ticker tape, along with every other transaction. Word of it would also go back to the brokerage house whence the order originated, and eventually back to the person who once held the stock that had now been sold.

Often many orders were received simultaneously. These were printed sequentially on the tape, however; there was no other way. When the pace of buying and selling exceeded the pace of putting transactions on the tape, the tape fell behind, was said to lag. When that happened, there was a discrepancy between what was actually happening at that moment in Charley Wright's presence on the floor and what the ticker tape said. A price that went by at minute number one might well be old hat by minute number five—wrong by a few points in either direction, and that difference could mean many dollars to people. Such a thing was, however, an ordinary occurrence, something that happened regularly every day, so the Exchange employed a number of other attendants who went around to people like Charley and asked them verbally for the latest price on ENX. Having gotten a quote, they would plug in their portable headsets at the phone jacks and relay these late figures to other clerks in rooms upstairs above the Exchange floor. The figures were, in turn, passed along by telephone to brokerage houses, where they were used as vital information in knowing what to buy or sell. On a day when the tape lagged, these quotes were all-important, because it was such quotes, rather than the ticker tape, which accurately reflected what was happening on the floor of the Exchange at a given moment.

Information was at the heart of the nerve center. Thirty-five thousand quotes were obtained in the above manner by 69 quote room employees and 127 floor collectors every day, to supplement the ticker tape. Would 323 phone lines have gone from quote room to brokers' offices, at $75 a month each, if the ticker tape had been enough? They would not. The quotes were the lifeblood.

There were other sources of information. On busy days the Exchange allowed the bond ticker to print the prices of leading stock issues every once in a while, as a service. Still more information could be obtained from the broad-tape tickers of the Dow-Jones news service. But these additional sources were not enjoyed by all. There may have been 8,000 stock tickers in operation throughout the country, but there were only 2,500 Dow-Jones tickers, in fewer than 100 cities.[3] Two years before there had been only half that number of D-J tickers; most of them were late installations. Worse, there were only 900 bond tickers throughout the country—and 680 of those were in New York! *There were no bond tickers at all in twenty-nine of the forty-eight states.* Some Dow-Jones tickers were scattered through all the states, but, in general, the folks in the hinterland, even though they might have been right at a broker's office, had to rely generally on the stock ticker, that old workhorse, for their stock prices. A new, high-speed ticker was being developed, but it wouldn't be ready for another year.

Right now it was the first moments of trading on October 24, and there were huge numbers of sell orders awaiting the floor brokers. These were, by and large, forced selling orders—instructions to sell X so that Y might be protected. It was a part of an account that had to go so margin could be maintained, or it was an entire account that had to go so that the brokerage house's loan to its customer could be recouped before it got entirely lost. At the opening gong, prices were steady, even going up a fraction here and there, but the volume was fantastically swollen. Within moments, there were orders to sell 20,000-share blocks of Kennecott Copper and General Motors.

These were shocking orders.

What could a broker do with such an order? Twenty thousand shares was a big lot, even if only a small percentage of 2 million shares a day (the average until then). Twenty thousand shares of General Motors, at 62½, was $1,250,000—a considerable fortune. Such blocks were usually not put up for sale early in the morning. Owners of such blocks usually waited until they saw how the market was doing on a given day, then threw in such a lot. When the trend of the day was known, the market's machinery could swallow such a big chunk. But at the opening? A 20,000-block at opening spelled trouble, plain and simple and obvious to those who knew of the blocks.

There were other blocks to be sold that morning. The GM and Kennecott were bought whole. But the others?

The trader with a 20,000 share block that he couldn't get rid of went to the specialist. He didn't necessarily want to—he had viewed the specialist as operating "licensed larceny" for years in the rising market. The specialists had sold things to him high, bought from him low. Should the specialist now get wind of the magnitude of his sell order, he might himself depress the price somewhat, perhaps buying it for his own trading account at a low price, and later selling it to another trader at the price the original broker might wish he had gotten. Trading with specialists was a risky business.

Perhaps the broker offered a thousand shares—and didn't tell how much he had in back of that. The price was down. Two thousand more. Still down. At this rate, getting rid of 20,000 shares would take the better part of an hour—but the broker didn't have an hour. There were those margin sellout orders waiting, and the feeling that many customers' fortunes might be lost if he spent too much time here. The 20,000-share block was simply too large to be gotten rid of in the accepted, cagey manner this day. But it couldn't be held back. What to do?

He perhaps tried to hold on for a while, let a few trades go by, but he couldn't do this forever. He might know, for instance, that other brokerage houses besides his own had finally decided they must raise their margin requirements to 60 and 70 percent, and that such new requirements were forcing many sales similar to his. The specialist probably knew that, too. Mike Meehan, Charley Wright, Buck Buchanan, Julian Bach, Arthur Gwynne— these folks didn't get their reps for nothing.

Coming clean, the trader had to list the stock with the specialist, having sold off only a fraction. The specialist agreed to sell off what he could, getting for each piece the best price possible. (What if he were lying? What if he already had other orders like our broker's?) The mere fact that the block could not be gotten rid of intact automatically meant that when it was sold off piece by piece, it would be for lower prices—the buyers, knowing the supply was great, could simply offer less for a piece.

Could the trader have done otherwise? Performed the Buddha-like feat of refusal? His judgment may have been unlimited, but his autonomy had severe constraints: his job was to execute orders. A customer's fortune, or his firm's, might have been at stake, and he was deluged with orders, all of possibly equal import. All around him on the floor was evidence of declining prices: brokers waiting with sell orders for different stocks. He looked to the screens, asked about of his fellow traders, and found out that within moments of the opening gong, the following huge orders had come through, all to sell: 15,000 Sinclair Oil; 15,000 Standard Brands; 13,000 Packard; 12,000 United Gas Improvement; 10,000 United Corporation; 10,000 Westinghouse; 10,000 Alleghany. All of these could now be seen moving across the large screen, all sold off at prices which were dropping steadily and continuously.

From the opening gong, the ticker ran late. The bunched-up orders at opening created a tremendous backlog; double, triple normal volume was trying to get pushed through. The trader saw his number flapping insistently on the call board and left the specialist with the 20,000-share block. He could have done nothing differently.

Something big was going on. It was the culmination of a terrible week.

Last Saturday's close was abominable, a half-day of trading in which stocks lost in a few short hours what they had taken months to gain. Monday, the twenty-first, was another bad day. Rails took a big beating as foreign capital started to be withdrawn: money was going back to London and Paris. The volume was the third greatest in history, and the tape was an hour and forty minutes late at the close. Not since March and the theatrics of Charlie Mitchell at the call-money corral had the ticker been that late on a losing day. Though Monday afternoon had seen a bit of a rally, the sum total was still bad. Tuesday brought an expected rally in the morning, but by afternoon stocks were heading down again and ran into many stop-loss orders. These were instructions to sell when a stock went down to a certain point. Many times these had been the instrument of destruction in a day's market. Way back in ancient history, on October 4, *The New York Times* had described what always happened with these orders:

> The catching of stop-loss orders pushed the decline along vigorously. The market has been honeycombed with these orders for many days, and as they were reached and touched off, the stocks thus brought into the open for sale found only feeble buying power below them.

The net result on Tuesday the twenty-second was the loss, in *one hour,* of all the gains of Monday and Tuesday.

This had happened before. But always, in the past, prices had rebounded after a day or two of bad breaks—always. After every break downward, there would be another sharp break upwards, which would invariably reach up to a new high for the market averages and make the losses of past days merely fleeting things of the moment—the "shaking out of the lunatic fringe," as Professor Irving Fisher of Yale was calling it in the morning's paper. If you held on or if you bought, went the prevailing opinion, you would do better. Those who sold in a panic were just giving in to the bears; had they the courage to stay in there, the bears would lose again as they had continually for several years: the bulls could be held in check for a while but would not be denied. There were more than enough people who could be counted on to buy at reduced prices, just to get in on the surely rebounding market. Weren't there signs that it would happen? Ivar Kreuger was lending Germany $125 million; he couldn't do that if his stocks and bonds weren't good, could he? Equitable Trust was planning $44 million of new capitalization—wasn't that a sign of health? The Pennsy announced orders for 100 new locomotives; Bethlehem steel's new subscription offer for stock was oversubscribed—everything gave "sure" signs of going back up.

"The ordinary human being," wrote Albert Einstein in the current issue of *Saturday Evening Post,*

> does not live long enough to draw any substantial benefit from his own experience. . . . We can try to transmit to them neither our knowledge of life nor of mathematics. Each must learn its lesson anew.[4]

That's what was happening on the stock market in this terrible week. Instead of the expected rally on Wednesday the twenty-third, there was a Niagara of liquidation. Six million shares—a new record—with the tape 104 minutes late at the close. *The New York Times* averages for fifty leading railroad and industrial stocks went down 18.24 points, a loss which made all previous declines look absurdly small.

People realized this was all bad but did not give up hope. They looked to the twenty-fourth to bring out organized buying support. They took to heart reports that many margin calls were being met speedily by additional funds. Surely those people whose large fortunes rested on the fact that their stocks—say Radio, or GM, or United Gas Improvement—were worth a certain amount of money could not afford to let the prices on these stocks drop too far. Could they? Such people would have to buy what was offered, to maintain reasonable price levels for their own stocks.

But as trading began on October 24, it wasn't happening that way. Those 20,000-share blocks, which only millionaires or bear raiders could afford to sell, were being offered lickety-split!

Where was the organized buying support? Where were the buyers?

At 10:15, when the outside world was seriously at work, or perhaps listening to Mary Hope Norris (founder of *Mother's Radio Round Table Club*)[5] broadcasting her talk on Hair Charm, the ticker was already badly late. Too many stocks were being traded at too great a pace, and the Exchange's recording mechanism could not keep up with the trading. At 10:22, WEAF interrupted Mrs. Norris with a bulletin: an unidentified ship off Newfoundland had seen the wreckage of an airplane believed to be that of cattleman Urban F. Diteman, who had set forth on the twenty-second from Harbor Grace, Maine, bound for London and glory. Diteman had been celebrated—and missed—by the papers for the past several days. Now he was more than presumed dead, another would-be hero of the aviation age come to naught. Mrs. Norris resumed. By 10:30, the stock ticker was telling the prices of 10:15, which were as much ancient history as Mrs. Norris's tips on hair care, and about as relevant.

No one, however, broadcast a bulletin about the lagging ticker, or the fact that at 10:30 the volume of shares was an incredible 1,676,300—almost as much in a half-hour as there was on an average day. Right at this time a divide opened. Those on one side began to have better information than the vast majority on the other side. We'll go into that shortly. One thing—the only thing—both sides had in common was the information on the ticker, and this information was very powerful. People became aware of the ticker, and something happened on both sides of the divide.

Inside many thousands of heads, all over the country, ideas, images, portents, whispers of mortality, dreams of ruination, totems of destruction began to overwhelm the acolytes of the new age. Their belief in the great bull market that never stopped going upwards was being shaken to its foundations.

As this change began to take hold, they remembered things they had heretofore pushed out of mind. Hatry. The Massachusetts Utilities Department ruling. Ominous stories. Roger Babson's whistlings in the wind. Now they thought of these again.

The great British swindler Clarence Hatry had started with the creation of the Austin Friars Investment Trust, capitalized with $1,500,000 in 1925. Austin promoted the Drapery and General Investment Trust which bought into department stores, then launched Corporation and General Securities in 1926. That concern floated fifteen loans for cities in England and Australia, then, in a sensational deal on the London Exchange, bought a coin-operated vending machine company which specialized in automatic pictures, and went big time. Pyramiding investment trusts and dummy companies, Hatry issued unauthorized stock, increased his assets by forging stock certificates, and committed other nefarious deeds. A classic swindle. Aiming for the topper, he formed Allied Ironfounders from various concerns manufacturing iron products, and used Allied to try for a $55-million take-over of virtually all steel production in Britain. On September 20, 1929, the whole shebang had collapsed, and the British market took a nosedive from which, the London *Economist* said, it would take months to recover: losses were suffered not only by those who owned stock, but by banks and others who had lent money on such stocks. Three brokerage firms failed, and the losses were running into the millions and still hadn't all been counted. Rumblings were felt in New York, but not seriously.

On October 11, the Massachusetts Department of Public Utilities denied the "petition of the Edison Electric Illuminating Company of Boston for approval of the change in the par value of its shares of capital stock from $100 per share to $25 per share." Many times before, the department said, it had approved such stock split-ups, which invariably had led afterwards to increases in the value of the stocks, but this time it seemed to them that the split-up was not warranted. They said that the present value of the stock was entirely due to the action of speculators, and that it had reached a level so high that "no one, in our judgment . . . on the basis of its earnings, would find it to his advantage to buy it."[6]

These were strong words, but then the state of Massachusetts was already in a bad depression, had gone for Smith in 1928, and had other similar aberrational qualities which allowed people in New York to discount what was seen as a real bombshell on the State Street Exchange in Boston. Boston Edison had been selling, prior to the ruling, at above $400 a share. It plummeted tremendously at the department's ruling.

Jay Busby, a student at the time at the nearby Harvard Business School, recalled an experience of the week before:

> Dean Wallace Donham called a general assembly of the school. He asked the students to heed their advice and get out of the stock market. He stated that the school authorities did not want anyone associated with the school, either as student or faculty, to be injured financially in what was to come. During that time I was taking a course in Investment Banking under Professor Clinton P. Biddle. . . . He suggested that we go to a brokerage house and wait for the event to happen which we might never see again in our lifetime. He suggested that we watch the papers for the death of a prominent businessman or possibly the failure of a large company, anything that could start the ball rolling.

Jay and his roommate went to a brokerage house on Milk Street and were there when the Boston Edison news broke. That, Biddle felt, was the catalyst. Biddle suspended classes and "went to New York to watch the fireworks."

In New York the market trembled at the Boston Edison news, but not badly. Now, two weeks later, people were remembering it, or Hatry, or any number of potentially terrifying stories they had buried under their intellectual rugs. On October 1, a spate of arrests in stock frauds had begun with the apprehension of nine people representing companies with the august-sounding names Wall Street Fiscal Corporation and Wall Street Financial Service, who were alleged to have obtained options on stock issues, then sold them at extra-inflated prices to the public.

Then there was W.J. Keyes, who jumped out of the Shelton Hotel, having lost a fortune in Chrysler and GM. His note said, "Last April I was worth $100,000. Today I am $24,000 in the hole."

One might have noted that Keyes was a vice-president of Earl Radio, and that another story in the same paper reported that Earl Radio had been acquired by the much larger Kolster Radio. (What one might not have known was that in private correspondence the deal had also been called off by Kolster that day.) Plans to regulate those mushrooming investment trusts, which many thought had boosted prices unduly, were bandied about on

October 4, as the market staged its worst day since March. And if these stories did nothing, what about the one about the run on the only bank left in Taylorville, Illinois? The run was stopped only by the dramatic delivery of a half-million dollars brought in by airplane—after the four other banks in the area had all failed in as many days.

Or maybe some people finally got around to listening to the Gloomy Gus of the financial soothsayer community, Roger Babson of Wellesley, Massachusetts. For a long time Babson had been saying that the bubble must burst. Back in January, in an article in *Collier's*, for instance, he said it loud and clear. And repeated it all the time. But Babson had been wrong for such a long time that few could take him seriously, as he pontificated from a point hundreds of miles away from the nerve center of Wall Street. Most prophets are not believed except in retrospect; it's one of the hazards of the trade. Doom-sayers are not pleasant to have about. How much nicer, for example, to listen to Dr. Paul V. Winslow telling the New York Curb Exchange that he attributed the "bulk of divorces and much insanity" to the noise level of New York City.

When U.S. Steel announced a production cutback in early September—a bad sign in anybody's book—everyone seemed to ignore it except Babson, who jumped on it as evidence that there would be a fifty-point drop in the Dow-Jones within a short time. Now, six weeks later on October 24, some people noted that, by God, the Dow-Jones had dropped fifty points in a month! Earlier in the week Babson urged people to sell stocks and buy gold, and some were now doing that. But, even at this late date, nobody wanted to believe him completely. His predictions were offset by other prophets' rosier pictures. Arthur Cutten, who'd made $150 million, said stocks would go higher. How much money had Babson made? Charlie Mitchell stepped off the boat from Europe and said stocks would go higher. Was Babson president of the largest bank in the country? If you wanted an academic, you could as easily believe Yale's Irving Fisher, who had been right more times so far than Babson. Fisher agreed with Mitchell and Cutten.

By 10:30 the ticker was already fifteen minutes late and the gloomy predictions were being proved, at the moment, terribly right. The portents, so long ignored, were recalled. They pressed in on the consciousness of many a stockholder. In a book of the day, Walter Lippmann was saying:

> The modern man who has ceased to believe, without ceasing to be credulous, hangs, as it were, between heaven and earth, and is at rest nowhere.[7]

That seemed to describe the state of mind at the moment. Lippmann further suggested:

> There is no theory of meaning and value of events which [the modern man] is compelled to accept, but *he is none the less compelled to accept the events.* . . . There are elaborate necessities, physical, political, economic. He does not feel himself to be an actor in a great and dramatic destiny, but he is subject to the massive powers of our civilization, forced to adopt their pace, bound to their routine, entangled in their conflicts. He can believe what he chooses about this civilization. He cannot, however, escape the compulsion of modern events.[8]

The modern event that compelled—what was it? Where could he find it as the world was shaking?

The fictions that investors had agreed to for so long were in the process of being revealed as fictions: one share of Stock A wasn't worth the $100 you said it was—it was worth only what it would bring on the market floor *at that very moment.* It wasn't worth what it said on the ticker, because the ticker had been superseded as it was late. When fictions such as these began to crumble, people looked for facts to hold on to. What were the facts, the incontrovertible facts?

Brokers' loans were a fact. The latest figure available, for October 16, showed $6.8 billion, the highest they had ever reached, up $88 million in a week. All those loans, one had to conclude, were now surely in the process of being called, which meant that many billions of dollars' worth of stocks would have to be sold on the market to protect the solvency of brokerage firms. What chance had your own share of Stock A got, a matchstick of $100, in a flood of billions of dollars? Another fact: the Federal Reserve's lending rate to member banks had been marching steadily upwards from 3.5 to 4, then 4.5, 5, and was now up to 6 percent. This was meant to stem speculation. What it meant right at this moment was that now, if the big boys wanted to borrow money to protect their already-made investments, it was going to cost them a lot more than usual to do so, and that fact might discourage even them. The rate had been made to deter speculation. Right now, ironically, it might have the effect of discouraging the possible saving of price levels.

Had the doom-sayers been right all along? Had the man who held Stock A at $100 been, not right, but incredibly wrong?

Again, the search for facts. The most imposing fact was the latest quote on his stock: 92, and dropping. It was a modern event that was completely compelling. Of a sudden it seemed to our stockholder that he had been, not right, but terribly wrong. The enormity of his mistake burst in upon his mind.

Heretofore his alignment had been upwards, a slant that mimicked those charts of averages he had long seen in the daily paper—up, up, for many moons. Now the alignment changed, in a single terrible moment, to a vision of the future wherein those little lines could be seen to be going down, down, down. And with this change in his vision of the future came a change in what he foresaw for that little piece of the future which he owned, his one share of Stock A. The great magnet had swept over his mind, reversing its polarity from Up to Down.

Now he wanted desperately to sell that stock, sell it for whatever it would bring. His fictions had been dissolved and replaced not by facts but by new fictions, fictions on the Down side. Now, all he wanted to do was get out while he still had something left.

A reasonable goal? Yes, but the times were, it seemed, no longer subject to reason. The investor's mind churned with additional thoughts, dark and encircling. What about Livermore? What about the great buying power of Cutten, Raskob, Durant, the Fisher Brothers? Why were they staying out? Did they know something he didn't know? Maybe they did! They always seemed to know more than he did when they were operating pools, riding a stock up and then bailing out at a high price and letting the ordinary suckers get hurt. Pools had been operating in 105 stocks that year. Maybe the big boys were entirely out now, maybe this was just a gigantic pool—a whirlpool to end all pools—and the little guys were going to get it in the neck again!

Yes, he concluded, the insiders probably knew something he didn't know. How could he find out the real information? He had already decided to sell Stock A, but what about the dozen others in which he had an interest? Should he sell everything? Hold on to some things? Should he even buy, if he could? Should he sell short? He must have facts, whatever facts could be found out, reliable information. The ticker recorded facts, but the ticker was behind, and lagging more with each passing second. What should he do?

He moved closer to the heartbeat. If he was out of town, he drove to a broker's office. If he was uptown in New York, he started downtown towards Wall Street. If he was in a broker's office in Wall Street, he inched closer to the quote board and called frantically to the customer's man to get him better and more accurate quotes from the trading floor. Eternity was flying by with each moment, his money was disappearing with every second. Information! He must have information!

Chapter Six

"IDOLS OF CONSUMPTION"
10:30 A.M.

Social critic James Truslow Adams, looking over America in the summer of 1929 from a vantage point of knowing both this country and England, tried to fathom the heart of the business ethic. Why did so many people, even the ones who didn't own stock, stand watching the tickers? Was it, as some suggested, because brokerage offices with their comfortable chairs, clublike atmospheres, brass spittoons, had replaced the lure of the old barroom with its swinging doors, that had gone underground during Prohibition? Or did the answer lie deeper, in the kind of country America was at that moment? England, said Adams, might be a nation of shopkeepers, but America was truly a businessman's civilization. We had no aristocracy to look up to, no gentry, no established church supported by the government (as was the Church of England), and, of the leaders in other spheres,

> Politics save in a few rare cases, have ceased to attract first-rate men as a career, and there is none in either diplomacy, which is usually only an episode, or in the civil service, which holds no position worth striving for. The rewards of a lifetime spent in the army or navy are negligible. On the other hand we have had the richest virgin continent in the world to exploit, and the prizes for a successful business career, measured in money and power, have been such as are undreamed of in European business.[1]

For many in America, even the unlimited vistas of business did not satisfy. They were too slow. The same American myth that said anyone could be rich seemed to imply that you could get rich quickly, more rapidly than the normal processes of work and modest savings made possible. As Max Lerner points out, stock speculation, which fed such a myth,

> also gives scope to the risk element that is being crowded out of the society, and it has a special appeal for those who lead humdrum lives on rarely fluctuating incomes. . . . In terms of ethnology, the fluctuating market has become the totem of business civilization, which has moved away from the fetishism of the commodity to the fetishism of "business conditions."[2]

The idea that business, and its symbol the ascendant stock market, had become accepted as the acme of American achievement permeated all levels of the social fabric, from the high to the low, from the New Yorker to the Californian. Even the most skeptical, such as Walter Lippmann, acknowledged

> The more or less unconscious and unplanned activities of business men are for once more novel, more daring, and in general more revolutionary than the theory of the progressives.[3]

Donald Richberg, social activist in Chicago, agreed, in the social worker's magazine *The Survey,* in October of 1929:

> Progressives believed we must "pass prosperity around" and that we must produce it with "social justice." We were not seeking a social goal—not a community experience—but a better individual life. Therefore social justice did not require us to ask "Why should we produce 20 million automobiles?" The question was "How shall we produce them?" And the progressives of my generation answered stoutly: "By well-paid workers able to raise healthy children and properly insured against hazards of accidents, disease, and old age."

Richberg's old idol, and Lippmann's old teacher and mentor, the fading Lincoln Steffens, agreed:

> Big business in America is producing what the Socialists held up as their goal: food, shelter, clothing for all. You will see it during the Hoover Administration.[4]

Leo Lowenthal studied the capsule biographies of interesting people printed in magazines such as the *Saturday Evening Post* and *Collier's,* to get an insight into American ideals.[5] In the early years of the century, the celebrated people were "idols of production" who had achieved success in workaday or enterprising ways—the immigrant scientist who had made good, the industrial or financial leader who built something out of an idea, the serious artist or writer, even a candidate for higher office whose strivings seemed especially worthy. These people were held up to be admired and emulated. "You, too," they seemed to say, "can rise in the ways we have risen." The conception of how people got to the top fit a schema as hackneyed and as true as some old film scripts: raised in obscurity or under a particular hardship (Teddy Roosevelt's asthma or George Washington Carver's race), they strove towards success through strength, intelligence, and skill, and, through perseverance and often in the face of adversity, achieved goals of worth. But, Lowenthal noted, in the twenties the script began seriously to change. The people celebrated in these same articles were ballplayers, stars and starlets, market millionaires. They may have been raised in obscurity, but they suddenly got a break and made good. Success was now not achieved, but somehow "happened" to them, through forces that were basically beyond their control. Instead of "idols of production," the models had become "idols of consumption."

One former idol of production saw this change graphically. Bernard Baruch, born poor and Jewish in America's South, had turned his intelligence into many millions in the stock market. In the early fall of 1929 he came back from grouse-hunting in Scotland and stopped in the financial district to give a beggar a coin. In gratitude, the beggar cited to Baruch a hot market tip then making the rounds. Hearing this, Baruch decided to complete his withdrawal from stock investments: too many people were trying to get something for nothing.[6]

To become what they beheld, millions of Americans believed they needed only a key, a cipher that could be decoded and used to produce the magnificence of a windfall. The stock market, with its magic ticker, was such a cipher. It was the up escalator.

For instance, stock and bond salesman Julian Sherrod divided the customers to whom he'd sold many millions' worth of securities in the past ten years, from 1919 to 1929, into four types of suckers. Number 1 was the *bony type.*

> You are easy to sell provided the salesman is patient and lets you think you are having your own way. Your strength is your weakness.[7]

Number 2 was the *blood type,* the emotional dynamo. All you had to do with this one was appeal to his feelings. Number 3 was the *meat type,* who liked his comfort and big chairs, such as were provided in customers' rooms. Sherrod avowed that you must never inconvenience a fat man; rather you should dip a pen in the ink for him, so he can sign on your dotted line. Number 4 was the *monkey type,* the kind that jumped all over the place. Sherrod's verdict on him: "A good candidate for a trust company."

This sort of salesman mentality could live only among a horde of willing customers. Edwin Lefèvre commented that

> The partners of reliable commission houses do not deliberately give wrong steers to their customers, but they all employ customers' men who, being human, are vitally concerned with earning their salaries. When a man is paid for getting business he is apt to lose his anxiety over the hazards of the game as they affect his customers. . . . The reason why nothing new ever happens in the stock market is that the game does not change.[8]

Lefèvre, who thought about the market and its problems deeply, believed that

> at the height of the boom imaginative Americans did what staid Dutchmen did in Holland 300 years ago when they

went crazy over tulip speculation and paid $5000 for a single specimen, or bought shares in the ownership of individual bulbs, or sold bulbs before they had come into being, or sold more bulbs than there were in Holland—or in the whole world, for that matter.[9]

By 10:30 on the morning of October 24, 1929, everyone knew it was an unusual day for stocks, if only in terms of volume. Prices were declining rapidly, and not merely by a point or two, but often by five and ten points at a clip, hitting what were called air holes, or spots where there were no buyers even at prices below the present market quotes. When there are air holes, a seller has to drop his asking price in great chunks, rather than a bit at a time.

The ripples were spreading out from the heartbeat. More people than ever before were here to watch the action in the Exchange's visitors' gallery. And down the street on the Curb Exchange, things were as bad as at the senior Exchange, and possibly worse. At the bell the Curb had had an enormous block to digest—a record-setting 150,000 shares of high-flying Cities Service. At the opening price of 55^{1}/$_{8}$, this represented well over $8 million in a single order. Electric Bond and Share was dropping, and so were other utilities and the newly listed investment trusts of Blue Ridge and Shenandoah.

Wiry Mike Kelley, twenty-one-year-old quote clerk, knew exactly how bad these numbers were: it was his job to go out on the floor and obtain quotes, then to plug in his headset underneath the shining globe at one of the posts and call such quotes up to the fourteenth floor, where they could be relayed back to the brokerage houses. Mike had been on the floor two years. He knew all the symbols, the posts, many of the brokers. Some of them tipped him $5 a week, apiece. On a good week, he'd augment his $15 salary by $100—big money for a young man.

He and the gang would spend most of it nightclubbing through Hoboken or Harlem, but he still had saved a tidy sum. Life was terrific for a young guy on the Street. In back of the Curb on Greenwich Street there were a dozen speakeasies: when he was sent into one of them to give a broker a message, he'd often get a free drink and lunch for his trouble. All of them were high livers, and even if quote clerks were low down on the pecking order, they enjoyed certain privileges just like the peacocks, such as eating breakfast at the neighborhood joint in the morning and signing their names on a chit to be paid on Fridays.

Today was something special. Today the brokers, even his friends, were pushing and shoving on the floor. A man with a 20,000-share order had knocked him down in his rush to get to a post and sell those shares. Some of these brokers were former college football players whose fathers had bought them seats; some were even ex-boxers who'd taken their winnings and somehow managed to get seats and become respectable. But today they were all acting like animals!

Things were getting hectic for Chuck Gabay, marking the board at Blyth and Bonner's 50 Broad Street office. Every trading day for a year Chuck had taken a piece of chalk and a wet chamois rag and marked the latest fractions for the various stocks. He and another guy got quotes from the Trans-Lux or the ticker and changed the numbers according to the latest sales. Ordinarily they only had to change a fraction, say from $1/2$ to $5/8$, because for the most part the whole numbers stayed the same. Not this morning. Changes were coming so fast that the third boy, the relief who usually only helped out when one of the main two went to lunch, was working steadily with them. A quote came across on Montgomery Ward—Monkey Ward, everyone called it—and it was down from 83 to 79, a huge drop. Chuck marked it up automatically. He had to do it fast, not think about them or his mind would get tripped out of the fast writing he had to do. But this quote produced a change in the room. People began to laugh. "That must've been a mistake," someone said. Then another Ward quote came over, and it was another drop. Chuck put it up, too, then heard a rough noise behind him: customers rushing to the selling windows, virtually trampling each other to get there quickly, because it had become obvious that every second counted.

Estelle McGovern, who worked the switchboard at Goldman, Sachs' 30 Pine Street office, had long understood that every second counted. Today she was glad she had been forced last year to memorize the names and numbers of hundreds of the firm's customers. Now, when senior partners such as Waddill Catchings (the genius behind Blue Ridge) wanted to call someone, she was able to save precious seconds by having the number in her memory and not having to look it up on a card. Business was frantic today, lots and lots of calls.

Estelle had been thinking that she had struck it rich: the company was good to her. Not only did it give Christmas bonuses of a year's salary, but of late it had been giving a bonus to employees whenever a new issue was floated—which, these days, seemed to be remarkably often.

A few yards away, Morton Jacobs sat on the runner's bench at Goldman, after coming over with a transaction from Hirsch, Lebenthal. To him the high-volume day meant just one thing: extra overtime and therefore extra pay. Half of the firm's runners were young (though not many were going to college at night as he was), and the others were retired police or firemen. One was even a retired actor. They were constantly on the run. Once Morty had to deliver an envelope with $10,000 in hundred-dollar bills in it; another time it was $100,000 worth of U.S. Steel stock certificates. Morton wished he held a few shares of "X," but thought, having heard the scuttlebutt today, that he'd be happy if the day's large volume helped to double his weekly salary to $30. There was a yell from somewhere in the office: "Blue Ridge dropping." A guy came by with a worried look on his face muttering something about automatic buy orders. Morton wasn't sure what all this was about, and he didn't care much, either. He simply waited for the ogre in the cage to call out his firm's name so he could get going to the next stop.

In the offices of Chase Securities Corporation, located with its parent bank at 70 Pine, Ruth Miller, the only secretary in the Trading Department, was doing something she'd never done in her life before: working on the trading desk. The switchboard was lit up like a Christmas tree, and every extra person counted. Ruth took a sell order on the phone—there were hardly any of the other kind, just now—and relayed it to the floor brokers for execution. This was so exciting, much more so than typing up confirmations of stock transactions: Ruth hoped it would keep up, at least for a while.

Some of the calls were about Chase Bank stock. "Where's Wiggin?" somebody was asking. "Why isn't he doing anything?" Ruth referred all such calls to the head trader of the department. Since the bank's stock was not listed on either Curb or Big

Board, the trading department here was constantly making a market for it, taking buy and sell orders in their own books. Ruth hoped the stock wouldn't fall. Just a week ago, on the advice of the vice-president of the department, she made her mother buy 10 shares of Chase at about $500 per. It was all the money Mother had in the world. Ruth wasn't too worried, though, because the veep had assured her that Chase was a good investment for "widows and orphans."

Alton Plunkett, who worked as an order clerk in a brokerage house, received a call from his brother, an employee of the National City Bank. The brother had heard that the firm's stock was dropping and asked Alton to sell his 25 shares of NCB for as close to last night's price of $450 as he could get. Alton got on the phone. NCB, being unlisted, was sold over-the-counter, which meant he was at the mercy of the various people who made a market in the stock. He called various brokers, trying to get a good price, then called his brother back—the best bid was $360, and he had been advised to take it or forget it.

"Take it. Get rid of it at any price," the brother said. Alton called back the broker who'd given him the price, but was only able to get rid of 10 shares at $300 each. It would be some time before they were able to get rid of the other 15 shares, and only God could tell what they'd bring.

Jack Ronger, who dealt in bank stocks for Normandie National Securities in a building near the Public Library uptown, had been getting calls from people like Alton since he got in this morning at 8:30. The market was thin, very thin, hardly any bidders at all—all sellers. Usually when one of his customers wanted to sell a bank stock, the fellows Jack worked with down the hall would take it in inventory if there wasn't an immediate buyer available. Not this morning. Normandie specialized in bank stocks, but even it couldn't take the kind of shellacking it would get if it took a stock in inventory today: with the market so thin, Normandie could get very badly stuck with a lot of stock for which there was no buyer.

Jack had lots of work to do. The company required 50 percent margin on bank stocks. This was regular practice on bank stocks. In past years when Jack worked for a NYSE brokerage firm, he had seen instances where, if a margin clerk knew you personally, you could put down much less on a stock—25 percent, 10 percent, even in some cases nothing, if you were well known to the firm. He himself had used 10 percent margin at times.

Now such small margins were collapsing back on their foundations. Jack was busy making margin calls, even at 50 percent. One was really important and difficult: a guy who had bought 100 shares of NCB at 480—and had thought it a bargain since it had been at 520 a few days before—hadn't yet paid a cent on the stock, which meant Normandie was currently $48,000 in debt on that purchase. NCB was dropping. Jack called the man to come over with the money, all of it, now, but the man stalled. Jack was forced to tell him that they would have to buy him in at whatever the market was, and sue him for the difference, if he didn't show up right away—a painful call, but absolutely necessary. Would he come in? Jack couldn't be sure.

Bank stocks were falling all over town: National City, Chase, Bank of U.S., Chatham-Phenix. Curiously, Transamerica, a holding company for banks that was listed on the Curb, was staying strong—old Amadeo P. Giannini out in San Francisco must have been buying like mad to keep the price up.

Jack's employer, A. E. Lefcourt the builder, had a dream he'd just announced: to build an edifice taller even than John J. Raskob's Empire State Building. It was an era of real estate dreams, of things rising straight up. Madison Square Garden was buying the rights to the air over part of Pennsylvania Station for an outdoor sports arena. Down on St. Marks in the Bouwerie, plans had been recently announced for four eighteen-story buildings of thirty-six duplex apartments each, to be designed by Frank Lloyd Wright in the shape of inverted cones, pyramids of glass, copper, and concrete with steel furnishings. National City Bank had announced plans to finance, in conjunction with the United States Realty and Improvement Company, new buildings, not by bonds but by shares of stock. Two apartment houses, at a cost of $3,937,500, were under construction with this plan, of which the staid *New York Journal of Commerce* had said: "A more arresting indication of the disfavor into which bond issues have fallen could hardly be conceived."[10]

So why shouldn't Lefcourt dream? The Brill Building sat on the corner of Forty-eighth and Broadway, and he would take possession of it from the brothers Brill in March. Then, using part of the income from Normandie's sale of bank stocks, he'd finance and erect the building. He'd done it with buildings in the garment center, so why not with a really magnificent skyscraper?

On the ground floor of a building in the garment district, in a branch office of Ira Haupt and Company, clerk Bill Gordon could hardly believe what he was seeing. People had been crowding themselves more and more into the customers' room, since the opening bell. Most of them were Jewish and worked in the area. They were standing with their eyes glued to the Trans-Lux and the board. More people were coming in every moment—how could there be any work getting done elsewhere, if everyone was in here? A steady line moved continually up to the selling windows where he and other clerks were taking orders. Today was Bill's twenty-eighth birthday, and he could see the evening's plans falling apart already. At the rate things were going, he'd be too exhausted for the party that was planned.

Edwin Lefèvre reports that

> Every one of the hundreds of branch offices in New York had its crowd. I paused by several of them that morning, and, on my word, not once did I hear a single victim tell his neighbor his tale of woe. This struck me as the unbelievable limit of suffering. . . . I visited a dozen offices and nowhere did I see the hysterical melodrama that people always expect . . . at such times. Perhaps the customers were packed too tightly to permit emotional outbursts. . . . Here and there some would grin (at bad news)—the only kind of grin that men can negotiate in public at such a time—and you somehow felt that these were married men, prematurely minimizing the damage, rehearsing for that evening at home.[11]

One of those not-so-silently rehearsing was Julian Sherrod, stocks and bonds salesman for the National City Company in Mobile, Alabama. He learned from a phone call that the over-the-counter price on the bank's own stock was dropping terribly, and he was heartsick. The ace salesman had held out as long as he could, but he had finally succumbed to the same mania he had so successfully transmitted to his own clients—he had bought four shares of NCB on time and was now on the hook for them. Just yesterday, the shares had been worth about $10,000, on an initial investment of about $1,000! But Sherrod hadn't paid them off—oh, no, not him. He had, by pledging the NCB shares as equity, pyramided a little empire: $75,000 worth of stocks on margin, plus an expensive home. Now, with one phone call, he could see his whole edifice of credit crumbling steadily, implacably. He made other calls, to see how the stock was doing. Down, ten, twenty points at each sale. He calculated swiftly in his head: he could easily lose everything—home, stocks, and all—by nightfall. The phone rang again, and he wasn't sure he wanted to pick it up.

Bea Hupp, from her post in the telephone company's headquarters in Chicago, was trying to be pleasant to the broker at the other end of the phone, but it wasn't easy. A flood of obscenities was coming through at her. On ordinary days these brokers were impatient, with their special calls that went to five or six people in Chicago at once ("Hello, Joe?"—"Hello, Bob?"—"Jim here."), but this was unbelievable! Bea was beginning to hate them all, for their uncouthness, for the way they would call up the supervisor and yell when one of their calls didn't get an answer. Bea's throat was parched from talking, yet she couldn't get a drink of water because it was too busy for her to leave her post. Was it her fault that people all over were too busy to answer the phone? There was nothing Bea could do about their complaints: the supervisor had forbidden any of them to talk back to the brokers, no matter how obnoxious the men became. Now that she thought of it, Bea was also angry at the huge sums of money the phone company was collecting from the brokers each month for these special lines, angry because the company paid her only $15 a week, and would hire her only after inquiring whether she could live with a relative who could help out financially. They knew darn well nobody could live in Chicago on $15 a week! A rumor came from one of the other girls that there were brokers jumping out the windows at the terrible market news. "Let 'em jump," Bea thought, "and don't stop 'em!"

Up in the brokerage house on the eleventh floor of the new Chicago Board of Trade building, accountant Don Himebaugh felt he was getting caught in an avalanche of paper work. There were so many accounts to be balanced. Everything was falling apart. Not only were stocks down on the New York exchanges,

but those on the Midwest Exchange downstairs and in the commodities pits were also down. Grigsby-Grünow, Ceco, Wextark,
even Zenith and Auburn Motors (one of the highflyers) were
dropping from moment to moment. Ceres, the Roman goddess
of agriculture whose statue adorned the building, must be completely shocked by the drop in wheat prices. Yesterday, the
worst day since the war ended, the price of December wheat futures dropped four cents on the whole day. Today, within a half
hour of opening it dropped another four points! Wild scenes were
taking place in the wheat pit, people who had been downstairs
said. It was the kind of trading that hadn't been seen since Cutten and Livermore were chasing each other around a few years
ago. For that matter, there was a strong rumor that Cutten was
at it again. In Winnipeg, a "well-known grain speculator" was
selling 10 million bushels, driving the price down. Right here in
Chicago, brokers were wrestling with several half-million bushel orders—indigestible hunks that had to come from big traders.
Silk, rubber, burlap, rawhide, coffee, cotton, sugar—all were
down, and everyone at Winthrop, Mitchell was running around
trying to keep up with the volume of the work. Maybe Mr. Illian,
the office manager, would come around to the eleventh floor tonight with handfuls of dollar bills to be awarded for staying late.

On the eleventh floor of the Terminal Tower Building in
Cleveland, the Paine, Webber office was busier than usual. People were rushing in and out all the time. Although the Cleveland
Stock Exchange was having a relatively quiet day—perhaps because of the requirement that all investment in stocks listed
only on that exchange be paid for in full, with no margin allowed—the Paine, Webber office, tied in to New York and Chicago, was busy. Every time teen-aged elevator operator Tommy
Murphy stopped at the floor, he noticed people moaning and
groaning about the news. At ten o'clock—eleven in New York—
the ticker was a half-hour behind the action. Such news didn't
sit well with Tommy—what was all the fuss about? Elevator
boys didn't make enough money to have anything to do with
stocks. Tommy had the glimmer of an idea. Now, each time he
stopped on the eleventh floor to pick up passengers from Paine,
Webber, he called out in a loud, clear voice, *"G O I N G
D O O O W W W W W N N N N N N N N !"* It wasn't
long before the brass sent word to him to keep quiet.

In the Union Trust building in downtown Pittsburgh, maintenance man Victor McClain was working as fast as he could. The building, which had many brokerage offices, was patterned architecturally after the cylindrical design of a Belgian cathedral: twelve floors high, with a large light well extending down the middle from skylight to lobby. On each floor, the boardrooms of the brokerage offices were like auditoriums, with long and wide-open exits going out towards the light well, which was bordered by a waist-high railing. The reason Vic was working so hard—aside from the fact that hard work ran in the family and that he was glad to have any job at all—was that yesterday, the employees of Moore, Leonard and Lynch had witnessed a tragedy: Homer Rossiter, fifty-six, stock speculator, after seeing his investments dissolved before his eyes, had fled the boardroom and had gone over the railing, to his death.

When Vic had come in early this morning, he and another maintenance man had been told to get to work with wire mesh and erect guards over the railings throughout the whole building so no one else could jump. It was slow work, but Vic was engrossed in it. Then a loud noise from the Key Richards office made him turn his head. A secretary came out screaming: one of the customers had put a bullet through his head! Vic wanted to stop what he was doing and go and see if anything could be done, but a glance exchanged with his partner told him he'd better keep on working. No telling what would happen next.

While waiting for his shift as a pharmacist to begin at noon at Kinsel's (largest-volume store in the States, open twenty-four hours, seven days), Art Garson had wandered down to the Paine, Webber office of Detroit to see what was doing. A small trader, he knew many of the office people there. The place was absurdly crowded.

Art saw something on the board that he liked: Inspiration Copper at 22. This summer it had been at 66—what a buy! He told the customers' man to get him 100 shares of Inspiration at the market, that he had the cash.

"We'll carry you for five points," said the customers' man. "Now get the hell outa here, this is no place for you today."

"Why not?"

"You see those two middle-aged ladies standing in the back? The ones in the blue coats?" '

"They seem very quiet," Art observed.

"You remember I got you in on Standard Gas and Electric at eighty last February, when it rose from twenty-one?" said the customers' man.

"Yup. I sold it at eighty-three—I was afraid of it, but I sure felt like a fool when it went to two hundred and forty-three."

"Right you are. Well, this lady, a retired schoolteacher by the way, the other one's her companion—we told her to get out of it at the end of the summer, but she wouldn't. She had a tremendous profit then, but it was all margined. Today we had to sell her out, and at that, she'll owe us plenty."

"Whew. What's the quote on Standard now?"

"One sixty-seven and dropping."

Art made his way back into the crowd, wondering what he'd get the Inspiration at. The ladies in blue coats just stood there, not saying a word, watching the Trans-Lux.

All over the country things were happening fast, and badly. In brokerage offices, board boys began to ignore the ticker—it was too far behind to help. Morse code was used to get information from New York. The bond tickers and Dow-Jones wires were slavishly followed where they were available. But help was, for the most part, not there. Telephone lines were down all over the Midwest from yesterday's ice storm, and people couldn't get through to their brokers, just as their brokers were having difficulty getting through to main offices in New York and Chicago. Information—that precious commodity in the midst of a crisis—was not getting through. In whole areas of the country, investors and stock speculators alike felt themselves to be working in the dark, unable to find out what was going on with their particular stocks on the faraway exchanges of New York and Chicago. Fortunes and life-styles might be slipping away, or they might not—it could be a temporary setback—but the point was, people didn't know.

The talk in most offices in the Midwest was not of the ice storm, or of the downed power and phone lines, but of the stock market. In most middle-class offices it seemed that everyone had money in the market in one way or another, and now everyone was miserable.

The sufferers could be divided into two groups. The first consisted of those whose brokers had already sold them out. They could be found commiserating with each other about the money they'd lost. Fifty thousand, twenty thousand. But wasn't much of that on paper? Yes and no. It was on paper if you had put in ten, had seen it go up to a hundred, and had been merely left with ten after the sale. But it was sure *not only* on paper if you had predicated on that money a life-style that was as real as a second car and/or a bigger house, and/or the money you'd been counting on to put the kids through college. It was not only paper if you had lost, through being sold out, the ninety in profits, but also—because you now owed the brokerage firm—that first ten, or a part of it. Suppose that ten was everything you had saved in your life thus far? Suppose it was your life's savings that was earmarked to tide you over for a time when you might be out of a job, or needed to get away for a vacation, or—anything? One might think oneself miserable, until one looked over at the second group.

In that other group were men (and some women) whose brokers had wired or phoned them for more margin money, and who were right now on the telephones busily trying to *borrow more money*—on their life insurance, on their homes, on whatever—in order to meet the margin calls. Bad as the first group's situation was, the people of the second group were far worse off because they were going deeper into debt! What if the darn stocks kept going down? What would those people do then? Where would they be? Maybe the first group wasn't so bad off after all. At least, most of them had a few bucks left after having been sold out. The ones on the phone right now might soon have nothing left at all.

The sun was up, now, all over the United States. The working day was well under way even in California, and the story was much the same. On the Los Angeles streets there was commotion; on the San Francisco stock exchanges—the city had a big one and a Curb—trading had not yet begun, but there was turmoil in brokerage offices where board boys had started writing at seven, and customers had come in before breakfast to see what was going on three thousand miles away. In North Dakota a billboard-space salesman read an electric sign in a newspaper's window that told him something was happening; in Texas, the head of the ice office for an oil company got in his car and frantically ran stoplights and eluded questioning policemen in a rush to get to a broker in Dallas before he was sold out. It was the same all over.

Glenn H. Elder, Jr., argues that the only meaningful transformations, in people or in groups, take place under the impact of profound events that cause crises. Crises, Elder says,

> reveal the inner workings of group life . . . the unquestioned premises and problematic features. To study crises . . . is to explore the incipient process of adaptation and change.[12]

At this moment in time, the unquestioned premises and problematic features of the United States' civilization were meeting head on with an event that was compelling to crisis, and the future of that civilization was hanging in the balance.

Chapter Seven

AFFAIRS OF THE CAPITAL
11:00 A.M.

In Washington, the nation's capital, at 11:00 A.M. on the morning of the twenty-fourth, it was business as usual—which, as far as the rest of the nation was concerned, meant quite a bit of talk and little action. The center was in New York, not in a provincial Southern town of great racial discrimination, a plethora of horses, and ineffectual governmental officials. The bureaucracy was small, centralized, and the city had not really spread beyond the tidy boundaries envisioned by architect L'Enfant.

At the Federal Reserve Board, an important meeting had begun at 10:45. Across the street from the White House, in a pile of stone with Victorian excesses, were the offices of Secretary of State Henry Stimson, Secretary of War James Good, and Secretary of the Navy Charles F. Adams, with their respective staffs, all under the same mansard roof.

At State, bags of mail from the more than four hundred overseas posts were being opened, having been rushed here off the decks of steamers by special trains from New York, ahead of ordinary mail. News from Russia would have told of the impending fiftieth birthday celebration for Joseph Stalin; today in Palestine a meeting was to be held about a bloody Arab-Jewish dispute that threatened to upset British sovereignty; things were heating up on the Sino-Soviet border, as well. Venezuela had become the fifty-fourth (out of sixty-four) nations to ratify the Kel-

119

logg-Briand pact to outlaw war, as earlier this morning Señor Don Carlos Grisanti had deposited his country's instrument at State. Secretary Good's department announced at an early conference that the Army Air Corps was that day ordering $1.5 million's worth of planes and parts from Douglass Aircraft, Curtiss Aircraft, and another smaller company. The Secretary of War—who was dying—and several other Cabinet members were concerned with plans for the afternoon's trip to New York by train for a special Republican party dinner that coming evening.

The House of Representatives was planning only a three-minute meeting at noon to disperse bills to committee. The Supreme Court, without a building of its own, was meeting in the old Senate chamber for one of its early fall sessions.

In the District of Columbia Supreme Court, Justice Hitz was charging the jury in the trial of former Secretary of the Interior Albert Bacon Fall, the wheelchair-ridden Westerner who, it was claimed, had taken a bribe from an emissary of Edward L. Doheny in 1921. The case was the parting shot in the Teapot Dome scandal. Fall, a friend of Teddy Roosevelt and a senator in the Wilson Administration, was appointed by Harding to Interior because the post was supposed to go to a Westerner and an out-of-doorsman. The Harding Cabinet did much business on the basis of old friends and companionable comrades, and Fall's bribe from Sinclair and Doheny had come easily and had sat well. Fall was not a wealthy man in 1921. His ranch at Three Rivers, New Mexico, to which he had hoped to retire, was run-down, and back taxes were owing from 1912. Soon the ranch started looking better, back taxes were paid, and new parcels added. The prosperity of Fall's ranch attracted attention, and, after two years in office, Fall resigned from the Cabinet. Then the storm broke: many people had been paid off, much had been done in secret, and someone had to be culpable. Fall and Doheny were first indicted in 1924. In 1927, when Fall and Sinclair were put on trial together, Fall became ill, and Sinclair was tried alone. This ended in a mistrial when Sinclair tried to influence the jury—an offense for which he was now serving a short sentence—but Sinclair was later acquitted of paying the bribe. So was Doheny. Was it possible that Fall could then be convicted of taking a bribe when the purported bribe-payers had been acquitted? On October 25, 1929, the jurors would answer: yes; it was the spirit of the times.

The day's other most interesting action was in the Senate, which had begun meeting at ten, with seventy-five members on the floor, a few in committee meetings where a famous lobbyist was shortly to be heard, three ill, one dying. The business was brisk: short mention of an ongoing investigation of the District of Columbia police, and a report on cancer research. Concerned about the hundred thousand cancer deaths annually—one out of every five women over forty, one out of every four men over forty—Senator Harris was begging the Senate to consider larger appropriations:

We spend hundreds of millions of dollars annually preparing for war and have spent millions to find a cure for hog cholera and other diseases of animals, but we have done nothing to find the cause and cure for cancer. . . . Even a small country like Belgium is spending more than $2 million annually.[1]

Then there was the request by C. S. Barrett, head of the National Farmers Union, to create an Industrial Art Commission under the aegis of the FTC, to regulate monopolistic practices of the motion picture industry. Motion picture industry? "The misleading impressions at times conveyed to the farmers' children of this country," wrote Mr. Barrett,

by pictures displayed in rural sections, show that one may walk off the farm and find in the city the luxuries and happiness unknown at home.[2]

Therefore, Mr. Barrett concluded, regulation was imperative.

Business continued. Senator Barkley begged leave to insert the President's important speech of last night into the *Record*. There was fulmination about a subsidiary of Electric Bond and Share doing nefarious work among the Flathead Indians in Montana to bamboozle them off a piece of property—nothing important, just what the FPC called "the most valuable undeveloped water power in the United States." This was left hanging, as was a nasty charge by Senator Wheeler about big grain operators being bolstered by the Department of Agriculture to the detriment of northwestern wheat growers.

The big question of the day—indeed, of the year—was the tariff. Senator Blaine picked up where he had left off yesterday, discussing a single line in Bill HH2267, regarding whether the duty on casein (a milk by-product) should be raised to eight cents a pound or left where the House had pegged it, at 3½ cents.

The debate was heated, but the larger issue was whether there should be any increase in tariffs at all. A coalition of antitariff forces had been trying to create enough of a bloc all summer and fall to prevent passage of HH2267. On October 2, the coalition had won a test vote, defeating a proposed increase in the chemical tariff. After all, they had argued, taxable profits in chemical companies had risen from $90 million to $1.6 billion in six years, so why did chemicals need *more* protection? But yesterday, October 23, the antitariff coalition seemed to be coming apart. They could not hold the line on carbide rates; a large increase was voted. News of that vote, transmitted to New York, was believed to have caused a lot of yesterday's distress selling. People believed the vote presaged passage of HH2267 intact, which would have a decided adverse affect on the future balance of trade. High tariffs meant blows to Europe's economy. This morning's Senate debate wound up allowing an 87 percent increase in the tariff for casein, another blow to the antitariff people. This, too, affected the market, though in the midst of turmoil in New York no one could be exactly sure to what degree.

Foreign affairs affecting the market? That might have seemed unlikely to most Americans, but enlightened thinkers had been saying it for years. It had been so since the war. Armageddon's most enduring and crippling legacy was not the millions dead, nor the hundreds of thousands of acres ruined, nor even the chaos of an age come to an end. It was the complex, unstable jumble of nation-states that was Europe after Versailles.

Two terrifying ideas had prevailed at Versailles. The first, *divide and conquer*, that the bogey of Prussian military might could never rise again. Estonia, Latvia, Lithuania were restored to independence; Czechoslovakia, Yugoslavia, Austria, and Hungary gained independence for the first time; France took back the Alsace; Poland gained a corridor to the sea and separated the giant from East Prussia. All were asked to be politically stable and economically mature. It was impossible. By 1929 dictators had taken power in Hungary, Italy, Spain, Poland, Lithuania, and Yugoslavia and were threatening elsewhere, and tariff barriers had gone up in such profusion it was almost impossible to export goods from one country to another.

The second principle was *extract revenge.* During the war, much money had been borrowed that the Prussian giant could be defeated; now, the war over, somebody had to pay that money back, and that somebody was Germany.

There was a horrendous tangle. Great Britain had lent money to Italy and France while simultaneously borrowing it from the United States. At the war's end everybody had screamed for repayment. Virtually no one except crackpots thought to suggest that all debts be forgiven and forgotten, so that a war-torn continent could start to rebuild without additional burdens.

Great Britain started to pay the United States but found she could not collect from Italy and France directly. Instead, the British were granted a one-quarter share of what was due the victors from Germany, in the form of reparations. *Reparations*— the word was to haunt the world until it went up again in flames. The sum of reparations after Versailles was far more than Germany could pay from the proceeds of its own economy. So Germany, with full cognizance of the other nations, performed the time-honored feat of borrowing from Peter (America) to pay Paul (England, France, Italy). Hundreds of loans were secured from American private business, and the dollars that flowed in went to pay the creditors and to rebuild the German economy. If America would not forgive, it would nevertheless loan money as long as it got a decent return.

A period of wild inflation wiped out much of the savings of the middle class all over Europe in country after country right after the war. Montagu Norman of England and Benjamin Strong of the Federal Reserve Bank of New York became fiduciary firemen, putting out the brush fires in different countries—but always, the basis of fiscal sanity was American loans. As the European economies grew, they had to have markets for their goods, and Americans loaned money to Latin American and Far Eastern countries to buy the European goods.

And all of these loans were, of course, resold to the American buying public, which lapped them up quickly. One Prussian finance minister was heard to remark that hardly a week passed when an agent of one American bank did not call on him to offer financial aid. Another Bavarian village that had need of $125,000 for municipal improvements was convinced not to be a piker, and instead borrowed from America a whopping $3 billion.

In Latin-American capitals, representatives of the Chase and the National City would battle each other for the right to provide money—and also for the right to make wonderful profits from bonds sold to the voracious customers in the United States.

However, when the American stock market had gotten into the meat of its upward ascent, in 1927 and 1928, the faucet had begun to shut off for Europe and especially for Germany, because it was more profitable to buy stocks than to buy bonds. American loans to Germany dried up. The British stepped in and replaced American loans with ones of British sterling. Now the Germans were borrowing from Paul to pay Paul, in an even more absurd and complex tangle.

In the midst of the bond surge, the United States had erected formidable trade barriers in 1922, and was now trying to raise them even higher in 1929. The shaky economies of postwar Europe had cried "foul," but to no avail. The question, the fundamental question, remained: how could countries pay their war debts but through sending goods to us? And how could these goods come through if there were tariffs too high to be absorbed? "By restricting foreigners' ability to sell their goods in the United States," writes Jude Wanniski,

> the Republicans were making it more difficult for foreigners to pay off their debts to the U.S. and import goods from us. Over time, tariffs would, in essence, have the same inhibiting impact on investment and commerce as an increase in taxes.[3]

So the tariff was of vital importance to the economy, and especially to the situation on Wall Street. In the face of such logic, who could really want regressive tariffs? Plenty of people. One of the most important was being interrogated on October 24 by Senators Blaine (Wisconsin), Walsh (Montana), Chairman Caraway (Arkansas), and antitariff coalition leader Borah (Idaho) in a committee meeting well attended by the press. His name was Joseph "Uncle Joe" Grundy, sixty-seven-year-old head of the Pennsylvania Manufacturers' Association and the nation's leading lobbyist. "He is a bachelor," said *The New York Times*,

> but taking the place of wife and children is the doctrine of protection for American industry. He possesses a fortune of

of perhaps $20 million, but he would spend it all in the furtherance of something upon which he has set his heart, which is the welfare of the Republican party, particularly in Pennsylvania.[4]

Grundy was a startlingly frank witness. He admitted to the senators that he had been instrumental in raising tariff duties in the present bill in favor of Pennsylvania industries by about $500 million. It was his opinion that the tariffs ought to be as high as possible, and that the consumers of the United States had wanted them to be so, because if they hadn't, they would have voted for Al Smith and not for Herbert Hoover.

Grundy had put his money where his mouth was, had raised a million for Hoover in 1928. He told the senators he saw nothing wrong in having done so, nor in believing that he had some influence with the present administration because of it. Nor did he think such influence undue or improper—rather, it was his due. Which also brought up a pet peeve of his: did the committee realize, Grundy wanted to know, that taking the states represented by his inquisitors, and adding fifteen others, their combined income-tax payments to the United States government were still $5 million a year less than that of Pennsylvania alone? The industrially "backward" states of the West and South ought therefore, he said, to have less to say in the matter of what tariff rates were to be raised than the representatives of those states most directly affected. Senator Caraway, apoplectic, asked whether Grundy would decide representation in the Senate on the basis of wealth, instead of by states. "I would not say wealth," Grundy responded,

> but national interest. I think these Western Senators should talk darn small. I don't think they ought to have as much to say as Pennsylvania.[5]

Grundy's views were applauded as candid, blunt, outspoken, and honest—only a few thought the tenor of his remarks would lead to the transformation of a democracy into a plutocracy. Grundy stood for the manufacturers and the tariff, and, as he definitely thought, for the same things as did the Chief Executive.

Those, like Grundy, who felt that Hoover was entirely in their corner, never took the measure of the President.

The greatest administrator of his generation, Hoover was the man who had saved millions from starvation at the end of the war and shortly thereafter in the postwar poverty that ran through Europe like a scythe. "You have saved from death," Maxim Gorki wrote him, "3,500,000 children, 5,500,000 adults." In the early twenties, Franklin Delano Roosevelt had been after Hoover to run for the presidency as a Democrat. He didn't take the bait. He entered the Cabinet as Secretary of Commerce in 1921. Within a year he had transformed an obscure and thoroughly belittled department into a powerhouse. When Harding died, and was succeeded by Coolidge, Hoover was considered the very backbone of the Cabinet. Hoover was an important factor in Coolidge's re-election of 1924. Though many professional Republicans shrank from him, Hoover dominated the 1928 convention and, through grass-roots support of a kind seldom seen in American politics, received nomination on the first ballot.

His opponent, wet, Catholic, son-of-an-immigrant, Tammany Hall denizen and New York State Governor Al Smith, had an incredible number of strikes going against him when he stepped into the batter's box of 1928. Social workers worried whether they should vote that half of their conscience which told them Smith understood poverty-in-the-midst-of-abundance, or the half that knew alcohol to be the scourge of the earth—and, like Jane Addams of Hull House, voted for Hoover. So did nearly everyone else. Farmers didn't like Smith because he was of the city. Protestants didn't like him because he was Catholic; Hoover's campaign theme song was "Onward Christian Soldiers." Such diverse people as Eleanor Roosevelt and Bernard Baruch, working for Smith, could not believe the depth of hatred and vitriol in the campaign. It appeared that on many issues Smith and Hoover were in substantial agreement—both believed in and were supported by some Wall Streeters and big businessmen— but the country had become prosperous under the Republicans, and there were all those reasons for *not* voting for Smith. The election turned on which side of the American dream you preferred: that of the hardworking, farm-raised boy, the son of pioneers; or that of the guy with the accent of the big-city streets who brilliantly clawed his way out of the urban jungle to the top. Hoover won all but eight states. America's voice was loud and clear in 1928, and it was the voice of Herbert Hoover. The "unparalleled rise of the American man and woman," Hoover said,

> was not alone the result of riches in lands or forests or mines; it sprang from ideas and ideals, which liberated the mind and stimulated the exertion of a people. . . . Capitalism . . . is but an instrument, not a master. In the American system, we train the runners; the winner is he who shows the most conscientious training, the greatest ability, the strongest character.[6]

There was no doubt Hoover considered himself among the winners.

He averaged over twenty conferences with individuals, groups, and aides a day—at breakfast and lunch, if working hours were not enough. He was, one of his five secretaries wrote,

> a walking encyclopedia of governmental, fiscal, and agricultural information, either national or international. I have seen many a conferee leave his office in a daze. And I have heard some say, "Why, he knows more about my business than I do myself."[7]

To get on with business in the best way possible, everything was to be put down on paper. Memoranda from the five secretaries were to be signed in the typewriter and then initialed by hand. The President held fifty-nine press conferences prior to October 24, 1929, nearly ten a month. They were of three sorts: 1) direct quotes, 2) wherein reporters could ascribe thoughts to a "White House source" or a "high official of the administration," and 3) straight background, with nothing for attribution. The President was accessible. And yet as early as September, contemporary reporters were finding a problem arising with Hoover's secretaries and aides:

> Ackerson and Richey and Newton . . . together they constitute a sort of Chinese Wall behind which the President sits hidden from contact or conversation with all but the nabobs of the Republican Party, the Congress, and the people of the United States. [They] are, in some respects, the

Presidential stimuli, and in many ways he's quite dependent on the unselfishness of their service.[8]

A curious story about Hoover's childhood was making the rounds in Washington, told by both admirers and detractors. It seems that when Hoover was a small boy in Iowa, and his father was operating a barbed-wire factory, the elder Hoover had hit on the idea of covering steel strands with tar, and had built machinery for that purpose. One day "Bertie" tossed a flaming stick into the tar to see if it would burn; the ensuing conflagration nearly wiped out the town, as well as the plant. His father told neighbors that evening that it was an accident. Bertie said nothing, principally because he was not asked. Yet that night he lay awake thinking. He had, writes Rose Wilder Lane,

> done a frightening thing; the shock of it was still in his nerves and the crime of it on his conscience, but he had not meant to do wrong. He had been innocently experimenting, and the result was not entirely disheartening.

> "Anyway, I found out what it would do," he thought. "I found it out all by myself." He wondered if he would be punished if he told. He thought not. But he decided it was better to keep his own counsel in the matter. And for forty years he did so.[9]

To some, this showed Hoover's ability to face the bald facts on an issue, to keep his own counsel, to make up his own mind. To others, it showed vacillation, indecision, hesitancy about facing issues bordering on cowardice. Hoover was a puzzlement.

There was no doubt what he thought about stock speculation. He deplored it and had warned against it as far back as 1926, that it could "only land us on the shore of overdepression." Up until the day he became President he had insistently repeated that the Federal Reserve Board was promoting easy credit under the delusion that the country had become immune to financial crises. He foresaw

> inflation with inevitable collapse that will bring the greatest calamities upon our farmers, our workers, and legitimate business.[10]

As soon as he had been inaugurated, Hoover had pressed Andrew Mellon, Secretary of the Treasury, to declare that "bonds are low in price compared to stocks," had replaced the chairman of the Fed and had made sure that the new chairman, Roy O. Young, followed Mellon's remarks with a public appeal to all banks to go slow on speculative loans. This had resulted in the March crisis, resolved in favor of speculation by Charles E. Mitchell's statements and actions. In April and May of 1929 Hoover communicated with the publishers of several leading newspapers and urged that they start campaigns in their columns warning the public against stock speculation. A few cooperated. In June he turned the wrath of the Department of Justice on the bucket shops and tip sheets operating on the fringes of the markets in New York, to stop them from using the mails to defraud customers and stimulate speculation. This was, Hoover believed, the only legitimate weapon he had to regulate the fever. He hoped the exposure of the bucket shops, whose heyday was actually long since past, would open the eyes of the public to the ills of the market. Telephone calls in New York City decreased by 150,000 a day, and the press attributed this gladly to Hoover's drying up of the bucket shops and tipsters. But Hoover felt he could not be overly concerned with stock speculation. He had set up long-range commissions to look into the pressing problems of America: prohibition; child care; the probable sociological, racial, and economic trends for the United States for the next half-century. There was a Farm Board to be set up. There was the reapportionment of the legislative branch that would come after the next census in 1930, which promised to revolutionize the country. There was the tariff. There was crime in the streets: "Life and property are relatively more unsafe here than in any other civilized country in the world." And, says Hoover biographer Eugene Lyons,

the legal authority to curb the stock market rested in Albany, not Washington, and there Governor Franklin D. Roosevelt brushed aside all pleas for moderation. Until the day he resigned from his Wall Street law firm to run for Governor, FDR had been personally involved in the speculative fury as a stock promoter. His closest associates were people who genuflected before the Stock Exchange.[11]

At 11:15 on the morning of the twenty-fourth, Governor Franklin D. Roosevelt of New York was in Salt Lake City addressing a governors' conference, and President Hoover was still aboard his train, speeding towards Washington. Before the speech in Cincinnati on the twenty-second, Martin Egan had delivered to him the memorandum on the stock market by Thomas W. Lamont, senior partner of J.P. Morgan's. He had not had time to read it then, nor even yesterday. Now, he would.

The genesis of the Lamont memorandum was convoluted. Lamont and Hoover had known each other through the twenties. As late as a month ago, Lamont had sent the President a confidential assessment of Ramsay MacDonald's character for use in negotiations; last year Lamont had been instrumental in getting all the Morgan partners firmly into line behind Hoover's candidacy, when some of them had been wavering. In late September of 1929 Hoover had sent to New York Harry Robinson, president of the First National Bank of Los Angeles, and a trusted personal confidant, as his emissary to Wall Street. Hoover and Robinson had been friends for many years, had worked side by side at the Peace Conference at Versailles in 1919. Robinson's visit had many purposes, among them to assess the situation with regard to international banking, holding companies, investment trusts, and other weighty financial matters. Also he had been sent specifically to tell the bankers and stock market people to slow down, to somehow check the ridiculous, overinflated posture of the market in any way they could.[12] In response to a Robinson visit, Lamont had promised to prepare a memo instantly. The preparation had stretched out more and more, with apologetic notes from Lamont to Robinson all the while, and was finally in Hoover's hand.

Hoover read a meticulously prepared, closely argued eighteen-page letter which downplayed the destructiveness of the stock market situation, and said that "nature will effect necessary cures" in the speculation craze, and that there was no need for official correctives of any sort. "At the outset," wrote Lamont,

I can express the belief that, although certainly there are elements in the situation that have given us all pause and real concern as well; nevertheless, there is nothing in the present situation to suggest that the normal economic forces, working to correct excesses and to restore the proper balance of affairs, are not still operative and adequate.[13]

Lamont, in almost schoolteacherish and simplistic language, continued to explain to Hoover why he had come to such conclusions:

> Taking first the so-called protracted bull market in stocks: Certainly this has been an extraordinary and at times very disturbing phenomenon. To many sound people it has been even alarming. Yet every protracted market on either the up or the down side of the stock market (or of commodity markets, for that matter) has its excesses. It is often said that speculation has diverted credit from business; and has also aroused a sort of gambling spirit in the public. Neither of these statements is capable of clear proof or disproof. The first is, I think, quite certainly erroneous. . . . [and] What proportion of the total activities of the stock markets represents mere gambling, and what proportion represents legitimate speculation in adequately margined accounts, it would be hard to say.[14]

Such soothing language had not always been the meat of this memorandum. Earlier drafts were more radical, more bearish (as Lamont called them), and more hard-hitting. For example, compare the above quote with an earlier draft of the same part:

> The protracted bull market in stocks seems to have passed all bounds. I think it is diverting too much credit from business but above all it is diverting the attention of the people from their work to gambling.[15]

Lamont's handwritten notes in the margins of that paragraph in an early draft, expressing doubt and modification of the radical, thought-provoking language therein, are prelude to the warm milk of the finished document.

Hoover read the memorandum carefully and noted that Lamont had sent a copy to Robinson. Hoover made a note to ask Robinson what he thought about it. The whole thing was obviously the result of a series of compromises and rewritings which had taken some time and which pre-dated the alarums of the past week. An addendum on the bottom of the last page said:

The developments of the last few days in the stock market would seem to indicate that nature is already operating pretty vigorously.[16]

The Morgan partners, then, viewed the losing of fifty points in a month from the Dow-Jones averages as something quite reasonable, inevitable, and not the sort of thing that should overly concern a President's problem-filled head.

It was an instance—once again, for the millionth time—of more experienced money-men telling the politician that he did not really understand the forces at work on Wall Street, nor was he equipped to deal with them. To a Harding, or a Coolidge, even to a Wilson, this might perhaps have been a reasonable thing to say—but to the former Secretary of Commerce, a well-known businessman before he had entered government service?

If Hoover took the memorandum calmly, it may have been because, in part, he agreed with its sentiments, and even its biases, including those which seemed to imply he knew little about money matters.

Although he had been Secretary of Commerce before becoming President, Hoover relied, as did most of Washington, on advice in the financial management of the country's affairs from Andrew W. Mellon, "the greatest Secretary of the Treasury since Alexander Hamilton." Before Harding had appointed him to Treasury in 1921, Mellon had been the head of about a hundred corporations, his wealth so large as to insure the grandest of lifestyles. He had long since become America's greatest patrician: austere, small, with slim hands, impeccably dressed in some Edwardian conception of nobility. Work was a necessary aspect of life in which he himself indulged to a great degree, and expected others to do the same. In his industries, twelve-hour days were the norm. Union Steel had but two shifts in a twenty-four-hour day. The aluminum companies operated similarly. Crews setting out at dawn to sink holes for Gulf Oil were relieved only at sundown. Gulf's service station men worked for $75 a month, plus small bonuses on oil and grease jobs. In the mining towns along the Alleghany and Monongahela rivers, where conditions were described politely as squalid, Mellon himself had remarked that "miners' housing was on a level with that of Southern slaves." Mellon's industries consistently refused to deal with unions unless they absolutely had to, and then often used spies and the plants' private police forces to vitiate their impact.

During the war emergency, the government had been taking a large percentage of very large incomes: $663,000 out of a million dollars. Mellon, once in office, recommended to Congress that it repeal the excess profits tax (which had helped to finance the war), cut the income tax on large incomes to 40 percent immediately (and later to 35 percent), and declared that the country could have its choice: repeal of the excess profits tax, or payment of the veterans' bonuses. It couldn't have both. On incomes of less than $66,000 he proposed no tax decreases. It was Mellon's theory—also widely held by others—that the only way to stimulate business was to let the big entrepreneurs make money, which would create jobs. If you took away the incentive to make big money, aspiring businessmen and big ones bent on expansion wouldn't bother putting in the time and energy that would, in the end, create jobs and buying power; so, therefore, you had to let the wealthy make lots of money.

Senator La Follette commented that

Brazenly and impudently Mellon has laid down the principle that wealth will not and cannot be made to bear its full share of taxation.[17]

Harding signed the revenue bill nonetheless in November of 1921, at an estimated personal savings to Secretary Mellon and his family in the millions, for 1922 alone. In the years to follow, the prosperous years of the twenties, taxes on big incomes decreased markedly, an aggregate of nearly two billion dollars:

1921	$663 million
1924	$519 million
1926	$422 million
1928	$222 million

As the twenties crept on, Mellon aged, gave up golf and horses in favor of a brisk walk four times a day to and from his apartment on Massachusetts Avenue (upkeep, $20,000 a year as against his salary of $15,000 a year) to his office, ate ever more sparsely, and puffed nervously on his little black cigars. He fumed at the efforts of the Progressive and Democratic coalitions of the midtwenties to foil his tax-cut programs for the wealthy:

> Assuming that all inheritances, large and small, were taxed at 40%, it could be only two or three generations until private ownership of property would cease to exist....Estate taxes, carried to an excess, in no way differ from the methods of the revolutionists of Russia.[18]

His senatorial opponent reminded him that fortune left to the children of millionaires had, in the children's lifetime, been tremendously expanded by investments: Alexis I. Du Pont had left $30 million, but his children now held half a billion. The more violent the attacks on Mellon from La Follette et al., the more adulation he got from the business leaders. Mellon had virtually outranked Harding. Mellon and Coolidge were close allies and perhaps even friends. He grew in popular stature and political clout.

In 1924, at the convention which selected Coolidge, delegates had risen to their feet to applaud Mellon as he came to the platform. He was the man behind prosperity, the symbol of an age of financial wizardry. Since then his prestige had grown, even as prosperity had grown (and just as his family's corporate assets had grown from $1,690,000,000 in 1921 to $6,091,000,000 in 1928). With Hoover, Mellon had long been a rival, a fellow Cabinet member competing with others for a president's time. Mellon had even flirted with the presidency in 1928, but had been badly betrayed at the convention when the Pennsylvania political bosses in a burst of independence threw their votes behind the obvious winner. Hoover had had to reappoint Mellon, but put his own man, Ogden L. Mills, in as Under-Secretary (to Mellon's chagrin) and consulted Mills quite a bit. He also appointed IRS and Federal Reserve people whom Mellon did not particularly like, and the powerful Secretary had progressively less and less to do with those departments. Perhaps Hoover had done this because he knew of Mellon's rather special relationship with IRS in the past: Gulf had paid $10 million in taxes during 1915–1919; Mellon had nearly $4 million of that quietly refunded. He also did some shady things with his own personal taxes. At Mellon's request an underling in IRS had prepared for the Secretary a list of a dozen ways in which the Mellons could avoid some taxes. Pleased with the list, Mellon then had a Treasury Department tax expert assigned to work on his personal returns, and used five of the recommendations from IRS, including the recording of fictitious gifts and losses, to reduce tax liability. He was also generous with his friends' corporations, which received tax rebates amounting to many hundreds of millions during the 1920s' great prosperity. An investigating committee later commented that

> the oil industry generally...has received excessive allowances for depletion, but the allowance to Gulf Oil Company...is so excessive as to constitute a gross discrimination against even the oil industry.[19]

When asked later about such things, Mellon said he was unaware that his companies had been the beneficiaries of tax rebates. While this may possibly have been true in the strictest sense, there is no doubt that Mellon understood point by point what good high tariffs were doing to his industries, especially aluminum: public outcries in 1924, 1925, and 1928 were unmistakable. Long before taking office, Mellon had set up a pattern of practice for companies which largely dominated one field and which were tending towards monopoly as a regular business practice. A complaint against the Aluminum Company of America charged that they were

1. acquiring all bauxite deposits where there might be competition.
2. acquiring water power or riparian rights that might furnish opportunity for competition.
3. preventing others from entering the aluminum business by representing itself as in total control of the market.
4. controlling the market for foreign aluminum in the United States by tariffs.
5. transferring aluminum to subsidiaries (such as those making household appliances) below cost of production to make competition impossible.
6. selling some aluminum alloy products at less than cost or less than competing producers can afford to sell and make a profit, in order to drive them out of business.

The Federal Trade Commission's investigation into Aluminum spanned the entire history of the Harding, Coolidge, and Hoover administrations up to this time. In October of 1929, six months after it had finished its last hearings, no report had yet been issued, but one was confidently expected very soon.

Things were looking ever better for the Secretary on October 24: Gulf would pay only about $5 million in taxes on profits of $44 million this year; Rockefeller's new Center in New York, shortly to be erected, was going to order 3 million pounds of aluminum to cover a sixth of the exterior surface of ten buildings; Mellon's nine major firms were going to report a gross profit of $230 million this year.

If Mellon was worried about the stock market—two years ago he had said that brokers' loans were a good indication of health, and they were now enormous and unhealthy—he said little about it in public, and in the corridors of power did virtually nothing to stem speculation. He did privately admit that speculation was going too high, but felt that a public admission of this would cause the bubble to burst disastrously. Privately he was worried more about inflation, but the curious thing was, in this era of prosperity, that prices seemed to stay stable—and that meant, to Mellon, that things were all right.

The Federal Reserve Board, of which Mellon was nominally the head, was meeting, and Mellon knew they were discussing the stock market situation. He did not attend the meeting. America was a nation of rugged individualists, in Mellon's view: you made your own decisions, took your profits when and where you could, suffered losses when they were inevitable, and rolled with the punches. He had done so, everyone else ought to do so.

If the Federal Reserve Board appeared to be doing little, there were numerous reasons. First, the Board had little power, even in regard to the few national banks it could, in some ways, regulate. The vast majority of banks in the country were state banks, which were not under the Board's aegis. Adolph Caspar Miller, a member of the Board since its inception under Wilson, was the Board's only professional economist. "Neither the Federal Reserve Board nor the Federal Reserve Banks," said Miller

are composed of men who are economists or financial statesmen in the sense that they have had much training that qualifies them to develop systematically, and long in advance of an actual urgent situation, the proper methods of dealing with them. For the most part what is done is done because someone feels uncomfortable about what is transpiring and what he thinks may develop. I should say that action by the Federal Reserve Board usually lies midway between a deliberate or calculated action, such as is taken with full appreciation of the consequences, and what you might call unconscious action.[20]

Other Board members were Charles S. Hamlin, George R. James, Edward Cunningham, Edmund Platt, and the new governor, Roy O. Young, recently appointed by Hoover. Young was fond of saying that he felt the Board did its work as well by silence as by crying wolf. The use of Federal Reserve credit for speculative purposes was specifically precluded by well-enumerated provisions of the Federal Reserve Act. Yet Federal Reserve Banks in many cities, and their own client banks, were—obviously to all—lending money right and left for speculative uses. Miller, who as far back as 1925 had said publicly that

It is not the duty of the Federal Reserve System to undertake to regulate stock speculation, or other speculation, or to interfere unnecessarily in the affairs of member banks.[21]

had just as publicly admitted that the Fed had no specific machinery with which to bring Federal Reserve Banks, or any others, into line. The Board's primary task was as an aid to industry, agriculture, and commerce by providing a system of liquid productive credits. The Board's stance against speculation was well known; or, at least, its apparent stance was known, as in the March episode of the shoot-out at Charlie Mitchell's corral. Adolph Miller and Herbert Hoover were old friends, S Street neighbors, confidants; Governor Young had been appointed by Hoover to kick out the old Harding crony who had previously held the job of titular head of the board.

With a concerted effort, it is possible that some combination of Chief Executive and Federal Reserve Board might have been able to persuade the Justice Department that if banks were specifically contravening the enabling statutes of the Board, there might be some prosecutable offense—with an end result of definitively curbing speculation by cutting off credit. Even a threat of prosecution might have moved things away from dead center. Impressive support in Congress might well have crystallized around a figure such as Senator Carter Glass, or Representative MacFadden, who knew the Board's machinery, and who knew how to get things done in Congress.

There is no evidence that any such course was considered at any time. The Board, though, had been contemplating the stock market situation for many months.

By 11:15 on October 24, the governor and other members were in virtual continuous telephonic communication with New York. And Dr. Goldenweisser, director of the Division of Research and Statistics, was leading a discussion which put the present problem into a long-term perspective. As Assistant Secretary McClelland noted down, Goldenweisser thought

the System should be more definitely guided by long time trends than by seasonal or other brief developments, predicating its actions upon its primary function . . . of providing a flow of bank credit adequate to meet legitimate demands, ordinarily at reasonable rates.[22]

Goldenweisser stressed the necessity of taking into consideration international as well as domestic developments, and pointed out that there was a worldwide shortage of capital, which ought to be the focus of the Board's concern. The fact that member banks were nearly constantly in the debt of Reserve banks worried him: that wasn't good, and the Board should take steps to prevent this from happening.

Goldenweisser's concerns were put aside for the moment to consider the news from New York, from bankers such as Lamont, and from Governor Harrison of the New York Federal Reserve Bank, who sounded especially worried. The Reserve Bank in New York wanted to do several things: reduce its buying rate on bank acceptances; purchase more government securities; and most importantly, reduce the discount rate of the bank, an action generally understood to mean an easing of credit.

Ease credit? It was widely assumed, both within the present Board and without, that the easing of credit by the Federal Reserve Board in the pre-Hoover years had led directly to speculation and the present bad situation. Other people merely pointed out that credit had been eased as an inevitable consequence of trying to deal with the international problems Goldenweisser had mentioned. On May 11, 1927, the Fed had held $253,896,000 in currency, and began easing credit to export gold and "help Europe." Bank acceptances were at $183,217,000 at that time. By January 4, 1928, banks held $627,403,000 as well as acceptances of $387,131,000, and Europe's gold situation was much better. But there was also more speculation, because the eased federal credit had enabled banks to ease their own credit to those who wanted to use the money in the market.

The loosening of credit had continued virtually until the time Hoover had been elected, and then tightening had begun. From 3½ the rate went to 4, 4½, 5, up to 6 percent in an effort to stem speculation. There were some who continually objected to this, who believed eased credit had nothing to do with speculation but that *tightening credit was badly hurting small businessmen and the basic economic structure.* Governor Harrison of New York had been tilting at the Board to get it to ease credit since much earlier in the year, ostensibly for these reasons. But every time the New York Bank would vote an easing of credit, their decision would be overridden by the Board as being a further stimulus to speculation, so credit stayed tight and even got tighter. The curious thing was that speculation seemed to grow anyhow. Now the New York Federal Reserve Bank was asking for credit to be eased—with alarm. Why? Wouldn't that send speculation through the ceiling? How could you do that in the midst of a crisis?

Because, the facts from New York argued, banks and brokerage houses were being squeezed and threatened: people were either 1) not answering their margin calls, or 2) defaulting on loans secured with stock.

Both of these happenstances meant that the banks and brokerage houses were losing money hand over fist, right that very second. Easing credit would enable local banks to borrow easily from the Federal Reserve Bank, and, in turn, to lend money more generously to brokerage houses, which in turn could lend more money to frazzled investors who needed it to protect their stocks.

Putting it another way, if $100,000 worth of Montgomery Ward was blowing away, half or three-quarters of that was a broker's money—and that broker had borrowed it from a bank, so it was in reality a bank's money. If such money were allowed to disappear, both the brokerage house's and the bank's financial security would be weakened. Those institutions, New York was arguing, could not be allowed to be hurt, and so, therefore, New York was urging the lowering of the bill rate.

But the New York people would not make a formal request until the afternoon. So amidst the reports of the air holes, and the reports that people all over the country were sending in virtually continuous sell orders, the Fed tabled the issue for a while.

Stacks of telegrams assaulted Andrew Mellon's desk; multitudinous phone calls from the important and the unimportant were turned away, but continuous telegraphic communication was established between the Secretary's office and a select group of men in New York's financial center.

Reporters had started to camp at Mellon's door, at the door of the Fed, at posts in Congress, at the train station to await Hoover. Senators and representatives took time out from their labors to call their own brokers, to look for tickers near the Hill. They asked questions of the reporters and began to issue statements of alarm and wonder.

Was anybody in Washington going to do anything? Could anything be done?

Chapter Eight

PANDEMONIUM EXPRESS
11:30 A.M.

"In all bull markets," Edwin Lefèvre writes,

> you will notice that promoters can and do sell to the public
> what they would not dream of trying to sell them in normal
> times, when they have to deal with investors. . . . Much
> more than people realize, the American imagination has
> been responsible for the excesses witnessed in every bull
> market. We cannot be the most imaginative people on earth
> and not pay for it.[1]

At 11:30 A.M. on the trading floor of the New York Stock Exchange there was pandemonium. Careful ties, pretty gardenias,
expensive handmade gray suits—all were being mangled as
brokers and clerks collided with one another, fought for split
seconds to get ahead, tried to conduct their urgent business as
the sky appeared to be falling in on them. Orders overflowed
their temporary containers by the posts, and wastebaskets were
brought in to handle the slips of paper. The ticker, the heartbeat,
was 48 minutes late, or, at this hectic moment, was registering
the prices of 10:42 A.M., a time when, compared to now, things
were still relatively stable. Air holes were all over the place.
Brokers cried out their sell orders, and for many moments at a
time there were no takers—none at all. Prices were dropping
faster than most could believe. Only a few on the floor had been

141

there in the panic of 1907. Nobody could believe this sort of thing was happening. Mass dumpings, panics, and chaos were all supposed to have been legislated out of existence. They had not been. They were here. Now.

At that moment, we were paying for our imagination. The battle was symbolized for many by the fight near Post 2, where U.S. Steel Common—"X" on the ticker—was being traded. Steel had opened at 205$^1/_2$, a reasonably strong price. But, since opening, it had been working its inexorable way down, by eighths and quarters—just as it had since a high of 245 in September—towards the magic figure of 200. Should the price drop below 200, many people believed the psychological impact would be disastrous. They argued that should this happen, the public would feel that the bottom of the American economy had dropped out, and everyone would sell indiscriminately, making values meaningless. If Steel crashed down through 200, the apocalypse was rumored near.

The twelve specialists in Steel had some discretionary powers, given them by large investors, to buy blocks of the stock if they felt the need to defend the price. That morning they bought, they defended, but by 11:30 their discretionary reserves seemed exhausted. Steel crashed through the 200 barrier to 199$^1/_2$ and kept going down.

The news traveled over the floor quickly, the frenzy intensified. People rushed to sell Steel and other stocks before they got hurt much more. Not only were the brokers selling the public's stocks at this hour, they were also selling their own. *Sell* was the order of the day, and sell they did.

Each event multiplied the previous one. People became frantic. A temporary annoyance of five minutes ago became a major source of pain; that pain became fright; that fright blossomed into panic. A weird roar surged from the trading floor and could be heard outside a block away from the Exchange: several thousand people, in a kind of extreme agony. A reporter described it as the cry of a mortally wounded beast. The aggregate market value of all the shares listed on the Exchange that morning at 10:00 A.M. had been over $80 billion—more than the total national wealth of many of the civilized nations of the world combined. Now, when the bottom was falling out, six or even eight of those billions had gone up in smoke—that was pain enough.

Richard Whitney, acting president of the Exchange at that moment, wrote later:

> In ordinary times, society is immersed in its detailed and momentary preoccupations; it placidly assumes that the economic forces of supply and demand which control both prices and production are in comfortable equipoise, and that—as the old song puts it—tomorrow will be as today. But when panic occurs, there is a sharp disillusionment of society as a whole, and a temporary absence of those customary assumptions upon the basis of which all normal life proceeds. All at once, the inconceivable terrors of the unknown and the unfamiliar are thrust upon the public mind; confidence is paralyzed, and until it is restored, chaos reigns.[2]

Above the floor, the visitors' gallery was jam-packed, as it had been since the opening, people waiting in lines four abreast to get in and see how fate wreaked havoc among the brokers—because, oh yes, they knew something exciting was going to be happening today. It had been in the air for the better part of a week. Some had taken in the Exchange's new public relations film *The Merchants of the Nation's Marketplace*, others had accepted one or several of the pamphlets prepared for visitors. It was a popular spot to be this day, more interesting than, say, Prospect Park Plaza where the one hundred and fiftieth anniversary of the first major engagement of the Revolutionary War, the Battle of Long Island, was being celebrated.

Ex-Chancellor of the British Exchequer Winston Churchill

> happened to be walking down Wall Street at the worst moment of the panic, and a perfect stranger who recognized me invited me to enter the gallery of the Stock Exchange. I expected to see pandemonium; but the spectacle that met my eyes was one of surprising calm and orderliness. There are only 1,200 members of the New York Stock Exchange, each of whom has paid over £100,000 for his ticket. These gentlemen are precluded by the strongest rules from running or raising their voices unduly. So there they were, walking to and fro like a slow-motion picture of a disturbed ant-heap, offering each other enormous blocks of securities at a third of their old prices and half their present value, and for many

minutes together finding no one strong enough to pick up
the sure fortunes they were compelled to order.[3]

Few observers agreed with Churchill's characterization of the
scene. Perhaps the Englishman's thoughts were conditioned by
what he had often seen happening in London's Anglo-American
Exchange, outdoors on Shorter's Court, where things were often
fairly wild. Had he been there instead of here at this moment,
however, Churchill might have thought differently: Shorter's
Court was an absolute madhouse at this exact hour, having begun trading at 4:00 P.M. (10:00 A.M. in New York), and continuing on into the early evening's gathering darkness, with the
brokers all frantic, hatless, rain-soaked, and completely at their
wits' end. Then, too, Churchill's observation may have been
only his well-known class prejudice, speaking as always in times
of stress. In any event, he reports that he shortly exchanged

> this scene of sombre and for the moment almost helpless
> liquidation for a window high in a titanic building. The au-
> tumn afternoon was bright and clear, and the noble scene
> stretched to the far horizons. Below lay the Hudson and the
> North Rivers, dotted with numerous tugs and shipping of
> all kinds, and traversed by ocean steamers from all over the
> world moving in and out of the endless row of docks.
> Beyond lay all the cities and workshops of the Jersey shore,
> pouring out their clouds of smoke and steam. Around tow-
> ered the mighty buildings of New York, with here and there
> glimpses far below of streets swarming with human life.

> No one who gazed on such a scene could doubt that this
> financial disaster, huge as it is, cruel as it is to thousands, is
> only a passing episode in the march of a valiant and service-
> able people who by fierce experiment are hewing new paths
> for man, and showing to all nations much that they should
> attempt and much that they should avoid.[4]

In the moments when Churchill quit the gallery—leaving behind his signature in the visitors' book, to be sure—Exchange
leaders were getting concerned about their noble scene. It was
decided that visitors ought not to be allowed to see the unseem-
ly things going on at the trading floor, and so machinery was set
in motion to close the gallery for the day at 12:30.

Torrential events were taking place on the trading floor at 11:35, events which were the culmination of months and even years of preparation. Eight million dollars was changing hands every minute. In the first hour and a half of trading, nearly 5 million shares had been exchanged, a figure that burst even the most extravagant predictions for volume on this day—a figure which sent the already strained mechanism of the Exchange into a virtual catatonic shiver. Here, together and in conflict, were meeting all the major economic forces responsible for the rise of the market—and its potential downfall. A cataclysmic event. Did anyone know what was really going on?

People knew in direct relation to where they stood geographically. The key was information—who had it, and when.

In the outer ring, the heartland of America, there was little information to be had. In the first hour this was but an annoyance; now it became a major factor. Board boys in Iowa, Kansas, Missouri were told to *forget the ticker*, to get their prices from the Dow-Jones, or the bond wire, or from what customers' men could get from offices in New York or Chicago. It became known that prices were dropping, and that people were obviously selling and selling heavily, but the dimensions of the earthquake were not known. Yet the Dow and the bond tickers were not much help—they gave only the prices of twenty leading stocks. Twenty, out of thousands!

What about all the others? There were not that many Curb tickers, for example, and over-the-counter stocks which were widely held, such as banks and some investment trusts, were usually only understood from closing prices in newspapers. Who could wait for the paper today?

Consider a man who held 200 shares of NYSE-listed Black-and-White Common, last seen on a ticker dated 10:45, quoted at 91 and dropping, after having opened the day at 100. It was 11:37 in New York. There were still nearly three and one-half hours of trading in which that man's stock, calculated at its present rate of dropping, could easily go to 70 by the end of the day! He couldn't find out accurately what the price was now—it wasn't on the Dow-Jones, or the bond ticker, and he couldn't get a quote on it from the floor—but he knew that the general trend of the leading stocks was absolutely disastrous.

If the leaders were going down, and Steel was below the magic

200—the Dow-Jones would print such news—could that man really decide to hold on and see what developed?

In many thousands of instances, the answer was no. Thousands of sell orders were transmitted over telegraphic wires, and thence eventually to the Exchange floor, giving instructions to sell all of those myriad stocks whose prices could not, at the moment, be ascertained. And sold at the market, or for whatever they could bring. In a certain ironic sense it was the revenge of the small investors, because the thousands of tiny droplets they were sending were making something bigger, an enormous wave that was gathering power with every passing moment. And of course the wave was sweeping them, as well as everything else, under its path by 11:40 in the morning.

The brokers and their customers near the center in New York had more information, but not enough. Jesse Livermore and hundreds of smaller fish began to drift downtown in the late morning. Livermore, to sell short, needed perfect information. Others, not so ambitious, still needed to know where they stood. Livermore's Rolls headed towards a place a hundred yards from the trading floor. As it inched its way downtown, the traffic got thicker, crowds of people thronged the street.

News of the events on the Street had been coming out all during the morning, and hundreds and possibly thousands of people were going to the area to see at firsthand the face of disaster. Across the street from the Exchange was "the Corner," 23 Wall Street, the offices of J.P. Morgan and Company. Across from that was the United States Subtreasury Building, the famous steps where Washington took the oath of office as first President of the country, where his larger-than-life statue now stood. The steps slowly filled with people, as did the streets. Newsreel cameramen, nearly a dozen of them, took positions near the statue, the best vantage point around. Reporters combed the crowd. Twenty mounted police were sent to the area, on the call for help from Captain Edward Quinn of the Old Slip Station. At the far end of Wall Street, the end called the Water Gate, Old Slip seemed to have been there since the days of the Street's first important resident, Captain Kidd. Usually there were no more than thirty men patrolling the area on foot. Quinn had to send these, plus mounties, plus ten more foot patrolmen and a squad of twenty detectives, to try and control pickpockets. The crowd was orderly but would not obey commands to move on, seemingly rooted to the small area bounded by the Subtreasury, Morgan's, and the Exchange. The cops were being harassed by bystanders: should they stop for a moment their ceaseless walking about, they were overwhelmed by questions to which they had no answers, and were themselves forced to move on.

Many visitors went into tall buildings to ask if they could use the windows to watch the scene below. There had been rumors of suicides. Ambulances responded to the rumors, screaming their way to the area. The crowd jostled to get out of their way, and there were scores of injuries, but no jumpers. One man spotted someone he thought was going to jump, on a high window; the crowd bunched and started calling for the man to end it all. It was just a window washer, and when he went back inside, the crowd was disappointed. A British reporter, however, unused to New York, took the suicide rumor for reality and cabled his newspaper that Lower Manhattan was littered with fallen bodies. Other rumors spread: the Exchange was going to close; exchanges in Boston, Chicago, and San Francisco had closed. The most persistent rumor, incapable of denial, was that something definitive was going to happen at noon.

At midmorning interest money was at its lowest rate of the entire year, but a fantastic thing had happened: no one wanted to try and borrow any money, even at the wonderful rates, in order to buy stocks. Also, there was virtually no short selling going on at the floor. The short sellers had all gotten out, except for a few fanatics throwing their fortunes into the whirlwind, such as Livermore. The small-timers on the short side had already bought and covered and made money, and were out. Now, there were only the *real* sellers, the distress sellers. Traders looked for buyers, any buyers at all, at any prices they might wish to suggest. U.S. Steel had sunk to 194; Bethlehem to 95; General Motors, which opened as a bargain at 62 1/2, was going begging at 50.

The usual volume was a million shares in three hours; now it was a million shares in fifteen minutes. But how could shares be sold if they were not bought? They were being bought! But who was buying? The brokers looked and looked with interest; the ticker-tape watchers pulled their chairs closer.

It was the investment trusts, at last.

The trusts, whose buying power had been looked to in vain for weeks, had carefully and protectively placed in certain brokers' files "automatic-buy" orders. These were the counterparts of "stop-loss" orders. Cash-rich and investment-poor, the trusts had been under heavy pressure to buy. Public criticism had reached a height, people were calling for investigation of the trusts, many said they were just fast-buck operators who had pushed up stock values in order to boost the value of their own portfolios and thus their own stocks' prices. It was hard to deny such accusations, especially when many of the trusts *had* indeed bailed out, *had* liquidated their portfolios in the past several months, *had* great gobs of cash and no stocks. Many had not been back in for six weeks.

To maintain their credibility with the stock-buying public, many of the trusts had placed these automatic-buy orders with brokers. When and if prices on certain well-known stocks dropped down to bargain-basement levels, these orders said, the brokers were to buy them for the trusts.

In the midmorning of the twenty-fourth, those heretofore unthinkable levels were reached. Perhaps the trusts never believed they would be, but, nevertheless, they were. Steel, at 245 a month ago, was going begging at 195; the Dow-Jones average of twenty industrials was down in the middle 270s, a 10 percent drop from the day's opening. It was the signal, and, whether they wanted to be bought in at this moment or not, the trusts were forced to honor their long-standing orders. Brokers for trusts began to buy in great clumps. A cheer went up from the knowledgeable: the savior had come at last!

In the hour between 11:15 and 12:15 on the morning of the twenty-fourth, several trusts were automatically forced into buying about $300 millions' worth of stock.

In the accepted theory of the Street, what should have happened next was that smaller investors, seeing that the big boys were buying and supporting the market—that is, preventing prices from slipping any lower—should follow the lead and buy for themselves at these bargain prices, thus starting a rally. But it didn't happen that way.

For all their buying power, for all the millions they were so quickly pouring into the market, the trusts were not enough. They seemed to be the only buyers around. Their automatic-buy orders were meeting thousands of smaller stop-loss orders, and prices were holding at the same awful low points and would not budge upwards. They seemed to be stuck, which sent another shock of fear through the market, because when a savior arrived, and *even he* produced no relief, then you knew you were in *real* trouble.

The Cuttens, Raskobs, Durants, Fishers seemed to be hiding. The trusts were doing what they could but it wasn't enough. Where were the banks with their huge reserves? The rumor had it that the banks would soon do something, and this rumor became the only glimmer of hope in an enshrouded world. J. P. Morgan, so the litany went, had stopped the panic of 1907 by bold action; in 1921 the bankers held the market up; as late as last spring there had been a bankers' consortium that had stopped a sudden decline before it had gotten out of hand. Now, they simply had to come to the rescue. But when?

Would they show their hand? And would showing their hand be enough? By 11:55, the market reflected the uncertainty in people's minds about what would happen next: it went up a point, down a point, up a point again, down again, hovering, waiting expectantly for a sign.

If the imagery was religious, that was because everything seemed to turn on a question of faith—faith in the saving power of the Street's most sacred institutions. Faith would persevere. And, in the meantime, some action was being taken. The Exchange issued orders to member firms that because of the large volume, the brokerage houses must keep their employees late and work through the night to clear the paper work for the next day. Stocks that had been traded this day would have to change hands physically by 2:15 the following afternoon. Phone calls went out to hotels as far away as midtown—several miles—and across the river to Brooklyn, and in a few minutes all accommodations within a five-mile radius of the epicenter were booked solid. The siege was on in earnest; the army had to be bivouacked.

Bill Seereiter, who had come over on his lunch hour from the AT&T divisional office on Rector Street to see what was doing at the Exchange, left the gallery shortly before noon, shocked at what he'd seen. They were always busy and seemingly wound up down on the floor, but this was something else. This was madness! Another shock greeted him as he got out into the street: the throng of people had grown by many thousands and was actively thirsting for something to happen.

At Arthur Lipper and Company, 50 Broad, board boy Charles Roesch noted with satisfaction that one of his favorite customers, the elegant Jesse Livermore, had come in and had taken a good seat near the action. Livermore had made a million, perhaps more, at this moment, but his outward manner showed nothing. Livermore had been good to Charles in the past: usually, each time he came in, he had given the young man a crisp, new one-dollar bill as a tip for writing quotes legibly.

Runner Joseph Coniglio couldn't believe his eyes as he brought a bunch of checks into a bank for certification. The checks were in payment for falling margins, and his firm, W. E. Burnet and Company, needed to confirm that the money was in their account, so the checks had to be certified rather than merely deposited. Today, instead of the ordinary scene, Joe saw a pack of runners like himself, all fighting to get in first. He asked, and was told it would take 45 minutes or so to certify the check. Forty-five minutes? That would put all his other tasks behind the eight ball. The boss would kill him! He started pushing and shoving to be first, just like all the others.

Joseph Jespersen, representing a firm of certified public accountants, was auditing the books of a well-known middle-sized brokerage house amidst the hubbub and confusion of the firm's overwhelming business of the moment. The books were a mess: innumerable cases where initials had been misinterpreted, where similar names had been confused (as American for Associated), where the distinction between common and preferred stocks had been ignored, where every possible mistake had been made. He had been working over these books since September 30, and wondered how long it would take him to sort things out and rectify them. If the mistakes of the less complicated days were this large, what would be the effect of what was going on right now, what he'd been hearing was the largest share-day ever? His gut feeling was that it would be awful.

Atop the construction work of the Bank of Manhattan building at 40 Wall, Walter Peterson noticed with surprise the thousands of dark-suited, light-hatted people on the streets below. What was going on? Nobody seemed to have a clue. It had to be lunchtime, but lunchtime never produced anything like this.

There were a fair number of women in the crowd, too. Curiously, there was very little noise coming from so large a mass of people; no wonder they hadn't noticed anything up here all morning. Why were they so silent? What could it all be about?

A junior clerk in a brokerage house, on his lunch break, was squirming his way through that crowd and reached the Subtreasury steps. He grabbed a position right next to the Pathé newsreel cameraman, who was grinding away. Many of those in the crowd seemed a bit in shock. He saw plenty who were adding and subtracting figures on small scraps of paper. Some women were crying—there seemed to be a lot of women. All the people seemed to be anxiously awaiting something. That was obvious because they all were facing the same way, all looking towards J.P. Morgan's, catty-corner from the Exchange's building and directly across from the Subtreasury's steps. It was nearly noon, and something was supposed to happen then. He strained to see what he could see.

A distinguished gentleman came out of the Guaranty Trust building and went in at the Morgan door, without much fanfare. Who was he? The face was not well known, but he was obviously somebody. A few in the crowd recognized the man as W. C. Potter, head of Guaranty Trust.[5] One or two might have known that he had gone from M.I.T. to spend many years with the Atchison, Topeka, and Santa Fe railroad, and from there had worked for the Guggenheim copper interests, before recently assuming the leadership of a bank whose capital structure outtopped that of any other American bank.

Now the crowd noticed another distinguished-looking man going towards Morgan's. Seward Prosser, president of Bankers Trust Company, and a more familiar face on the Street. It must have been quite a walk for Prosser: nine years ago, at noon on September 16, 1920, he had been coming out of his office when there had been a tremendous explosion that had killed many people and had nearly done him in. That explosion outside Morgan's had never been solved or explained; the scars were still in the building—and in Prosser's own body. He completed his short walk and went inside the Morgan door.

A dozen newsreel cameramen waited for more bigwigs. Murmurs began in the crowd, and the cameramen strained for the shots. Two of the most famous bankers on the Street approached. Charles Mitchell, of National City, and Albert Wiggin, of the Chase. They, too, headed for Morgan's. Half an hour ago all of these bankers had decided on a meeting, and further decided that they should all come to it separately, and publicly, for the good psychological effect such a demonstration would have on the public. Now, as they walked, and felt the excitement of the crowd, the decision seemed to have been a good one. Ripples of approval could be heard.

As the bells of Trinity Church chimed out high noon, the last of 6 billion dollars' worth of banking power disappeared into the mysterious and imposing edifice of the House of Morgan. At long last, the bankers were meeting.

Chapter Nine

FIVE BANKERS MEET
Noon

In the circuitous domain of high finance, it is sometimes difficult to tell the heroes from the villains, or both from those who
are innocent of either term of opprobrium. All heroes are villains, all villains scapegoats, all scapegoats martyrs, all martyr-
doms the figments of a public's imagination. From time im-
memorial it had been a banker's highest wish to attain that sort
of circumspect invisibility which allowed him to maneuver and
influence the course of affairs behind the stalking-horse figures
of kings, admirals, and railroad barons. A banker must never
catch the public eye, because therein one could either be celebrated or vilified, neither of which brought in 8 percent on an investment. In the United States' era of perceived prosperity, however, this had all rather suddenly changed; bankers, as licensed
priests of a religion shared by many, became themselves worthy
of reverence.

The famous bankers' conference at noon on the twenty-fourth
of October, 1929, took all of twenty minutes, and the ensuing
press conference but an additional five. The controversy about it
has lasted fifty years. There are no real records. It was not the
style of any of the participants to leave revealing memoirs; neither did the participants, it seems, take notes. Money is a curious fluid which washes much from a man's life. Yet it is altogether fitting and just that there are no real records, for what

went on was far too convoluted to have been adequately noted by the group of graying, distinguished gentlemen who participated in this event at this moment in time.

Consider the cast of characters: Prosser, Potter, Mitchell, Wiggin, and host Thomas W. Lamont of J. P. Morgan's. In their fifties, bankers all and proud to be so, their professional careers predated the formation of the Federal Reserve System in 1913, and were forged in the crucible of a time when private banking held unchallenged sway over both public and private money. This was not their first panic, not their first crash. Indeed, they had met earlier this year, in the spring of 1929, and by concerted action avoided a crash then. Each had been apprenticed for many years to more senior men who taught them the ropes. At Morgan's, Lamont sat in a special corner office now, but he had been in view of that office for many years: at each step up the pecking order, his desk had been moved closer and closer to its goal. The hierarchy, and the way one was supposed to act, was well known to gentlemen of this sort. Similarly, the setting was comfortable. The second-floor boardroom was a quiet space much on the order of an English clubroom, with many dark woods, a fireplace to take the chill off the day, great comfortable chairs, and uncomfortable portraits of the ghosts of the past.

In Morgan meetings among the partners, which took place every morning, seldom were notes taken or papers discussed. One knew one's job, one laid out succinctly the problems facing one to the others, one was given an assignment or a suggestion and carried it out with a minimum of fuss and bother. No one got agitated; no one pored over annual reports to discern what was happening. Everything was clear, unhurried, and the making of money was of the quiet sort, not spoken or stated but taken for granted. The same would hold true in this meeting. The men were rather close associates. Potter and Lamont families exchanged gifts: in two weeks the former would send the latter a brace of live turkeys for Thanksgiving use. The style of all was English gentlemen of the Victorian era. If this could not always be attained, it could quite well be approached in the Corner's rarefied atmosphere. We may venture to guess that in this room there were no desk plaques suggesting "the buck stops here," or even "think"; not even paper or sharpened pencils as would in modern times be *de rigeur* for a board meeting. All the participants knew this was going to be a short one. Therefore, no lunch would be offered or served. This was to be a meeting of the minds.

Reality has many levels. This meeting seems to have had no less than six, and one cannot say which was dominant, or even more real than the others. Intelligent men all, the participants knew many of the levels.

A first level was the *popular conception of what went on,* what those people gathered about in the street outside, and those frantically working on the floor of the Exchange, thought the bankers must be doing. A hint of this level had already come in the decision to have gone to the meeting publicly. A second level was in *what the press conference said they had done.* This was not the same as what was actually said and done in the meeting. A third level, on which we must admittedly speculate, was *what they probably did discuss in the meeting,* as deduced from contemporary and later records, statements, and a bit of metaphysical hijinks.

The remaining levels differ radically from the three above. Fourth: *what the bankers' representative did publicly that afternoon.* Fifth: *what the bankers did in concert privately* as opposed to publicly. Last: *what the bankers did individually during and after the meeting.* These last two levels probably never entered the conversation during the twenty minutes, but later evidence shows that thoughts of them permeated the minds of the participants throughout.

First level. The scene was a cosmic poker game. In this conception, the players, all in green eyeshades, agreed in the opening moments that the stock market situation was gravely serious, that stock values were collapsing, that they were all being hurt, and that it was incumbent upon themselves to do something about it. What they were supposed to do, in this popular conception, was ante up many millions which would go to buy shares of stocks and support the market, that is, ensure that prices would go no lower than they presently were; these millions would possibly even (on the basis of the bankers' involvement) begin the process of recovery. Thus, the conversation was believed to have gone as follows:

"I'm in for twenty million. You in?"

"See that and raise you five."

"I'll match that."

"Me, too."

This was a palpable version of reality, possibly even a workable one. In fact, as the bankers were meeting, it was this version which was believed to be valid and which was used as a working hypothesis by many. On its basis, stock prices began to inch up. The ticker was more than an hour late, however, and all over the country people were seeing the devastation of 11:00 A.M. There was a block of 40,000 shares of a big-name stock stuck in the craw at the floor; the volume at noon was a whopping 5,711,200 shares and was rising with every passing second—but prices were, indeed, inching up, on the good news that five men were talking to one another. Level one was having a marketplace effect. Good. The bankers understood that the public was honoring the supposed reality of this version, since they had deliberately fostered it by their manner of coming to the meeting. It was, however, only one version of the truth.

To perpetuate that version, to exacerbate and augment it, the bankers' press conference, shortly to be held, would say, from the mouth of spokesman Lamont, *precisely the opposite*, that is, that there was no bankers' pool to support the market. Of this ploy, more anon.

For the moment, an attempt to reconstruct something of what actually was said. Remember: informed conjecture, here, based on later records.

Level Three. To begin, the bankers probably did agree the market was in serious trouble, and that they were expected to do something. Lamont, as leader of Morgan's—Jack was still in Europe—took the lead and suggested that the Corner would show its hand, do some buying. A reason for this—and nobody would have said so, though they all knew it—was that Morgan's, as with several of the other banking institutions represented in the room, was in the midst of floating some new issues. Should the market collapse completely, they would be stuck with those new issues, unable to sell them to the buyers. Therefore, the market had need of some support.

From this they passed swiftly on to the core of the matter, the clear and present danger not only of a collapse in stocks, but of a collapse in the supporting institutions, the brokerage houses and the banks themselves. Many of the banks had huge amounts out on loan to brokers, who in turn had the money out to margin and other customers. All morning long a great need had been shown, not to reduce these loans to brokers but, rather, to *increase* them, that is, to create a monetary cushion so that the stocks, which underlie the edifice of credit, could be supported with buying power from the general public. At each of the banks, for example, there had been that morning and for some days previous calls from out-of-town banks, and from corporate lenders (remember the bootleg loans?), begging the New York banks to take over loans which these others had outstanding to brokerage houses and stock speculators. Evidence of this: for the past week, out-of-town deposits in the New York banks had been rising: the Podunk Company, calling in its money from Sam Speculator, stipulated that the man must deposit the money in Podunk's account at the Chase, forthwith. A mass movement has been going on, with out-of-town and nonbanking sources pulling their call money, in effect, out of the market. And this has, the bankers know, accelerated the downfall in prices. What to do? The answer was not only plain, but incontrovertible: the more the out-of-towners took out, the more the in-town banks were going to have to pour in, in the form of additional loans to brokers, or else there would be a real collapse.

It had long been axiomatic in high banking circles that the worst thing that could happen in a stock panic was if it pyramided to a point where people were afraid for their own money in the banks, those banks that had lent it to the brokers who had lent it to the speculators who were losing it. The whole chain must not be allowed to collapse back on itself. If Better Brokers called National City and pleaded for more money, National City *had* to give it to them, had to keep things liquid, had to keep the juice of credit flowing, because if Better Brokers saw a stone wall, they might panic too. And call in their loans. And sell out more customers. And force thereby lower prices.

Where was the money going to come from, to make these loans to brokers now? Part of it could come from their newly increasing deposits, but not enough.

The rest must come from their own source of credit, the Federal Reserve Bank of New York. The bankers were hoping—discussing—betting—that the Reserve Bank would open its floodgates to them, so they could keep the whole chain from collapse.

In this hope they were fairly certain. Governor Harrison of the Federal Reserve Bank had consistently sided with them, in the March call-money occurrence, he had even stated that his reason for supporting Mitchell had been to provide liquidity and avoid a crisis. Many in the room had spoken to Harrison that morning, and several were due for a meeting with him shortly, as directors of the Bank.

Lamont and perhaps some of the others had spoken with the higher authority, the Federal Reserve Board in Washington, which was still meeting and which knew of their needs; indeed, Lamont and others may have even spoken to Mellon directly, for certainly the Secretary and Under-Secretary were informed. Such being the case, conversation turned on whether the Federal Reserve Bank of New York would make credit easier for them now, or not. In order to make that credit easier, the Bank would have to buy large quantities of "governments," or government securities, now held individually by the banks. Harrison had been pleading with Washington and the Board for weeks for the authority to do so, but thus far his authority had been limited to buying only $25 million's worth of governments a week, far below what was now needed.

This phase of the discussion was inconclusive. It waited on the decision from the Board in Washington, which was itself waiting to hear from the Federal Reserve Bank in New York, which meeting had not yet been held. No matter: money was going to cost the banks something, and the basic question was whether it would be more or less dear. One thing they could do on their own was ease margin requirements on their own loans to brokers. Recently, those had been tightened from 30 percent to, in some cases, 75 percent. Now, in the midst of the panic, the bankers were forced to decide—seemingly paradoxically—*to lower* margins to brokerage houses. Why? So that the brokers could, in turn, lower them to customers, who could then have more buying power of their own to support the market. The point was that no one wanted to sell out a customer, neither a brokerage house nor a bank, because sold-out customers always cumulated towards disaster. To lower margin requirements was a calculated gamble that counted on a recovery that would soon start. The scenario was this: lower the margin, let the customer put money into the market which would raise the prices, and then everything would be stable, after which margins could come back up to a reasonable level. This gamble—and it was a gamble—was not perceived as such at that moment, but rather was seen as a necessary movement in order to prevent further collapse. Buying power must be provided.

What about the banks' own buying power support? Mitchell, Wiggin, and the others were indeed interested in supporting *portions* of the market. In particular, those portions labeled National City Bank stock and Chase Bank stock, which were dropping precipitously. On the highest plane, this was tied in with the idea of not allowing those banks to fail, as one failing bank of national stature would undoubtedly affect all the others. Yes, there was substantial pool agreement on shoring up the bank stocks. But those were not listed on the Exchange. What of the stocks that were listed? What of General Motors? Steel? Montgomery Ward?

An agreement to support the entire market was never considered. It would have been meaningless, as well as impossible. Too many stocks, too many shares. If the pool had at its disposal $240 million, that was still a drop in the bucket of $80 *billion* of valuation. At best, only certain selected stocks could be shored up, if any could.* Horse trading started. Morgan's wanted Alleghany supported. Someone else countered that the Van Sweringens could darn well look after their own interests, and Alleghany was crossed off any potential list. But, in return, U. S. Steel, which had been put together by Morgan, surely needed to be supported, and would be. Certain other stocks could be crossed off a potential list. For instance, the great rival private banking firm of Kuhn, Loeb was not represented in this room—let their baby, the Pennsylvania Railroad, go hang! Nobody in the room was seriously into Montgomery Ward right now, so the heck with them. But Bethlehem and General Motors, on whose boards many of those here (and their associates) sat, would get votes of confidence. Then there were more difficult problems, such as Anaconda Copper.

Anaconda and National City had long been linked. John D. Ryan, chairman of the board of Anaconda, was also on the NCB

---

*A list of possible buys, which correlates with actual transactions on the Exchange later in the day, is on an undated, unsigned scrap of paper in the Lamont collection.

board. So was Cornelius Kelley, president of the copper company. On the Street for the past two years, Anaconda had been a
speculative favorite.

In 1928 the National City Company had bought 300,000
shares of Anaconda at an insider's very good price, below the
market level. The bank's security affiliate was thus sitting pretty in March of 1929, when copper was at 24 cents a pound. But in
April of 1929 the buy had no longer looked so hot: copper
dropped to 18 cents a pound, and NCC wanted to get rid of its
shares. But they couldn't dump them all at once, or else the price
would have gone down. So, during May and June, NCC performed the hydraulic feat of selling its 300,000 shares while simultaneously buying a million shares. The activity thereby generated caused a predictable upward shift in the stock's price—
whereupon, in September, when everybody was interested in active Anaconda, NCC had coolly sold out all its remaining shares
and made $20 million in profits.

But that was September. Now, October 24, the National City
was out of Anaconda almost entirely, and so were its friends.
They could let it be, and $100 million of other people's money
could go down the drain if it folded—*it was that shaky*—but, for
old times' sake, the pool decided to buy a bit of Anaconda to
keep up appearances, say, 8,000 shares.

Support would also go to AT&T, General Electric, Du Pont,
General Motors, Steel. But weren't those the sorts of stocks that
needed help least? What about Auburn Motors, Montgomery
Ward, the new aviation stocks? Nothing was said about them.

But then, support was not exactly the name of the game. The
point was that all of the banks in the room had a need to do what
National City had just finished doing with Anaconda: get out of
certain stocks. Should the market collapse quickly, they could
be caught with a lot of worthless paper, so what they had to do to
save their necks was buy certain strategic stocks which might
lead an advance, to give themselves that precious commodity in
a panic, *time.* They were not going to buy, necessarily, at current
market levels. Oh, no. Rather, they determined to buy at prices
just below those levels. Why? To stop further decline for a moment, thus gaining time. During that gained time, they would,
as prices held for a while, get themselves out of many other
stocks without suffering losses too great to be borne. While the

pool was buying, in other words, its members, the individual banks, might be selling. Yes, indeed, the market would be propped up if at all possible, but basically for the health of the pool members, not for the welfare of the general investing public. Some would have called this "holding up the rug in order to sweep the dirt underneath it."

To put the worst face on it, this was a version of a con game: you knew the public thought you were supporting the market, so you made a strong feint in that direction, hoping the market would follow, while in reality you were doing precisely the opposite with your strong hand. To put a better face on it, you were making the best of a very rough game while protecting the interests of your own stockholders and the solvency of your own bank. Which stocks to support, then? Obviously, only those which can be seen on the Dow-Jones ticker—quickly.

Little of the above was probably discussed. All understood the unsaid implications of their actions. They weren't lambs, they were survival-of-the-fittest wolves who'd been through crises before. The talk likely ranged to how much for Steel, how much for GM, and so on.

For that matter, there were myriad things not discussed at this meeting which nevertheless echoed through it as palpable forces. Suppose, in a moment of passion, the erudite Lamont were to have said, as he later did for a Senate investigating session, something on the order of, "Gentlemen, we know you to be our true friends, and we always support our friends." What did this mean? Most probably it was a way of reinforcing a fact known to most of the participants individually, though perhaps not collectively, and that was that they were all (with the possible exception of Wiggin) in hock to J. P. Morgan's for substantial amounts of money personally, ranging up into the millions of dollars—each.

One wanted to refurbish a yacht. Another wanted to buy a controlling interest in a stock. Charlie Mitchell was in deep because he had bought his own gospel.

Mitchell, no less than a minor figure such as Julian Sherrod, had got the disease: both owned NCB stock. By the lights of the day, Mitchell appeared to have more to lose because he had, of course, far more stock than a salesman in Mobile. Mitchell was one of the largest single stockholders of NCB and had many millions to lose that day.

Such happenstance was encouraged by the bank itself. A time-honored custom in American industry said that one paid a chief executive modestly, but gave him great incentive to make the company do well by giving him a share of the profits as a bonus only to be paid if success were achieved. Mitchell had such an arrangement. His salary was only $25,000 a year, but he was given the lion's share of profits from the work of the security affiliate, and from the management fund of the bank, reserved for officers. Those latter compensations had made him rich: from them, in 1927, and 1929, Mitchell made a total of $3,481,732 above his salary. Ferdinand Pecora says that this sort of pay arrangement had much to do with

the reckless, anything-for-profit mood in which the National City was operating. The officers had nothing to gain and everything to lose, individually, by a conservative policy. Merely to make eight per cent on the stockholders' money—surely an adequate return for a banking institution eschewing unsound and speculative ventures—would have left them, under these arrangements, with a bare $25,000 to $50,000 a year as salary. Their own participation was only in the superprofits. No superprofits, no "management funds."[1]

The bonuses, Pecora later found out, were paid by checks drawn on other banks, to avoid disclosure which might enable someone to find out who was making money, and where, and how. Such simple but effective deception was part of a pattern of dealings that were an accepted part of the game of stocks and bonds and higher finance in 1929. Mitchell had avoided disclosure with Anaconda Copper. He had done the same in 1927 with the bond issues from the Republic of Peru, based on their nitrate holdings which Mitchell knew full well were growing rapidly worthless because of the development of synthetic nitrogen fertilizers. Others in this room had done the same: they thought this neither deceptive nor unusual; it was accepted practice. As John Brooks suggests, banking had changed:

Imagine an old-style American banker in a Midwest farm town—one who eschewed stock speculation on principle as his father and grandfather had always done, who lent cautiously in local mortgages, who never solicited business because he believed that salesmanship was alien to the fiduciary aspect of his profession, and who scrupulously absented himself from the board room when his own remuneration was under discussion—considering the doings of Charles E. Mitchell. He might have found himself confused. He might have had a sense of the world gone mad and of himself as a caricature of a fuddy-duddy, goody-goody old fool.[2]

This day, Mitchell personally had to commit himself to purchase huge quantities of NCB stock, to keep the price up and himself afloat. To do this—and possibly the arrangements were started now—he would go into debt to J. P. Morgan's *another* $12 million in the next week.

Consider, for a moment, an important distinction in the matter of Charles E. Mitchell, a distinction that was being made on a small scale in banking offices all over the country as the Morgan meeting was going on. It was a decision on who was worthy of a loan right now, and who was not.

A man to whom your bank lent money was in deep trouble. The trouble was getting worse. What to do? The answer was that what you did depended on how much the man owed you. There was a double standard. If he owed you a small amount—the price of a house or farm—you said no and let him go bump. But if he owed you a whole lot—the entire worth of a Main Street, or Madison Square Garden, or a director's seat on the board of U. S. Steel—you couldn't do that. Why? Because if you let him fail, his failure might make your bank fail. In Denmark, at this very hour, the failure of butter magnate Harold Plum had, in direct chain action, caused the failure of a major Copenhagen bank, and had caused a financial crisis that was taking the resources of the entire Danish government to stem. That must not be allowed to happen to your bank and country. With the small fry, you could absorb the loss, even sue the guy for back payment and garnishee his wages from here to retirement. But with the big roller you couldn't do that, because he'd just declare bankruptcy and you'd have to stand in line with the other creditors—

if you were still standing by that time. Therefore the rule was when the big fish got in trouble you loaned them more. Charlie Mitchell's case, in spades.

The purported pool had a top, the Street said then and later, of $240 or $250 million. Let's call it $240—$40 million each from the five banks represented in the room, and an additional $40 million from First National's George F. Baker, who had been unable to attend the meeting but who was known to be in agreement with the goals. It was not entirely clear, then or now, that there were $240 million in the pot; some knowledgeable people at the time thought there might have been only half of that.

Looking at the liquidity figures of the banks in the room, $240 million seems a doubtful total. Much available cash had to go to brokers to take up the out-of-town slack. And there were other factors.

It appears that if there were a real discretionary account for the pool, on October 24 it probably totaled in the area of $120 million rather than a full $240 million. To be on the generous side, let's say $60 million for Steel, NCB, Chase, AT&T, and others mentioned above, and another $60 million for fooling around. Not all of this money could be applied to the market at once. Some had to be held in reserve in case of further drops. Remember that the investment trusts, which had been bought in to the tune of about $300 million in the hour from 11:15 to 12:15, had not really been able to stem the tide; the bankers' pool would commit resources that were no greater than that, and possibly far slighter.

At best, it seems to have been a hedged and uncertain pool which the five bankers put together in this meeting. Then, too, the bankers were not basically about the risky business of support, but rather of propping things up for a while so they could get out.

If banker Mitchell was valiantly trying to support his bank's stock, for personal as well as altruistic motives, what fellow-banker Albert H. Wiggin was doing was considerably more intricate, convoluted, and devious. The two men seemed superficially alike but were quite different. Both had been raised in Massachusetts, had started their careers at the bottom of the ladder in business, had become presidents of rival institutions at an early age. Mitchell, the younger by nine years, was thickset and, according to Morgan partner George Whitney, "looked like a prizefighter." And Mitchell, according to Whitney and James Paul Warburg, was not a banker at all; he was a salesman and a very good one, but never, in the old sense, a banker. Wiggin, on the other hand, was the most respected banker in the Wall Street area. Whitney refers to him, in this time of financial magnates, as "the only fellow downtown who was really top-notch" as a banker, and Warburg remembers that his own father, Paul Warburg, a fiscal conservative who had foreseen the Crash and had been vilified for suggesting it, thought Wiggin to be an excellent manager and "a very reliable man . . . a man who would never go back on a friend."

Albert H. Wiggin, Thomas Lamont later told Wiggin's daughter, "had the courage of a lion" during those trying days in 1929. According to Marjorie Wiggin Prescott,

> By the end of October when thousands of people were selling rapidly, my father's one thought was to remain outwardly calm and to show confidence in the future of American business by buying and buying . . . irrespective of the downward trend of prices. . . . My sister said that she knew things were at their worst when Father was calm . . . and Father was frighteningly calm.[3]

Mrs. Prescott's was only one view. Wiggin may have been buying and buying, but he was also selling and selling.

For several years the Chase had been growing by leaps, bounds, and mergers. Wiggin was the driving force behind these events. Unlike Mitchell, he did not take a small salary, but a generous one: $175,000 a year, plus a bonus of $100,000. In addition Wiggin was a director of 59 other corporations, some of which added to his income as well. From the BMT he got $20,000 a year; from Armour, $40,000; from American Express, $3,000; from Western Union, only $2,000. The greater part of his wealth, however, came not from these sources but from family corporations. These were sentimentally named for his daughters and their husbands: Shermar and Murlyn. Another was named Clingston. In addition to these—all quite legal—Wiggin owned three Canadian corporations. "There were few stranger blossoms in the corporate garden," says Frederick Lewis Allen, than the private corporation. It enabled one to engage in transactions with which one would not care to have one's personal connection generally known; and it also enabled one to put one's profits beyond the reach of the income-tax collector.[4]

Shermar had participated in the Sinclair Oil pool of October 24, 1928, and in many another pool, and made a great deal of money for Wiggin, his children, and other officers of Chase who were simultaneously officers of his private corporations. As one of the biggest banks in the country, Chase was in on the financing of many dozens of new issues, at very good prices. From his privileged insider's position, Wiggin made money hand over fist. And he endeavored to keep more of it than he might otherwise, by having Canadian corporations. Because of a loophole in Canadian law, it was possible to buy some shares of Stock A for $100,000 and wait for it to go up to $150,000. Then, when you wanted to sell it, and to avoid paying capital-gains tax on $50,000, you simply transferred it to your Canadian Corporation where you recorded it on the books as having cost $150,000— and then you sold it for the same price, thus making and keeping $50,000 tax-free. Wiggin's private corporations did this regularly, as did the private corporations of many another bigwig including Cabinet officers under both Hoover and Franklin Roosevelt. There were further dodges that could be used if a man had several corporations rather than only one. In a neat operation, Shermar sold some stock short; Murlyn then bought some of that same stock and lent it to Shermar to cover. As Ferdinand Pecora points out,

> Shermar could now say that it had not yet realized any profit, as it had not yet completed the transaction by an actual covering *purchase.* Murlyn, on the other hand, had surely realized no profit, for it had merely purchased some stock and then *loaned* it. And Mr. Wiggin could say that he himself had not realized any profit, because in the eyes of the law, he and his corporations were entirely distinct entities from one another.[5]

Therefore, Shermar and Murlyn paid no taxes at all on this successful short sale. This, too, was not unusual; many millionaires were using the same dodges. What was unusual was the fact that the stock which Shermar, Murlyn, and Wiggin were selling short was the stock of the Chase bank of which Wiggin was the chief operating officer. And the transactions were taking place as Wiggin was sitting in the hallowed chairs of J. P. Morgan's on October 24.

In fact, for several years Wiggin had been actively about the business of selling Chase short in this manner and making money for his family corporations by doing so. But the biggest caper came at the time of the Crash. Wiggin had, with no one in the room the wiser, started selling Chase short, that is, selling it down, on September 19, 1929. He continued doing so through the Crash and afterwards, until he covered on December 11, 1929 (using, by the way, borrowed money from the Chase to buy the stocks to cover), to the tune of making $4,008,538, on which, as shown above, he paid no taxes.

We are thus confronted with the wonderful duplicity of a man stoutly suggesting to the others in the Morgan office that the Chase would support certain stocks, such as that of the Chase itself, while his corporate amanuensis was busily selling short the same stock. In a nicely honed move, Shermar even sold 5,000 shares of Chase—short, of course—to the pool!

Bankers Whitney and Warburg tell us that what Wiggin did was far from unusual. Taking a participation in underwriting stock was "supposed to be creditable . . . you put your money alongside your bank's," said Whitney: it was accepted practice. The younger Warburg reports that his father looked a little askance at Wiggin's buccaneering, but found it only a minor defect in a character of major import. As his daughter and biographer says of Wiggin, "his triumphs and his mistakes are a slice of pure Americana."

So twenty minutes were gone, the meeting at an end. Wiggin, Mitchell, Prosser, and Potter departed for their offices, or for the Federal Reserve Bank meeting. Lamont invited waiting reporters into his chambers for a moment to meet the demand for information.

To begin with, Lamont, once of the *Herald Tribune*, a man who had faced innumerable questions before, said he was not going to make a statement. Silver-haired, aristocratic, pince-nez in hand, he was the Establishment completely. He said:

There has been a little distress selling on the Stock Exchange, and we have held a meeting of the heads of several financial institutions to discuss the situation.

Lamont expanded on this by telling the reporters that there were no brokerage houses in difficulty, and that reports as to the maintenance of margin were satisfactory. Had the worst been reached? "I do not think we tried to analyze that situation." Was there a pool in existence? "When it comes to talking about united action and pools and all that sort of thing," said Lamont, "I really can't say anything." By saying this, he reinforced the idea that the pool was, indeed, in existence; the discreet denial brought smiles.

A dozen reporters threw questions simultaneously: had he been in touch with the Federal Reserve Bank? The Board? Going up or down? Stock prices? Things got confused. Lamont said it was his opinion that some action would be taken on the rediscount rate—or, at least, this was how he was later quoted, to much consternation including his own. He continued. It was the consensus of the bankers that many of the quotes of stock prices did not fairly represent the situation, by which reporters took Lamont to mean that he was saying that stocks were below their real value. What had caused the situation? "Air pockets." And what caused the air pockets? Lamont conferred with the firm's partners for a moment, then turned back to the reporters. "We consider the situation this morning a technical one rather than fundamental, and that it will result in a betterment." Nobody was quite sure what that meant, but the reporters took it down verbatim.

The overall impression conveyed was that very little was wrong that could not be fixed, and that the powers that be were actively about fixing them. Lamont dismissed the reporters, and it was over.

Chapter Ten

ORDINARY BUSINESS
12:25 P.M.

In New York at this hour, shortly after noon, most people were going about their ordinary business. The Advertising Club of New York was honoring the captain of the liner *America,* who had taken their delegation to an international meeting, and who had, on the way, rescued several people from a downed ship. On Park Row, banker Paul Mazur of Lehman Brothers was suggesting to the Board of Trade luncheon that the stock slide might halt mergers for a while. Lucius Beebe had returned to the Museum of Natural History just yesterday, with over a hundred thousand specimens from Bermuda, and was already starting to catalog them. Word came in to newspapers that up in Northampton, Massachusetts, Calvin Coolidge had hurried to the bedside of his mother-in-law, who was dying. In the paper one read that there were 1,976 prisoners now at Sing Sing. During the morning there had been two fires at a Du Pont plant in Leominster, Massachusetts. From Atlanta, the wire service was reporting that W. D. Manley, former president of Bankers Trust Company and head of a chain of more than eighty banks in Florida and Georgia which had failed, had just been found guilty of using the mails to defraud the banks' customers, for which he received a sentence of seven years in jail plus a $10,000 fine.

In restaurants all over town, the tomato juice cocktail had replaced the clam juice cocktail, though some people preferred the new sensation of pineapple juice. After a century's obscurity, broccoli had returned to the American table. People lamented that there was no unsweetened chocolate anymore. Foods were as modish and shifting as women's dresses. Why, it was only a few years ago, said a contemporary magazine, that

> every stenographer in New York, wearing a smock to pro-
> tect her dress, and, like as not, a Helen Wills eyeshade to
> protect her eyes, spent the noon hour munching raisins be-
> cause the ads had taught her that her system needed iron.
> Next came the daily apples, driving the doctor away. Now
> the girls cultivate yeast gardens in their patient stomachs.
> And then, having done their hygienic duty, they rush out to
> fill up on Eskimo pies—undoubtedly, with the airplane and
> the radio, one of the chief characteristics of American civili-
> zation in this decade—and Baby Ruths and Oh Henrys.[1]

Ruth, the Sultan of Swat, was at this moment perhaps contemplating the recent death of Miller Huggins and today's an-
nouncement that Bob Shawkey would replace Hug as the Yanks'
manager next year. He was also sitting pretty economically, as
his own manager had just recently, and over his violent objections, put the Babe's money in an irrevocable trust from which
he could enjoy the interest and never touch the principal.

In California, one read, male bathers were arrested when they
appeared on a popular beach without their "uppers." Paul Partridge of the University of Oklahoma tried to breakfast in the
university cafeteria in purple pajamas; not only was he led gent-
ly out by the ear, but the college's paper was threatened with
confiscation should the editors print even so much as a picture
of Partridge in said pajamas.

One read also of Jean Acme LeRoy and Eugene Augustin
Lauste, both now in their midseventies. LeRoy had designed and
invented the first motion picture projection machine, the cine-
matograph, which had preceded the better-advertised Edison Vi-
tascope by a year. Lauste had invented a way of recording and re-
producing sound photographically. These pioneers were now
destitute. They petitioned the motion picture giants: LeRoy was
partially paralyzed and needed a stipend, Lauste begged for work
of any sort. Nothing was forthcoming for either.

The ILGWU was meeting at 12:30 at the Hotel McAlpin to try

to avoid a strike at the end of the year. Ben Schlesinger and David Dubinsky were sitting with the wholesale dress manufacturers to try to find ways of satisfying the city's 45,000 dressmakers. At the Grand Central Palace all this week was the twenty-sixth annual National Business Show, "America's Efficiency Exposition." The *Bremen* set a new world's record for the Atlantic crossing yesterday, and a Japanese liner did the same for the Pacific at virtually the same time. Japanese scientist Dr. Yusaboro Noguchi was reporting success in changing people's color through skin manipulation. Thirty-six-hour zeppelin service was being contemplated from San Francisco to Hawaii. The Daughters of the American Revolution had just dedicated Constitution Hall in Washington. The papers told of a one-billion-dollar traffic plan for the city of New York just presented to Mayor Jimmy Walker.

The plan was visionary, an attempt to combat New York's horrendous traffic problems: roads, tunnels, freeways, all across the outer boroughs and linking up with the new Triborough Bridge, construction of which was due to start tomorrow with appropriate fanfare. It was, after all, an election year for Walker.

"Beau James" was the Democratic candidate and enjoyed the support of Governor Roosevelt, ex-governor Smith, *The New York Times,* and the people. Though his vacation periods rivaled in duration his days in office, he was immensely popular. A former Broadway songwriter ("Will You Love Me in December As You Do in May?"), he was often seen in the company of his mistress Betty Compton, an actress currently rehearsing for the opening of *Fifty Million Frenchmen.* The Mayor—witty, charming, well dressed—was the focal point for the corruption which flourished so openly that everyone seemed to take it as a matter of course, nothing to be upset about. The city's business, it was said, was conducted over a table in the back of the recently reconstructed Central Park Casino. Two days ago the Bar Association had labeled the Walker-Tammany candidates for judgeships as, one and all, unqualified for such positions—but nobody cared.

Though Walker's election seemed assured—there were 1.2 million registered Democrats to 600,000 Republicans—the Mayor had begun to campaign actively two weeks before the voting. He had a full day of speaking, including an address this evening to 4,500 at the Odd Fellows Hall on One-hundred-sixth Street.

This morning, the *Herald Tribune* had come out for Republican candidate Representative Fiorello H. LaGuardia. Why had the *Trib*, a Republican paper, waited so long to endorse him? Perhaps because the paper's own editorials had earlier excoriated the Little Flower as the wrong candidate at the wrong time for the wrong job. It was symbolic of the man's difficulties in the campaign.

He was a radical. A "foreigner." Almost a socialist. True, during the war he had been a heroic Air Force major, and afterwards an aggressive and important Congressman, but he had been sniping at Hoover this last year and was unpalatable to the Republicans of New York who had learned to live with Tammany and like it. What could a respectable Republican do with a man who, when asked to trace his descent, had replied

I have no family tree. . . . The only member of my family who has is my dog Yank. He is the son of Doughboy, who was the son of Siegfried, who was the son of Tannhäuser, who was the son of Wotan. A distinguished family tree, to be sure—but after all—he's only a son of a bitch.[2]

As a Congressman, LaGuardia had examined speakeasies in New York, meat trusts in Chicago, coal strikes in Pennsylvania; he had fought to legalize sex education, make Columbus Day a national holiday, and break the baseball trust, and had introduced a bill to provide free transportation for Gold Star mothers to visit the graves of their sons in Europe.

But that was yesterday. Now the fun had gone out of Washington, and LaGuardia very much wanted to be mayor. He even proposed taking Charlie Mitchell on the ticket as comptroller to get the nod, but fortunately that wasn't necessary. Today he was running hard, spending the day in the Bronx, which he admitted was "an uphill battle." He vowed to beat Walker on the corruption issue, though his real opposition came not from Beau James, but from his own longtime friend and fellow liberal, the Socialist candidate for mayor, Norman Thomas.

A paradox. LaGuardia had supported Thomas's bid for the mayoralty in 1925; how could he run against him now? He couldn't. Socialist Thomas, with his intellectual coalition, wild ideas, his pastor's eloquence, was splitting the liberal vote and refusing to get out of his friend's way—as usual, on principle.

Thomas, who had been a neighbor of Warren Harding's in their youth, had done the worst of any Socialist candidate thus far in the century when he ran for President in 1928. Nonetheless, a quarter of his votes in that election had come from New York City, so people thought he might have a shot at City Hall. Nineteen-twenty-nine was a difficult year for him: his wife Vi had suffered her first serious heart seizure, and the Socialist party was running out of gas under the continued prosperity of the country. Thomas campaigned for mayor, he said, not for Marxism but for Progressivism, not for revolution but for reform. His program included unification of a patchwork transit system; rent control; a merit system for all civil appointments; the razing of slums in Brooklyn, the Bronx, and lower Manhattan; and the municipal erection of housing. Yesterday he had promised to roll back the price of milk. His vision of the future had appeared in last Sunday's *New York Times*:

> We Socialists look at this city of great luxury and greater poverty, a little beauty and immense ugliness, the market-place where everything, even justice, is bought and sold, and we say: Nevertheless those who toil with hand and brain can, if they will, by intelligent, collective action, by building their own party, make this marvelous city the dwelling place of comfort and beauty, justice and peace.[3]

At the moment, Thomas was at the Hotel Bossert talking to the Brooklyn Rotary. He railed against the way in which the present directors of the IRT subway line were running the company while controlling only 112 shares out of 350,000, but nobody much cared.

In Manhattan, the Association of Railway Executives was lunching. Atterbury of the Pennsylvania, Crowley of the New York Central, and others were meeting to discuss a rail-and-water "unity" which would charge similar rates for moving goods by water or rail. Hoover's grand canal plan had the iron horsers worried; if water transport got too cheap, they might lose business.

Everything seemed to be conspiring against them. Planes were going to put a dent in mail-carrying. The birthrate of cars and trucks, which now exceeded that of people, was taking freight from them.

It was a different era from the heyday of the railroad barons. Atterbury and Crowley were not magnates, but corporate executives. There were still some titanic railroad battles going on, but in a new mode: now was the time of the battle of the holding companies. Among the executives conspicuously absent from the day's meeting were Otis P. and Mantis J. Van Sweringen of Cleveland, Ohio, who controlled more track at this moment than anyone else in the country.

The Van Sweringen brothers were as alike as two peas in a pod. Bachelors, they worked and planned together, slept in twin beds in the same room. Neither had gone beyond the eighth grade. At twenty-one and nineteen, they had gone into real estate in Cleveland, starting with virtually nothing. They bought land in Shaker Heights, borrowing to do so, using a holding company to sell off enough to pay their debts but still retain control. By 1910 they were acquiring, with the help of banks, their first railroad, the small Cleveland and Youngstown, which ran through Shaker Heights and spurred development there.

In 1912 they formed their first big holding company to get control of the Nickel Plate, as the New York, Chicago, and St. Louis railroad was generally called. The price put on this road by the New York Central was $8.5 million. Using $500,000 of their own money, they convinced associates to put up another $1.5 million, and signed a note for the other $6. 5 million to the Central. The New York giant transferred able executive J. J. Bernet to the line as a favor to the buyers, and looked well on it, considering it in "friendly" hands. The line prospered: by 1916 it had earned 6 percent on its common stock; by 1920, 10 percent; by 1921—in the depth of the slump—over 25 percent. These earnings enabled the Van Sweringens to issue more stock, more bonds, pay off most of their debt to the New York Central, and begin the purchase of three more railroads. In 1925, with the Morgan interests looking on benevolently and not, as they could have done, blocking the way, the brothers bought the Huntington interest in the Chesapeake and Ohio. By 1927 they had bought the Pere Marquette and were knocking on old George F.

Baker's door to ask his permission, as the largest and most influential stockholder, to buy into the Erie. Baker reportedly asked them two questions: did they work hard, and did they sleep well. Apparently satisfied with their answers, he allowed them, with the potent help of the Morgan bank, to acquire control. By the end of 1927 they controlled a system with many thousands of miles of track from Chicago all over the Atlantic Coast, over a hundred thousand employees, and assets in the neighborhood of $2 billion. On this they owed $35 million but believed themselves to be worth three times that, because the stocks they controlled had risen every time they had gotten involved in a new road.

In 1927, for virtually the first time in their career, the Van Sweringens found themselves combatants in a railroad war. The Morgan interests, with the Van Sweringens holding company, Alleghany, were at war with the Kuhn, Loeb interests who controlled the Pennsy. In order to protect their territories, each of the giants had to buy more. Stock prices for all railroads started going up. A man named Frank Taplin bought control of the piddling Pittsburgh and West Virginia, at a price of $52^{1}/_{2}$ a share, and finally sold them to the highest bidder, the Pennsy, at $170 a share. This single purchase cost the Pennroad Corporation about $38 million, almost half of its original capital, but succeeded in blocking any serious invasion of its territory. That was September of 1929.

In 1929 Alleghany had begun trying for its biggest prize, the road that Jay Gould had built, the Missouri Pacific, which would give the Van Sweringens (for the first time) tracks west of the Mississippi and down as far as the Mexican border. By this year, although they controlled 51.8 percent of Alleghany, the Van Sweringens' actual financial stakes in their railroads were minuscule: less than one percent, for example, of the Chesapeake and Ohio, and less than a quarter of one percent in the small Hocking Valley line. Yet they controlled these railroads as surely as if they owned 100 percent of their common stock.

However, because of the intricate structure of their financial pyramid, it was essential that all of the railroads they controlled should have rising stocks and pay good dividends on a regular basis, or else the huge debt structure the Van Sweringens had built up would come crashing down to bankruptcy. As long as things kept going up, they were the fair-haired young men of the Morgan interests, the greatest railroaders of the century.

Today, at their farm called Daisy Hill, outside Cleveland, the brothers' private long-distance operator was receiving bad news on a very regular basis. The stock of Alleghany was in serious trouble on the floor of the New York Stock Exchange. The brothers, knowing the whole pyramid depended on it, sent large buy orders to prop up the stock, and hoped the Morgan interests would realize how much there would be to lose if they didn't help prop it up as well. All the brothers could do, right now, multimillionaires or not, was hope and buy.

At the main offices of another pyramid, the news from the stock market was causing even more uncertainty. The Bank of United States was in very deep trouble, even if only a handful of people knew it at this moment.

On the corner of Orchard and Delancey streets in the pushcart neighborhood of the Lower East Side, on July 1, 1913, Joseph Marcus had opened the Bank of United States, with a small capital outlay. The many immigrants in the area, whose native tongues were other than English, perceived the private institution as a veritable arm of the government because of its name. In six months Marcus had to have a new building. In five years the assets had grown to nearly $4.5 million and the offices moved uptown to the garment center. By 1923 the assets had jumped to over $45 million. In 1927, when the elder Marcus died and left the business to his son Bernard, the Bank of United States was a solid, respectable institution which served well the Jewish "little people" of New York. That was when the trouble began, because if the elder Marcus had wanted to make money, the younger Marcus wanted power. In the words of the biographer of the bank, M. R. Werner, Bernie Marcus, at thirty-seven, fancied himself "a Napoleon of New York's jewry." He took as a partner Saul Singer, president of the Cloak, Suit, and Shirt Manufacturers Association and the chief promoter of the Garment Center Capitol Building.

On the first of September, 1927, Marcus and Singer formed the City Financial Corporation, CFC, to buy and sell stocks. The capital offering was oversubscribed 14$^1/_2$ times: if these boys who had done so well in banking wanted to do bigger things, people were with them. By December the partners had formed a syndicate to speculate in CFC stock, that is, to manipulate it upwards. To do so, they borrowed money from the bank itself. The scheme worked. By May of 1928, Bank of United States stock was so high that they were able to take over the Central Mercantile Bank on an exchange of stock plan. Now their assets were $60 million and the stock was selling for $600 a share.

While pushing up their stock, they went into real estate, establishing some twenty dummy corporations. They made many questionable loans. A friend of Singer's, who owed the bank $250,000, was given an additional loan of $400,000; he used it to pay off the first loan, and then, since his credit had thus been established as good, borrowed an additional $500,000. The pattern of holding companies was now an accepted practice. The bank lent the money of its depositors to Marcus and Singer's "security affiliates," in the same way as the Chase and the National City had done, to deal in securities. But if Wiggin and Mitchell knew what they were doing, Marcus and Singer didn't. The real estate continued shaky, and that was where most of the loans of the parent bank went. And they were after power, not money. On January 1, 1929, they offered Alex Walker, a Scot who had built up a profitable banking business on Manhattan's upper West Side, $19 million for the stock of his bank which was then worth only $6.4 million. How could he refuse? He couldn't. They borrowed money for the purchase from their own bank, and from Wiggin and Mitchell. Then they turned around and bought the large Municipal Bank and Trust Company of Brooklyn.

By May of 1929 the empire had 57 branches, 440,000 depositors, deposits of $220 million, and resources of $314 million. It was estimated that $100 million of this was in small accounts. Marcus and Singer controlled Jewish banking completely and were, in fact, in terms of depositors served, the largest bank in the largest city in the country. "One can imagine," writes M. R. Werner,

the depositors of the Municipal Bank and of the Bank of United States going in the evenings to their homes in Brownsville, the Bronx, the upper West Side and the lower East Side and discussing with their friends and their families what smart fellows Bernie Marcus, Samuel Barnett, Saul Singer, and Morris Diamond were, and how Lawyer

Kresel and Lawyer Kugel were connected with them, and what tons of money they must all be making. If these workers and small tradesmen had profits or savings, they probably decided that it would be foolish of them not to put them into shares in these men's enterprises. [4]

Which, of course, is what Marcus and Singer wanted. While inflating their stock before the mergers, the men had purchased a great deal of their own stock, taking, of course, loans from their own bank to do so. Now they were going to unload it, at enormous profit, on the public. There was, however, a small worm in the apple. In early July, just as they were starting their selling campaign, a hundred examiners from the New York State Banking Department and the Federal Reserve Bank of New York descended upon them for a semiannual examination. Not waiting for the results, which they knew would be bad, Marcus and Singer hastily sold to their own bank's depositors (some 30,000 of them) $6 million of the bank's stock. Many savings accounts were liquidated in this cause; the stock even went up, for a while.

On August 9, Superintendent of Banks Joseph A. Broderick got the report and sent an examiner to meet with Marcus and Singer on August 19, to tell them 1) they were not qualified to run such a large bank, 2) that $70 million in shaky real-estate loans had to be curtailed, and 3) that they had better merge with a well-run institution. Marcus and Singer denounced the examiner and his ilk as "crooks," though they admitted that if news of the real-estate blunders got out, "there would certainly be a run on the bank."

As Broderick started to get nasty, Marcus and Singer did two things. First they took an additional loan of $11 million from their bank; second, they started negotiations with the firm of respected Wall Street securities brokers, J. W. Seligman and Company, for the purchase of 115,000 units of their own stock at $185 a share, four times what they had paid for it. Hearing that they were meeting with Seligman, Broderick called off the hounds. Inquisitions of this sort brought up the nasty idea that perhaps his department had not been doing its job and was only jumping on the prosecutorial bandwagon after the damage was done. It would be so much better if Seligman would just take the whole mess off his hands. While the hiatus thus created went on, Marcus and Singer continued to try desperately to sell stock to the public. On September 22, however, the Seligman people found out about the examiners' report in detail and called off the deal. Broderick reluctantly began his actions.

So, a bare month later, when stock prices started falling and bank stocks headed for the cellar, Marcus and Singer knew they and the Bank of United States were in deep, deep trouble. At any moment, they might have to close their doors.

Down near the Bank of United States' old neighborhood, on St. Mark's Place, Mr. Zero was serving lunch in his soup kitchen, called The Tub, to homeless derelicts and chronically unemployed men. Mr. Zero was the name by which the unfortunates called Urbain J. Ledoux, who, before turning to social work, had been American consul in Prague from 1903 to 1907.[5] As with most social work and welfare in the country, Mr. Zero's soup kitchen was a private charity.

For centuries, following the old English common law and traditions, poverty in America had been looked on as a condition of disgrace. Poor men were branded as unworthy and shiftless. In several states the laws still provided for the letting of contracts to private charities for all taking care of the poor, and a few states even authorized the old pattern of indemniture or apprenticeship of children to pay off debts. Practically every state had laws providing for almshouses for the poor, but less than a third had any provision for keeping poor people in their homes and providing any sort of relief for them there. Twenty states deprived relief recipients of the right to vote. Though 70 percent of relief money in the country came from the various governments, there was a deep distrust of governmental work in the area. Private charities were the norm of the day and they "took care" of the situation. Federal relief was limited mostly to disaster sufferers, and, on a state basis, officials mostly handled relief as a secondary function. Most states required recipients to be absolutely destitute before they could receive governmental help.

This situation reflected the belief of most Americans, including President Hoover and business leaders, that welfare was a private affair, a shameful one best handled without too many people knowing about it. One of the most persistent problems in welfare management was that there were no accurate statistics on the poor or the unemployed, or, for that matter, on the economy in general.

The Bureau of Social Statistics was first established by Hoover. Most of the money spent by governments seemed to be in mothers' pensions, or aid to dependent children. A peak of expenditures was thought to have been reached in the 1920–1922 depression, but money outlays had actually been rising since 1924.

Usually in the spring of the year, expenditures would drop for a while, then pick up again. In spring 1929 they didn't drop. There were 2,860,000 unemployed. Throughout the summer, figures collected by the Children's Bureau from 120 cities showed that the numbers of people needing help were seriously higher than corresponding figures for 1928. Figures for September were even worse. In Buffalo, considered one of the cities where relief was well administered, unemployment was over 10 percent and rising. Cleveland, Baltimore, and Philadelphia—considered backward by social workers—were even worse. And New York's latest study put the unemployment figure at close to 17 percent.

Teen-ager Marie E., in Chicago, knew what it was to be on the receiving end of this kind of charity. When her father had been ill for a time, a few years ago, she and the whole family had been on welfare. Dad's job as a motorman working for the city hadn't provided a dime in sick benefits. When he became ill, so ill he had to receive the last rites, all they could do was hold out their hands. It was embarrassing, humiliating, even a young girl felt that. You never got a dime in cash, Mom would complain, just staples—flour, sugar, hardly ever any meat. Chicago had no city assistance. You just went to the charity place with a coaster wagon, once a week, and picked up the groceries, which were wrapped in a particular kind of brown paper. That paper was well known in poor neighborhoods; when people saw you with groceries wrapped in it, they knew you were on welfare. The E. family stayed on for about a year, or until Dad got well enough to have some strength for work. The fellows at the car barn took up a collection for him when he returned, which was nice. Mom wasn't so lucky: during the time on welfare, she caught sick and died within a year, at the age of thirty-four.

Down in Gastonia, North Carolina, at this hour, some people

were upset over the death of a twenty-nine-year-old woman, a cotton mill worker named Ella May Wiggins. On the other hand, some people were far from upset over her death. For both, today was an important day, the day of the trial of her alleged murderers.

Gastonia was the obverse of the coin of American prosperity, as much a symbol and a token as was the stock market in New York City. Thirty years ago Gastonia had been a hamlet on a crossroads. Then came the mills. The Loray, a mile west of the city, was the largest mill in the world entirely under one roof. Owned by Manville-Jenckes Company of Rhode Island, it had been making fabric for automobile and truck tires for some years. At the height of the boom, it was going full blast. And it had wrought much. In Gastonia, Mary Heaton Vorse reported at the time,

> nothing I had read prepared me for what I saw. The industrial revolution had here run its completed cycle in thirty years. I found myself in the presence of an industrial development which was so gigantic and had been encompassed in so brief a time, that it had the terror of incalculable energy. . . . The transformation of North Carolina, within a period of thirty years, from a sleepy agricultural state still struggling with the problems of reconstruction to one of the richest states in the Union, is a miracle.[6]

Now there was a new city hall, courthouse, high school, a widely known orthopedic hospital where much of the work was performed free of charge, many fine homes and new churches. Yet, Sinclair Lewis's reports in the Scripps-Howard papers were saying,

> The mills control the banks, the banks control the loans to small businessmen, the small businessmen are the best customers of the professional men—even when the latter are professional men of God—and so the mills can back up the whole human train, down to the clerical caboose.[7]

But while the rest of the country was booming, the textile industry had already begun to feel a cord about its neck as early as 1924. Pressure to cut production costs gave rise to a speeding up of the work process known as the "stretch-out," which meant, one worker said, that

> they cut my wages and increased my work. I used to tend 48 looms, while under the stretch-out I have to tend 90 looms, and I couldn't do it. Three years ago I was making over $19 a week. Now I make $17.70. I ain't a-bragging. I'm an experienced weaver. I don't believe there's many can beat me. I make a hundred per cent, the most any weaver can make.[8]

It didn't seem to matter. Senators investigating the mills in 1929 concluded that the industry's wages were the lowest in all of the country: less than half as much as the average manufacturing wage. That this would mean worker unrest did not seem to occur to the management. The Loray mill did as all the others did: cut workers, and cut the salaries of those who remained. It was the standard way of doing business.

Fred E. Beal arrived in North Carolina on January 1, 1929. Wide-shouldered, heavily built, boyish, with blue eyes and light hair, he was quintessentially American, come from Yankee dirt-farmer stock. He had begun working in the textile mills of Lawrence when he was a teen-ager. Inspired by Big Bill Haywood, he walked out with the Wobblies in 1912. After the war, he moved from one left-wing organization to another, led the New Bedford strike, and came into the Communist fold when disillusioned over the moderates response to Sacco-Vanzetti. The Communists sent him to Carolina.

He worked in Charlotte for two months, then went to Gastonia in March, quickly building an underground organization among the downtrodden mill workers. Beal, interested primarily in trade-union objectives, feared from the outset that the Party might use whatever he did to stir up a revolt far wider than it needed to be, but the conditions were so bad—far worse than those in the North—that he decided to endure the risk.

On March 30, the underground activity was discovered. Next day, Beal led almost everyone at Loray out, both day and night shifts. His demands were for the elimination of piecework, a minimum wage of $20 a week (far below the national average), a 40-hour week, abolishment of the stretch-out, equal pay for all, union recognition, and certain changes in sanitary and housing conditions. The demands were rejected in three minutes. As was usual in the area's strikes, Governor O. Max Gardner sent a division of the National Guard to maintain order. This generally meant the breaking of a strike. Seeing this, the Party sent great reinforcements in the form of people to assist and publicize the strike. Much violence and militancy obtained. A young worker at the mill, twenty-nine-year-old hillbilly Ella May Wiggins, expressed much of the hurt:

> I'm the mother of nine. Four of them died with whooping cough, all at once. I was working nights and nobody to do for them, only Myrtle. She's eleven and a sight of help. I asked the super to put me on day shift so's I could tend 'em, but he refused. I don't know why. So I had to quit my job and then there wasn't any money for medicines so they just died. I never could do anything for my children. Not even keep 'em alive, it seems. That's why I'm for the union. So's I can do better for them.[9]

Pictures show Ella May as a frazzled, used-up woman, shockingly old at twenty-nine—not unusual for this area, as Mary Heaton Vorse had observed. But Ella May was something special, a composer and singer of "ballets," or ballads. Folk-song collector Margaret Larkin noted

> a clear, true tone in her untaught voice. She sang from the chest. Full-throated, unmodulated, her voice rang out in the simple monotonous tunes.[10]

What she sang about at union meetings were the consequences of what the Brookings Institution was finding in a 1929 study: that three-quarters of the people in the country didn't really have enough money for an adequate diet for themselves and their children; that pellagra was unconquered among the mill people; that death at forty-five was an everyday occurrence:

> We leave our home in the morning,
> We kiss our children goodbye,
> While we slave for the bosses
> Our children scream and cry.
>
> It is for our little children
> That seem to us so dear,

> But for us nor them, dear workers,
> The bosses do not care.
>
> But understand, all workers,
> Our union they do fear,
> Let's stand together, workers,
> And have a union here.[11]

All over the country, union membership was down in the face of widespread prosperity, down though advances in wages had in no way kept pace with the enormous advances in profits to the big companies. The AFL had lost members steadily through the decade, and the forefront of labor agitation had passed to the Communists, replacing the "dry rot of aristocracy" that seemed to have affected the more moderate leadership of the organized forces.

Communists from twenty-three different organizations converged on Gastonia. By the time the second week of April had arrived, Fred Beal thought the strikers were being used as "cat's paws for the world revolution which every Communist sees just around the corner." But the problem was that no one but the Communists seemed to be noting the plight of the mill workers—and so the Communists expanded into the vacuum, mounting an attack on Gastonia's culture that opened not only the question of economics, but of race as well. The confrontation was looked for more and more openly by the town and state authorities, too. "With the aid of adroit propaganda from the employers," writes Liston Pope,

> the Communists were forced from the original position of opposition primarily to the employers, into a position of open conflict with the community and the police power. The strike moved from the economic sphere into the political sphere and assumed the character of a revolt.[12]

On April 15 striking pickets failed to prevent strikebreakers from entering the mill. On the eighteenth, armed and masked men demolished the union's headquarters. By April 20 the governor was recalling the Guard because of the general belief that the strike had been broken.

On June 7 some hard-core strikers, reduced to two hundred

from two thousand, went towards the mill to persuade workers to a second walkout. The police bashed heads and turned them back; then, led by Chief O. F. Aderholt, they attacked a tent where strikers were living after being kicked out of company housing. There was shooting from both sides; four police and one striker were wounded, and Aderholt died of wounds the next day. Beal and fourteen others were indicted for murder.

The trial began in late August. The charge may have been murder, but, a Carolina newspaperman wrote,

> To the resident Gastonian there is but one issue. By all the sacred bugs and beasts of ancient Egypt he is determined that no organization which denies God, defies the American flag, and makes a mock marriage shall gain a foothold among 18,000 of the "most contented workers in the country." . . . All else about the industrial disagreement is a snowflake upon the river. The resident Gastonian knows he is defending his home, his God, and his country.[13]

The trial of Fred Beal and his compatriots, and the trial later for the accused murderers of Ella May Wiggins, attracted national attention. If the stock market's majestic rise was proof of the attainability of the best parts of the American dream, these Gastonia trials were proof of the darker hues of that dream: of the possibilities in the American system for the perversion of our stated lofty ideals. As with all paradoxes, both parts existed simultaneously.

The proceedings for Beal and the others were moved to Charlotte, and a jury which satisfied both sides was picked. Then rare shenanigans began. A life-sized mannikin of Aderholt dressed in a blood-stained uniform was rolled into the courtroom. The chief's daughter and wife burst into tears, the judge ordered the monstrosity instantly removed, but three days later a juror went violently insane from the shock he had suffered seeing the "ghost," and there was a mistrial. A new trial was ordered.

Released jurors told the press that on the evidence thus far presented to them, they would have acquitted the defendants.

Riots ensued. A hundred men kidnapped a visiting British Communist, flogged him and two others. The mob then tore up a hotel where "sympathizers" were staying. A large meeting was scheduled near the Loray mill for Saturday, September 14: members of the American Legion were deputized to close all roads to it.

A truck filled with workers was turned back as it tried to approach the meeting place, then was pursued and forced off the road by an automobile filled with "faithful employees" of the Loray mill. Shots were fired into the truck and at occupants who had deserted it and were running across the fields. Ella May Wiggins, struck in the chest, had time to cry, "Lord-a-mercy, they done shot and killed me!" and then she died. Fifty people witnessed the attack, made in broad daylight. Beal and others heard of it in their prison cells and cried.

Seven men were arrested. In the interim between their trial and Beal's second trial, scores of strikers were killed in nearby Marion, and in Kentucky and Tennessee. The second Beal trial began.

At that trial, the prosecution team included the governor's brother-in-law, Clyde Hoey, the stentorian Major Bulwinkle, and "Wallowing John" Carpenter. The prosecutor spoke of "scenes of debauchery" among the strikers and gave a summation which crystallized the real issues:

> Do you believe in the flag of your country, floating in the breeze, kissing the sunlight, singing the song of freedom? . . . Do you believe in . . . the good roads of North Carolina on which the heaven-bannered hosts could walk as far as San Francisco? . . . The union organizers came, fiends incarnate . . . into peaceful, contented Gastonia, with its flowers, birds, churches . . . sweeping like a cyclone and tornado to sink damnable fangs into the heart and lifeblood of my community . . . [14]

Some evidence was presented showing that it was possible Aderholt had been shot by his own men. The jury returned on Monday, October 21, after deliberating less than an hour, with verdicts of guilty of conspiracy to murder. The defendants were sentenced, then freed on bail pending appeal.

The bitterness of Monday's decision was still in the air on the twenty-fourth, for the Wiggins trial. Beal and the others, convinced that justice could no longer be had in America, were clandestinely on their way to the Soviet Union. Attention turned to the Wiggins murder case. Heywood Broun, the columnist for *The Nation,* said he was all for combating communism and had no desire to see the Russian experiment tried out in the United States, but

> There was deep cancerous trouble in the Carolina mills before any alien agitator set foot on the premises. It is tragic that the mother of five children should be shot down by an anti-Communist mob, but it is a fantastic perversion of logic to attribute her death to the people who organized the strike. Any woman with five small children to care for does not go bustling off to a strike meeting upon some mere caprice. If there had not been the deadly pressure of a grinding and torturing poverty upon Mrs. Ella May Wiggins she would not have been in the truck with the other workers.[15]

Seven men, all workers or minor officials at the mill, were in the dock on the morning of October 24 for Ella May's murder. At 12:30, without much ado, the judge threw out the case against them, and they walked out of the courthouse, free.

Chapter Eleven

EL DORADO PASSES
12:45 P.M.

At 12:45, young Cecil Cannon, an employee of Brooklyn Edison Company, was in Wall Street on a special assignment. As he had never been down here before, he didn't know whether the crowds in the streets were unusual or not. There were men crying and raising their arms to the sky—something was wrong, but, as a recent arrival to the metropolis from Augusta, Georgia, Cecil couldn't be sure what it was. He saw the number he was looking for, Twenty-three, and entered the building. After looking again at the cards of people he was supposed to see, he told the secretary he was here to talk to Mr. John P. Morgan about a contribution to the Boy Scouts of America. The secretary tried to control her laughter, then looked grave, said Mr. Morgan was extremely busy and would Mr. Cannon please come back another day.

Frank Ayers, the Packard dealer in Port Jefferson, called his customer, Mr. Woody, and told him he'd found just the car they'd been looking for. Mr. Woody said would he please just hold the order a bit, as he had had some bad news from Wall Street this morning. Frank wondered how long he'd have to hold the deal.

In Poughkeepsie, calendar salesman Irv Wolfe nosed his Ford into a space near the Smith Brothers Restaurant and hoped he'd be able to get a seat in the popular place during the lunch rush.

Usually he had to stand in line to get served at the counter of the restaurant connected with the famous Smith Brothers Cough Drop factory. But today the joint was well near empty. What was going on? The counterman told him that the broker's office next door was where all the people were, and that it was a madhouse. Before eating lunch, Irv decided to investigate. Just yesterday he'd told the broker in there to sell his few shares of Anaconda. Irv had to fight his way in through a crowd of men and women in turmoil. Some were crying, others had looks of abject personal disaster and terror on their faces. The broker who had sold the Anaconda saw him and rushed through the crowd, screaming, "Why didn't you tell me you knew the market was going to crash?" The guy looked so terrifying, Irv thought he was about to be attacked and beat a hasty retreat into the crowd and out the door. The place really had gone mad.

At the H. Company brokerage firm in St. Louis, there was a barely controlled pandemonium. Insull's Midwest Utilities, and such other "go-go" stocks as Eisler Electric, Nehi Corporation, Prince and Whitely, were gyrating wildly on the Midwest. Paul M., the firm's treasurer, was having a hard time keeping up with what was going on. Hallgarten, their New York wire house, had called them for $50,000 to cover stocks they had in their own margin and cost accounts. The company couldn't dig up that kind of money that fast, and so Hallgarten had sold out their underlying stock that morning at ridiculous figures. This created a backwards-collapsing mess, for in St. Louis it meant that H. Company had difficulty calling its *own* customers for more margin—because, if the customers didn't deliver, the threat of selling out their underlying stocks had lost its bite. The company had to place buy orders for, in essence, duplicates of the underlying stocks Hallgarten had sold, and had to do this at current prices, which were even lower than the ones H. Company had taken a beating on earlier in the day. Also, communications between St. Louis, Chicago, and New York were breaking down under the heavy load of messages. Things were getting sloppy. Paul wondered if his firm would go the route of the one upstairs in the building, which had closed its doors, despite the boom, a couple of months ago. If so, he'd be out of a job, which wasn't a pleasant prospect.

Auto road man Earl P. showed up at his wife's podiatry office in Buffalo shortly after midday on his thirty-fifth birthday and cried. Everything was going down the drain, all the money he'd made in the market on the $10,000 she'd loaned to him. What a fool he'd been, he said, for telling his friends to get out and not getting out himself. Was everything gone yet? No, not quite, he said. There might still be time to prop up the faltering stocks, to prevent them from being sold out, but that would, of course, take more money, money which he didn't have. His wife looked at him: it was heartbreaking to see a grown man cry, a man who had exuded confidence and strength and the attitude of a winner just this morning. There was still some money left over from Mother's estate; unhesitatingly, she made arrangements so that he could use it. There was no question but that it had to be done—if not only for the stocks and the money, then for him: he needed it now, needed it badly.

In black Chicago there were two big banks. One, the Douglass, had been organized by Anthony Overton, who also owned the Victory Life Insurance Company. The other, less extensive but more influential, was owned and operated by Jesse Binga, the man responsible for the development of the Thirty-fifth Street Arcade. The high-ceilinged, marble-floored Binga Bank was an institution so solid and beautiful that many people swore by it, and by tall, slightly stoop-shouldered, graying, steely Jesse Binga himself.

Binga was outspoken and self-assertive, couldn't be bluffed or frightened. In the terrible summer of 1919, when blacks were being killed in race riots all over the country (and especially in Chicago), he wanted to move out to where he thought he belonged, in a better section of town; Jesse moved out there despite bomb threats that kept others away. Binga was a success, and, more than that, he was the kind of man, according to W. E. B. DuBois, whites did not like to see being a success, because "he did not bend his neck nor kowtow when he spoke to white men or about them; he represented the self-assertive Negro and was at times rough and dictatorial."

According to a contemporary, he was not worried about the race problem because he was too busy trying to fulfill a black banker's primary function, to give good mortgages to his community. "Lots of people criticize me," Binga said. "They don't like my methods and offer me suggestions. I always tell them, 'Jesse Binga knows what he's doing and he's doing it like Jesse Binga wants it done.'" He was the epitome of black Chicago.

There were 170,000 blacks in the city, 90 percent of them living in well-defined areas that constituted portions of the city that were, as was Harlem in New York City, separate and divorced from the main city. Three newspapers, the *Defender*, the *Bee*, and the *Whip*, served the community. There were great differences between the blacks in Chicago and those in New York. The Harlemites

> charged Chicago Negroes with being a group of money getters without any sense for the finer things in life; while Chicago has retorted that the "homeless ones" of New York float in the clouds of spirit without any sound economic basis for their culture.[1]

Black Chicago was hardly without resources. As a matter of fact, the one black Congressman from a Northern state, Oscar De Priest, thought his congressional district in Chicago to be the second richest in the country. In October, people in the district were still talking about the incident that had been caused when Mrs. Hoover invited the congressman's wife to tea at the White House. Newspapers all over the South had erupted with dire predictions as to the future of the white race, but Mrs. Hoover and Mrs. De Priest had sipped and chatted nonetheless. Perhaps, people mused, that was because they were both Republicans.

De Priest and other black officials of city and county government were the results of an unusual political alliance with Mayor and Cook County boss Big Bill Thompson, which resulted in patronage and favors being effectively swapped for black ballots. In the recent 1927 election, Ralph Bunche reported, the opposition even suggested that Thompson was wholly the candidate of the blacks, going so far as even to kiss dark-hued babies. In the black wards, Big Bill's pluralities ran as high as sixteen to one. The black influence in political circles was beginning to spill over a bit into industry—but just a bit.

Since the war, Southern blacks had been pouring into the Northern cities at phenomenal rates. Most of Chicago's new workers came from Georgia, Mississippi, and Alabama, right off plantations and cotton farms in states that had been notorious for their low wages. In the early years of the decade, turnover was great in industry among these migrants. Many went into the manual labor areas, especially in the stockyards where they slaughtered and packed meat, and in the iron mills, and in servicing the great railroads that pulled into and out of the metropolis. Determined opposition to blacks in the unions, especially in the high-paying building trades, kept them only in outdoor positions of this industry such as bricklaying and plastering, which still commanded relatively low wages. The number of black people in middle to high positions in white-controlled business could be counted on the fingers of both hands. Most employment was unsteady, at best. When unemployment came along, as in the Stop and Shop Food Shops throughout Chicago,

> all the colored employees were given sterling recommendations as to their ability and character, with the added statement that they were being replaced because the policy of the stores was to employ white help.[2]

Throughout the country, blacks, as a class of workers, were continually being thrown into competition with new immigrants from foreign shores. An article in the Urban League's journal, *Opportunity*, early in 1929 worried about certain trends which seemed to be emerging in black employment. In addition to serious competition from new immigrants, the blacks were troubled by many industries which were slumping, precisely in those fields in which blacks had found their largest employment: agriculture, bituminous coal mining, lumber, iron and steel, building. Textiles were in serious decline as were food products, and, although the latter had not employed blacks in high numbers, the fact it was in decline would preclude future black employment there. The result of all of this was that

> All of these industries in their suspended activity have thrown labor upon the market. Add to these factors the rapid introduction of labor saving devices during the past 10 years, and as one economist has pointed out, the rearrangement in plant layout, the simplified routing of materials which under the old system required common labor, and

the substition of machinery for hand labor—the problem of
excess labor begins to assert itself.[3]

Blacks were already showing up in unemployment statistics in
increasingly higher numbers. As T. Arnold Hill put it:

> white men are driving trucks and express wagons in the
> South, repairing streets, doing scavenger work, delivering
> ice on their backs where formerly Negroes delivered and
> white men collected for deliveries. [4]

Another consequence was that black insurance companies, fra-
ternal orders, and even banks were complaining that their reve-
nues were being cut because of the decreased earning power of
their constituents. Already, in the fall of 1929, the Binga bank's
mortgages were getting shaky as black men and women were being fired and were having difficulty meeting payments.

There was a paradox: high wages were appearing right alongside increasing unemployment. Many blacks attributed the up-
swing in black unemployment to the demonstrable fact that racial attitudes had hardly changed an inch in half a century, that
discrimination operated openly and continually in the marketplace as it did in the social life of the community. Of the million
black men employed in heavy industry, nearly all did strictly
manual labor; of the million-and-a-half black women employed
full or part time, the greatest number did domestic and personal
service, or worked in agriculture—which meant picking cotton,
mostly—or in tobacco factories, or dressmaking; no other cate-
gory had as many as 10,000 individuals. It was not only discrimination. The blacks, Hill said in May of 1929,

> made entrance into industry when there was a strike to be
> broken, a shortage of labor for which white men could not
> be found, something onerous to be done, when pay was less
> than that paid others, or when some emergency made his
> labor expedient. And when emergencies subsided he was
> discharged and left to find his way as best he could.[5]

Now people were praying it wouldn't happen that way again, but
things didn't look good. Sure, Detroit could boast that 15,000
blacks were employed in the auto plants, but demand for autos

had been slackening all year. Too many cars had been produced; now dealers were unable to sell them at the rate the factories were making them. People all had their "first" cars and were waiting for those to get older before obtaining new ones, and auto jobs were dropping like flies. In cities other than Detroit, Ford plants had gone back to employing blacks only as janitors, porters, and truckers. Herbert Seligmann of the NAACP concluded a 1929 article by noting that

> Grave tensions and terrible maladjustments persist. A period of economic depression, with intensified competition for work, would undoubtedly throw a dangerous strain on relations between the races.[6]

During recess in a St. Louis school, while all the other kids were playing and running around, eight-year-old Bert Louis thought about his family. His father, formerly a machinist with American Can, had been laid off nearly a year ago, and, after drinking a lot, seemed to have gone away and disappeared. Bert and his family had to move to the third floor of an old flat. When it was cold, they had to carry coal up to the floor from a shed in the yard. The attic was actually just across the hall, and they did the wash there. Mom went to work in a grocery store across the street to try and make some money for a down payment on a rooming house she had her eye on. Every morning Bert, on his way to school, would drop off his brother and sister at the house of an "aunt," who would watch them until he got out of school. In the afternoons he'd pick them up again and take them home, up to the third floor. If they needed Mom, they could always lean out the window and yell for her. It gave her apoplexy to see them inching precariously out over the sidewalk, but at least she was nearby in case of emergencies. Bert wondered whether his father would ever come back.

In another industrial city about this time, writer Stuart Chase was having a shave when a workman entered the barber shop, dressed neatly in newly pressed suit. He was a little stooped and his eyes were tired; his hair was grizzled at the sides, but he moved briskly.

"Shoot the works, George," he says. "Gimme everything

you've got—haircut, shave, shampoo, massage, violet light, and George, just touch up this gray hair a little.'"[7]

The whole process took about an hour, and when it was over, the man handed George a five-dollar bill, squared his shoulders, and headed confidently for the door. George shook his head.

"He'll never fool that woman . . . that blamed personnel manager over at the National Brass Industries. He'll lie about his age, but she won't let him by. The poor devil has been out of work for God knows how long. Good machinist too. The people he was with pulled off a merger. Let the older men out. Lord, how I hated to take that five dollars—it was just thrown away. He'll never fool that woman, never in the world."[8]

Chase saw this event as one more bit of evidence that the mirror of American prosperity was cracked, if not completely flawed. The National Association of Manufacturers, surveying its members, found that 30 percent of them had maximum-age hiring limits running from twenty-five to seventy years; the most frequent limit for skilled workers was fifty, and forty-five for the unskilled. The age limit for firing was called the "dead line," and in many companies it was rapidly approached after forty. This dead line and the concept that went with it—that men were no longer productive workers at a certain age—was a relatively new phenomenon, introduced with the full flush of the machine age. The 1920 census showed that 8.8 percent of the farmers in the country were over sixty-five, and 5.4 percent of bankers and brokers—but barely more than one percent of the bookkeepers, machinists, coal miners, clothing workers, and so on. In the factories, the older the average age of the work force, the higher the premiums under group insurance schedules; with 6 million workers insured, this translated into reason for letting go of older workers as quickly as possible, and even more reason for not hiring an older man when a younger one was available.

Another rationale given for favoring younger workers was the result of old-age pension systems of private plants, which covered 4 million workers. In Europe such pensions were funded by the government, but not in America. Here, companies which had pension plans looked long and hard at a man over forty who came seeking a job, because entrance into the plans usually called for twenty-five years of service, and if an older man got sick or was forced to retire before completing those many years, the resultant fuss always made the company look bad.

James Truslow Adams commented that

There is no prospect of comfortable retirement in old age. For many who never thought of it in the old days there is the ever-present specter of illness and incapacity. Our prosperity can be maintained only by making people want more, and work more, all the time. Those, and there are many, who believe that our recent prosperity has been mainly caused by the phenomenal expansion of the automobile business, tell us that it will soon be necessary to find some other article which will similarly take the public fancy and create billions in sales—and billions of expense to men already tired of doing nothing but meeting new expenses.[9]

According to an ad paid for by *True Story Magazine* in *The New York Times*,

America's Greatest Discovery Was—That a millionaire cannot wear 10,000 pairs of $10 shoes. But a hundred thousand others can if they've got the $10 to pay for them, and the leisure to show them off. This discovery was made less than ten years ago. But it has been responsible in these ten years for a greater measure of success of American business than any other factor. . . . You Business Executives sitting at your desks, you have been making a fairy tale come true. Within ten years you have done more toward the sum total of human happiness than has ever been done before in all the centuries of historical time.[10]

It was not entirely untrue. Per capita income had increased nearly 20 percent during the decade. The installment buying system created $6 billion of new buying, but the consumers had to pay that money eventually, plus an average of 15 percent interest. This, it appeared, they were doing with relative happiness. A British psychologist, studying the phenomenon of installment buying—the British called it "hire-purchase"—concluded that it was another instance of the emergence of America's national myth, a belief in El Dorado, the city of Gold:

In a community large enough to be essentially self-support-
ing an unquestioning faith in prosperity does produce it,
provided the necessary energy is put into industry. . . .
Any business system which is "American" is sure to
furnish gold in dreamed-of volume . . . since El Dorado
belongs to the community as a whole . . . the
wealth . . . justifies the expansion of production. Similarly the distributor encourages the consumer to buy more
than he can afford, on the strength of that faith, which they
both share, the certainty of catching up with the rainbow's
end tomorrow.[11]

Toward this end, the standard of living had visibly shifted—
again, urged by the realm of the imagination. It had been in former days a luxury to have a car; now it was a necessity, and an
expensive one. In 1920 the Department of Labor had estimated
that 80 percent of American families lived below the line of
health and decency that an income of $2,000 would give to
them. By 1929, even with the 20 percent jump in income, Brookings was still estimating the poverty group as near 75 percent.
Why? Probably because the new wants had taken up most of the
new money: out of twenty-six families in Middletown who had
no bathrooms in their houses, twenty-one did manage to have
cars.

As the Lynds said, among such families,

The poorer workingman coming home after his nine and a
half hours on the job, walks up the frequently unpaved
street, turns in at a bare yard littered with a rusty veloci-
pede or wornout automobile tires, opens a sagging door, and
enters the living-room of the house. From the room the
whole house is visible—the kitchen with table and floor
swarming with flies and often strewn with bread crusts,
orange skins, torn papers, and lumps of coal and wood; the
bedrooms with soiled, heavy quilts falling off the beds. The
worn green shades hanging down at a tipsy angle admit only
a flecked half-light upon the ornate calendars or enlarged
color portraits of the children in heavy gilt frames tilted out
at a precarious angle just below the ceiling. The whole interior is musty with stale odors of food, clothing, and tobacco.
On the brown varnished shelf of the sideboard, a wooden-
backed family hairbrush, with the baby bottle, a worn

purse, and yesterday's newspaper, may be half stuffed out of sight behind a bright blue glass cake dish. Rust spots the base-burner. A baby in wet, dirty clothes crawls about the bare floor among the odd pieces of furniture.[12]

The Lynds found these conditions in from a quarter to a half of all the workingmen's homes surveyed. Their research convinced them that installment buying, along with the heavy promoting of new needs by industries such as motion pictures and electric utilities, were facilitating the wish for higher standards of living.

The result, said the Lynds, was that life now was not, as it had been in 1890 in Middletown, a series of economic plateaus. No longer did you "arrive" at a station in life. You didn't hear people saying that making X or Y a year was "pretty good for people in our circumstances." Today, everybody in town could see what the families above them on the economic ladder had, and they all, rich and poor, lived "on a slope from any point of which desirable things belonging to people all the way to the top are in view."

Not everything that was visible was attainable, and there lay the rub. This was true in Middletown, and in many another part of the country. In the summer of 1929 the New York Department of Labor, under Frances Perkins, studied 536 working-class families where the wife worked at some task inside the home which added to the family income. The husbands averaged $28.86 a week, or $1,470 a year, well below the poverty line, and *17 percent of them were unemployed at the time of the survey.* The women's work brought in about $6 additional per week. Not a single family of the 536 surveyed made enough money, in the state's eyes, to maintain a family of five at what was considered the minimum comfort level.

It was true all over. Hourly wages, in an average of 23 different industries, had been up to 61 cents per hour in 1920 before the slump. By 1922 this had shrunk to 49 cents; though it had been edging up ever since, in 1929 it had climbed back only to the same level it had been at the beginning of the decade, before the "greatest era of prosperity the country has ever known."

Relative poverty spread beyond the hourly-wage worker. Of the independent storekeepers in the country, 750,000 did business of less than $25,000 a year accrued turnover, with profits in the 5 to 10 percent area; in one survey, more than a third of the retailers in a large city did total business of less than $7 a day. Teachers earned $1,200 a year; department store clerks, $1,800; the one million government service workers averaged $1,585 each. On top of this, about 20,000 businesses a year had been failing through the decade, most of them middle-sized enterprises.[13]

Earlier in the year, engineer Ray Schroeder, in Cleveland, had been thrown out of a job by one of those business failures. He had been out of work a few months, but fortunately, the signing of an agreement between Arthur S. McGee's International Engineers and the Russian government had given him back his livelihood. On October 24 he was busily at work helping to create plans for what was to be the world's largest steel plant. It was a monumental project. There were five Russians permanently in the office, to help in translating English into Russian, and feet into meters. They were reasonable sorts of fellows, even if they kept mostly to themselves. Ray used his own drafting instruments, of which he was very proud. But it wasn't work that interested him so much these days, or the discussion by the Russians about their ambitious Five-Year Plan of which the steel plant was an important part—it was a young girl who lived down the block from him. In the afternoons, after work, on the way home, he'd see Hazel swinging on the gate of the fence in front of her parents' house, and they'd stop to talk. It was curious that they had the same last name and weren't related, but Ray was aiming to fix that. They planned to get married next summer. Maybe they'd even get a chance to go to Russia when the plant was built. That would be quite a honeymoon.

Paul Edwards was taking a lot of heat from the other guys at the Brunswick Radio factory in Muskegon, Michigan, where he assembled the iron cores for the power transformers of the radios. That was because he had gone over to show the new Swedish girl from Minnesota exactly how the cores were put together—and hadn't tried getting a date with her. Now, with all the pressure from the guys, he had to go over and ask her. In the background, he could hear over the airwaves, which were constantly being tested, a story about one of the Lake Michigan ferries being given up for lost. Fifty-seven people dead! It reminded him of his own narrow escape. This past summer he'd been employed by Captain Anderson on board the old whaleback cargo ship *Andaste*. It was a good job, but what with being on the lake all the time it was hard to date girls, so he'd taken the radio factory job instead. He was glad he had, because a few weeks after he'd said goodbye to the old scow, she'd sunk in a storm, and old Captain Anderson's body had washed up on the shore with a $400 roll of bills still in the pocket. He told the story to the Swedish girl and—what do you know!—she said she'd give him a date after work on Saturday. The guys looked at him with new respect.

Up in Sargent, North Dakota, blacksmith Bert H. was working as hard as he could, as he always did in the fall before the winter's slack season set in and there was nothing for a smith to do but sharpen plow lathes and replace sled runners. Now there were lots of wagon and buggy wheels to be redone; he took off the bad spokes and the old rims, and heated up new iron rims in the forge to replace the old ones. Later, he'd bring the wood from the old wheels home; it burned steady and long. His shop had a large forge, an anvil, benches with vises, and a trip-hammer and polisher powered by a small gas engine. A lot of work this time of year was out in the fields, in the evenings, mending the flues of the threshing machine engines. As soon as the machines had cooled from the day's work, Bert would work with them in an enormous boiler, as a foundry all night, and he'd be covered with soot in the morning, but it paid reasonably well. The drought had hurt the crops in the area this year, as it had for the past several years. Many of the farmers weren't able to pay on time, but Bert hoped that during the winter they'd be able to pay something, so he could keep his family in food and together under one roof.

The fall of 1929 reminded young Hazel Cardozo, a farmer's daughter in Lawton, Oklahoma, of the terrible falls of 1919 and 1920. The family had been in Texas then. When her father and mother got married around the turn of the century, they'd each had a farm. By the time the war came along they were down to one farm. The war gave good prices for a while, but not very evenly. Some years it was good, some, bad. Prices for cotton varied tremendously, and so did the crops. It seemed that every year that her father would decide not to plant but to move the whole family into town to work for somebody else, there'd be a good crop, and it would fire him up to plant the next year; then that next year would come, and it would be a bad one.

Little by little he was reduced from owner-farmer to cropper. Although 1920 promised to be a good year, and the crops of peanuts and cotton looked real fine, in the fall the rains came and continued for six weeks. At the end of them, the cotton stalks had just about turned to trees, and the peanuts, turned over to dry in the air, were all moldy. The land couldn't even be cleared easily for next year's planting: those stalks had to be hewn down as if they were wood. With seven cotton pickers on his hands, Father had taken up the family and moved to Oklahoma, where there was work and farming for a time. Even this got too hard, though, and Father left the family in 1922 and hadn't been seen since. It was a blow, but nobody had much of a chance to go and find him, either, what with work six days a week for the older ones, and school for Hazel and the younger ones. Somehow Ma managed to scrape by, taking her pay for washing and mending in chickens or a few eggs. By 1929 Hazel was in the ninth grade at Lawton High School, and she was doing "A" work in every subject. Her Latin teacher was especially proud of her. But crops in the area were bringing such low prices that the farmers were telling Ma they had no more work for her coming up, and it was going to be a strain to get through the winter. So, one day in late fall, Hazel walked downtown and into the Woolworth's to see about a job helping out after school from now until after the Christmas season. To her surprise, she got the job. It was a relief to know there'd be some extra money to help the family.

Things were bad for farmers all over the country. Up in Boise, Idaho, Fred Fletcher had decided he was fed up enough to be called an extremist. "If a farmer plants four rows of potatoes," he wrote angrily to *The Nation,*

> he must give the product of three of them to the railroad to haul the crop to the market. . . . If he plants apples he must give for freight the product of two out of three rows. We get about 60¢ a box—the Idaho Delicious sells for about 10¢ each on the stalls. . . . A million tons of hay rotted in the stack in Idaho three years ago. Freight on hay is ten dollars a ton to points of market (stockyards fifteen dollars) and as these cities are closer to hay fields of Iowa, Nebraska,

Kansas, the Western farmer can't compete, for they cut the price when the Westerner ships and he gets a net amount less than cost—under five dollars, and it costs to harvest the bale and haul to the depot about seven dollars per ton. . . . Legislate? We have tried and failed. Write it up, broadcast it? We get—indifference.[14]

During the early twenties new high farm taxes were adding to the burden by absorbing in some cases one-third to two-thirds of net farm income. During the decade, a million farmers left their homesteads, and by 1929 only 6 million remained. The new machinery, the tractors and combines, required large acreages to work effectively and efficiently. In some ways these machines were the farmers' worst enemies: during the decade, they helped to eliminate millions of horses and mules from farms, and, in the process, eliminated the markets for hay and grain which fed those animals. Yet land prices continued for a while ruinously high, and mortgage payments were difficult. Fred Fletcher remarked that in his valley near Boise, homes were selling in 1929 for half of what they ought to have been bringing. Many of the farmers were being forced to sell out to pay off their debts. Some ended up as sharecropping tenants on lands they once used to own; others lost everything through bankruptcy. These farm failures led in turn to the failing of several thousand rural banks during the decade, a trend which seemed to reach its peak in 1926, when 976 banks went under.

Iowa was the state with the most severe number of failures; about five hundred closed their doors in the state during the decade. H. Mac Bohlman suggests that

Iowa bankers tended to believe that the land was a superior form of security and often they were unduly suspicious of loans except to farmers and were interested in getting mortgages on the farm lands of Iowa in return. . . . Iowa was cursed with bank failures. . . . Stockholders of defunct banks were required to "dig up" an assessment of 100 per cent upon their respective capital stock holdings so that depositors could receive back a larger percentage of their deposits. There was *no* government guarantee of deposits. This meant that many stockholders could not do this or if they did their savings and assets were depleted.[15]

In this manner the farmers, bankers, and businessmen all suffered from the plight of the farms. It was a vicious cycle.

In a sense, farms suffered in the twenties from lack of attention by a government and a people caught up in the glamorous and exciting advance of business. Manufacturing and distribution of industrial and commercial products seemed to be everywhere and everything. Business bought itself high tariffs behind which to grow; business consolidated and controlled railroads which squeezed the farmers dry; business controlled needed mortgage money; business even controlled farm prices because grain speculators acting in a few cities set the prices for crops before they even got into the ground—and there seemed little that farmers could do about any of this. They might curse the grain wheeler-dealers; they might agree with Will Roger's definition of a holding company: something akin to handing the stolen goods to an accomplice while the policeman searched you. This did little good; few heard their protests. It was, after all, a new refrain.

In the preceding half-century, agricultural discontent about these forces had organized to some degree, primarily in the use of cooperatives to get better prices for crops and lower prices for needed supplies and staples. By the early twenties, these cooperatives had been able to muster enough political power to crystallize an incipient revolt in the form of the La Follette candidacy of 1924, but La Follette was soundly defeated along with Democrat John W. Davis, and the political power of the farmers dwindled in consequence.

The discontents of the farmers crystallized into the successive versions of the McNary-Haugen farm bill, about which discussion raged throughout the twenties. At its most radical, this bill would have operated farms in the same way, and with the same help, as businesses in the country were getting. There would have been attempts to control the disposition of crop surpluses and to minimize speculation, thus insuring prices. To further aid the farmer, loans would have been readily available through farmer-run cooperatives. Farm Bureau spokesmen from the western Midwest states took the leading role in promoting McNary-Haugen. The position this organization took became increasingly radical: regulations on the foodstuffs industry; the return of railroads to private control so competition would lower rates; vast calls for economy in public expenditures, as well as specific farm-oriented proposals such as export debentures, domestic acreage allotment plans, price fixing, and other similar and radical measures. All of these were threats to a business-oriented culture. McNary-Haugen was vetoed twice by Coolidge, in extreme form in 1927 and in watered-down form in 1928, despite the support of over two hundred farm organizations. The veto the second time, which was strongly applauded by Secretary Mellon and Secretary Hoover,

> was taken to mean that American industry would not tolerate any attempt to tamper with the protective system. Industry was the political and economic boss and it intended to remain thus.[16]

As antidote to the parity arguments of McNary-Haugen, the Hoover presidential administration could offer only the Agricultural Marketing Act of 1929, which relied for help to the farmers on loans for consolidating and coordinating the marketing activities of farm co-ops. Its major action arm was the Farm Board, chaired by International Harvester President Alexander Legge. Although the language of the enabling act suggested that the Farm Board's specific purpose was to encourage the cooperative marketing organizations that had long been in existence, the Board viewed its own fiat differently and was proceeding with the setting up of *new* cooperatives, to be run by "professionals" which would presumably do better than such organizations had done in the past.

The entire farm problem in the fall of 1929 was seen in terms of one facet only: crop surpluses. By handling these more effectively, Farm Board logic went, farm problems would clear themselves up. That exports had dropped, that farm values were unreal, that millions of farm laborers had deserted the homesteads, that farm commodities did not command equitable prices when compared to the goods farmers needed: none of these myriad and complex facets held any sway with Chairman Legge, nor with Vice-chairman Stone or Commissioners Teague and Denman.

At this moment on October 24, 1929, those gentlemen were in Chicago, discussing how the Farmers National Grain Corporation and the Grain Stabilization Corporation—two of their new cooperatives—ought to be set up. They had just offered the chairmanships of these new organizations to James H. Murray, vice-president of Quaker Oats and current president of the Chicago Board of Trade—precisely the sort of person farmers had long viewed as the enemy incarnate. With great foresight, Murray turned down the job. The commissioners continued the search.

By sheer chance, they were met this day at the center of action for commodities trading in the United States, that is, at the single most farm-sensitive spot on the continent, above the wheat and corn pits of the Chicago Board of Trade—at precisely that moment in time when farm products were crashing down precipitously. The Farm Board was the legally constituted body who could have done the most to fend off the disaster occurring floors below them, or ameliorate its impact. Wheat was down 8, 9, 10 cents the bushel, the worst calamity in that grain in Chicago's history. The city's bankers, desperate to help, had offered virtually unlimited loans to their brokerage and commodity customers, to prevent further collapse at this hour. Such news, combined with that of the bankers' meeting in New York, had let some small rays of sunshine into the pits' gloom. What should the Farm Board's commissioners do? Many farmers and grain merchants could have told them, instanter: make outright purchases of corn and wheat and stabilize prices. As simple as that. Just two days ago, the Farm Board voted $100 million to prop up the price of cotton in the South. Couldn't it do the same for wheat?

It could, but it didn't, though that fact had not yet become known in Chicago at noon, or one o'clock in New York. However, on the strength of the fact that the Board was meeting (even if to consider wrong action), wheat began to inch back up slowly in the grain pit.

In San Francisco, it was nearing ten in the morning, but the day seemed already to have gone on forever. Word had gotten out that the market in New York was collapsing. Monroe Bloom, unable to obtain by telephone the latest market quotations in order to check on the margins of his bank's collateral loans, went out of his office and walked to the nearest brokerage house two blocks away to look at the board. The streets were swarming with people, excited and grave-looking, and he had to fight to get a glimpse of the board in the office. A few blocks beyond, at the second-largest exchange in the country, stocks were collapsing just as surely and steadily as they were doing in New York and in Chicago.

In one of the outlying San Francisco business districts, board-boy Jack Simpson was already covered with glistening sweat that had mixed with the fine dust of the chalk from the figures he was putting on the board.

Usually in the mornings, starting at six, he got the figures from the tape, but the ticker was so hopelessly behind this morning that he had long since donned a pair of earphones. The main office downtown fed him quotations in a steady drone. The numbers were coming in so quickly now that he couldn't get all of them. The blue chips were acting queerly, prices were dropping, the ticker was useless, and nothing that came over the Dow-Jones seemed to explain why it all was happening.

People who had come in for just a glance were staying on; the room was getting more and more crowded. Along with the regulars, there were others this morning: waitresses, icemen in their long aprons, a cop on rest from his beat, several bankers, small businessmen from what seemed to be every shop in the area. For such a large crowd they were, it seemed to Jack, unusually still. Instead of the daily jocular comments, exchanges, and greetings he was used to, there were only dour, tight-lipped expressions of concern, reflecting general amazement at the steady downward pull in values. At the order desk the telephone rang constantly; those rings, and the continual chatter of the lame ticker, were all that could be heard in the room. No one spoke a word.

Using the headset was giving Jack a headache. He removed the earphones and switched the broadcast from downtown to the loudspeaker system. Now everyone could hear it. No one would miss a quote this way. Jack thought rather gloomily that the people here were sure entitled to that right now. The broadcast seemed to stir people to keener attentiveness while it added to the tension. The voice coming over the speaker was so steady that the speech often seemed blurred; only a practiced ear and a sharp mind could make out most of the quotes. Once in a while, when there was a big drop in a stock, Jack could hear the muffled gasps of the crowd. Though it was nearly one o'clock in New York, as far as the ticker was concerned it still showed the eleven o'clock valley of despond. Jack worked on:

> All eyes attentively followed my movements as I continually chalked down the price changes, mostly on the downside. All ears were straining to decipher the jumble being broadcast over the speakers, and Lord! was I getting tired. Both in my arms and legs, not to mention eye strain and my long-empty stomach. . . . The strong-smelling, swirling clouds of smoke from countless cigars and cigarettes were especially heavy on the platform where my dashing, rising and stooping quotation-making gymnastics made me breathe heavily in the thick haze; growing increasingly weary and breathing heavier, the atmosphere caused me to cough often.[17]

At the windows, which normally could be opened for ventilation, faces pressed in from outside, straining to hear something of hope. There was nothing. And every moment, the quotations seemed to be getting lower and lower. How much longer could it go on like this?

Chapter Twelve

ON THE COUNTRY'S WEALTH
1:00 P.M.

It was a peak year for travel among those who had money. Ocean liners, filled to capacity, steamed across the Atlantic, the Pacific, and the route between New York and the South American ports with regularity, loaded with Americans going abroad, then returning home after holidays. In the past few years it had become a trial to these shipbound people to be away from the stock market for the length of time their crossings took, and they would linger in the wire rooms for news of their favorite stocks. This soon became more than the wire rooms could handle along with their regular work, and requests for stock reports were kept to hourly listings by some ships. In the fall of 1929, on the liners *Berengaria* and *Leviathan*, the enterprising Michael J. Meehan and Company had recently set up modest stock brokerage offices which relayed orders and prices to and from New York on the Atlantic crossings. These offices also offered another function: they performed as miniature exchanges themselves, encouraging trading among the passengers in the stocks they held.

At one in the afternoon of October 24, the *Berengaria*, several hundred miles east of Southampton and heading in towards New York, was making good time. But in the small Meehan and Company offices, there was a state of panic. Several hundred of the ship's 1,414 passengers had crowded in to find out what was doing and, once they found out, to hurry buy and sell orders to

New York. One woman had already lost $160,000, and losses from many another person were acknowledged as heavy, if not as bad as that. Approximately 20,000 shares, with a market value of over $2 million, had been traded thus far during the day in the *Berengaria*'s stock office. The luxury pleasure cruise had, for many, turned into a bad trip. One passenger described the scene at the Meehan office as a death watch which kept people from their meals.

Carl Fisher hoped that one day ocean liners such as the *Berengaria* would dock in Fort Pond Bay in Montauk on their way to and from Europe, so that rich passengers would be able to come and go on vacation from his own coastal resort at Montauk, even now abuilding. In October of 1929, Carl Fisher owned nine thousand acres of Montauk Point, the entire eastern tip of Long Island.

An extraordinary man, Carl Fisher. An Iowan, he owned a bicycle shop and saw the value of a vacuum-sealed headlight when one was presented to him. He bought the patent, made the Prestolite, and coined money with it. He had become a millionaire by the time he was twenty-two. He soon owned the speedway at Indianapolis, and in 1911 he broke the auto world speed record for one mile. After a fling at trying to build the country's first coast-to-coast paved highway, Fisher had gone south. By the end of the war, he was heavily involved in a risky enterprise with his money: the building of an entirely new city out of the mangrove jungles on Florida's eastern coast, a city he called Miami Beach. But by 1925, when most of the country was just diving into the Florida real-estate boom, Fisher was pulling out. Miami Beach was well under way, and he was restless. "There's nothing left for me to do . . . but sit around in white pants looking pretty like the rest of you goddamn winter loafers," he told friends. So he decided to build a new Miami Beach on the eastern tip of Long Island.

With great secrecy, so as not to raise prices, he and cohorts Jim Allison, Albert Champion (spark plugs), Howard E. Coffin (Hudson Motors), Richard Hoyt and Charles Hayden (bankers), paid $2.5 million for nine thousand acres of farm land and deserted beach coast to build a resort and a transatlantic harbor. It was Fisher's conceit that the city and surrounds he would build there—he conceived all the plans in an afternoon on the deck of his yacht—would have old-world charm: medieval cottages with thatched roofs and windmills, blooded sheep with shepherds, hunters, and hounds. The prevailing architectural style was English Tudor. There would be moors and dunes, horse trails, and a yacht basin second to none. Work started in early 1926. Eight hundred workmen built roads, electrified miles of property, built a three-hundred-room Tudor hotel, a yacht club, a polo field, a race track, a glass-enclosed tennis area. On Star Island a casino was built: Fisher planned eventually to have a hospital and a college on the island, which he would connect to the mainland by means of a causeway. By 1928, the Manor (hotel), Surf Club, and the exclusive Shepherd's Neck housing development, as well as Montauk Chalet and Fisher's own seven-story-high skyscraper, were completed. A Protestant church, a movie theater building, and other such edifices were coming along well. Plots of land were reserved for Woolworth, Goodyear, Champion, and Chrysler. All building plans were to be subject to Fisher's approval. Several hundred houses had been built; plans were afoot for two new skyscrapers and for a new five-hundred-room hotel.

By August of 1929 Montauk was active. People with money came out to watch professional tennis matches in the glass-enclosed courts. Yachts filled the club marina. Crowds watched auto races on Fairview Avenue. Fisher magnanimously gave the first house built at Montauk to an old benefactor, a man who had given him a start years before. People were eager to buy the bonds Fisher floated for the project, and he let only certain people take them, asking for one-third of the money down and making generous payment schedules for the rest. Borrowing millions from friendly New York banks, Fisher operated Montauk essentially on margin. By 1929, $10,000 was a usual asking price for one acre of his paradise.

In September of 1929 the Star Island Casino was raided by the district attorney. One story had New York's Mayor Jimmy Walker posing as a waiter in order to escape the D.A.'s dragnet in this raid. Fisher had already sold the property to a New York developer and was reportedly unhappy about the gambling, loose women, and liquor. A teetotaler for years, Fisher was proud that his own Montauk Yacht Club was not raided, though *The New York Times* casually reported that it was well known that bootleg liquor was regularly unloaded there. Fisher survived this scandal, but then worse things hove into view.

By October 1, 1929, Fisher had $40 million invested in Montauk's future, and that money was balanced on bonds due in November, December, January. His own money would come out only when other people bought the cottages and the office buildings and took places in the yacht basin he had dredged at enormous cost. He was on the cusp of success when, a week later, he received word by telegram that a hurricane had done tremendous damage to Miami Beach. This wasn't precisely true, but Fisher had no way of knowing that. He suspended all work at Montauk and shot right down to Florida to see what he could do there. Money that was supposed to go towards completing Montauk and paying off those bonds went instead to shoring up his Miami Beach holdings, which were already shaky, undermined by unwise real-estate sales he had made to others around his own holdings. Would Montauk have to be sacrificed to Miami? No, Fisher said. He would personally guarantee the Montauk bonds with his Miami holdings, which were as good as gold.

October 23, 1929, was an anniversary of sorts for Fisher, the anniversary of his first marriage, the one to the woman who had nurtured him and who would be his biographer. He had left her when he had left Miami. Now he was married for a second time, and both new couples were friends of a sort. Fisher magnanimously built houses for both families in Montauk and Miami— he liked to do that for old helpmeets.

On October 24, then, Carl Fisher hovered between Miami and Montauk, between old and new loves, as the stock market crashed and $40 million of his money was stretched to the breaking point.

Fisher was trying to attract the very rich but succeeded in attracting only what one might call the second tier, those wealthy enough by ordinary standards, but not wealthy beyond the power of crashes to change. Along the northern shore of Nassau County were these immensely wealthier people. They pursued a way of life so fabulous it seemed not of the same world as the rest of humanity. They owned more than six hundred estates along the Gold Coast of Nassau: most of which were more than fifty acres. Some had hundreds of acres, and more than a few ran even larger. They held parties with swimming pools that had thousands of orchids in them, and cigarettes wrapped and designed to be smoked in hundred-dollar bills.

Many of those who lived in these estates had ties to the stock market, and to that portion of the country's wealth—the far larger part—which remained in the hands of a very few families. At the cornerstone of the Glen Cove peninsula, then, it was fitting to find the estates of J. P. Morgan and his partners, their yachts riding side by side. In October of 1929, Morgan had donated his old yacht to the President of the United States and was busily building a new one which would be the largest in the world. Nearby was the estate of George F. Baker the elder, who had ridden at the side of Morgan the elder in the bloody wars of the turn of the century. Baker, eighty-nine in 1929, ill and permanently in bed, was the largest single stockholder of both AT&T and U.S. Steel. He was in many ways the epitome of the very, very rich. He had a custom-built car with a built-in toilet and carried an ancient canvas bag in which he kept one-dollar gold pieces for tips. His silence was as legendary as his wealth. His two public speeches consisted of "thank you" and "God bless." His one interview contained this gem:

> Everything is all right. The country is on the road to prosperity, perhaps the greatest prosperity any country ever attained. But I shouldn't be talking about it. Business men of America should reduce their talk at least two-thirds. Everyone should reduce his talk. There is rarely ever a good reason for anybody to talk. Silence—it uses up less energy.[1]

On July 18, 1929, Baker's holdings appreciated $11 million in one day. On October 24, 1929, by 1:30 P.M., he had lost approximately $11 million. Did it make any difference? It was hard to tell.

Things were going similarly with many others of the Gold Coasters. Near Baker and the Morganeers were Charles Pratt and Stephen Harkness, early partners of Rockefeller; Henry Phipps, the partner of Andrew Carnegie; Clarence Mackay of Postal Telegraph; the Fricks; Claus Spreckels of sugar trust fame; Payne Whitney of Standard Oil; the Vanderbilts. The F. W. Woolworth house contained solid gold bathroom fixtures and doorknobs and a dining room ceiling gilded with fifteen hundred square feet of fourteen-carat gold. The Tiffany estate in Laurel Hollow had eighty-two rooms. The Phippses had a private golf course, the Marshall Fields had polo, golf, squash, tennis, badminton, indoor and outdoor pools, sailboats, motorboats, a skeet range, a seaplane landing area, and a thousand-acre hunting preserve.

The Phipps estate, one of seven owned by the family, was modeled on a large English eighteenth-century manor house of cherry-red brick, limestone, and a pale gold roof. It had separate rooms for glasses, china, luggage, silver. Original Chippendale furniture, an armoire which belonged to James II, and a desk used by Cromwell to sign the death warrant of Charles I. Mrs. Phipps played no political favorites; she liked all manner of English things.

Otto Kahn's place was the stuff of dreams. He built a mountain in country that was no more than rolling, and had to make a railroad to bring in the supplies. This was fitting: senior partner in Kuhn, Loeb, he had helped to reorganize the Union Pacific, the Baltimore and Ohio, the Missouri Pacific, and other railroads. He made enormous amounts of money and spent enormous amounts. Unlike many of the other Gold Coasters, Kahn was a serious philanthropist. He was the major supporter of the Metropolitan Opera for a third of a century, and also supported the New York Philharmonic and opera companies all over the globe. He sponsored the first appearances in this country of Toscanini, and the theaters of Max Reinhardt and Stanislavski. In 1922 he paid Enrico Caruso $20,000 to sing one song at his daughter's wedding. His estate adjoined the grounds of the Morristown Club. When the club wanted to expand their golf course, they asked Kahn if they could buy some of his land. He donated it to them, and they felt obliged to offer him a membership even though he was a Jew. He accepted it, then never used it. That was the gentlemanly thing to do.

It was a grand gesture, one of many in a grand age, but such gestures were not always the hallmark of the very wealthy. They more commonly used their wealth to maintain and protect their interests. Many villages were incorporated by the estate owners in order to lower their own taxes and control the areas. Morgan, Baker, Mackay, and others founded Lattingtown and kept it under tight control. Roads not used for access to the estates were allowed to fall into disrepair. Local police acted as private guards. In another instance, Mrs. August Belmont stationed her own uniformed employees at entrance routes to public beaches and told people the beaches were private property. Pratt bought and held control of the Long Island Railroad in order to keep it rickety and antiquated, the better to prevent the riffraff from flooding out of the wicked city too near the estates of the mighty. Lest this have the unwanted side effect of cutting down on the supply of servants for the estates, the owners simply imported them wholesale from abroad. Mrs. Phipps, of course, would have only English servants near Cromwell's desk.

Robert Moses, protégé of Al Smith and builder of Jones Beach State Park on Long Island's south shore, a facility for the people, was in the process of building a highway near the north shore, the Northern State Parkway. To do so he had to do battle with the estate owners. And it was in this battle that the estate owners' style of life was clashing most directly with the public interest, in October of 1929.

At issue was the sanctity of a Wheatley Hills private golf course. For several years Robert Moses had been jockeying with the power barons of the area—Kahn, Stimson, Mills, Winthrop, De Forest—for a right-of-way for his route that would not unduly irritate them. So far he had done all right. He touched little of their property though he had run roughshod over small farmers in place of disturbing their serenity. But when the Northern State got to a place between North Hills and Dix Hills, things got more difficult. Here the names were Morgan, Whitney, Grace, Garvan, and Phipps, and the route could take no more twists and turns. He had to go through them and their golf course; there was no other way. But the barons refused to give an inch, and they threw into the battle against the Master Builder a masterpiece of monkey-wrenching, attorney Grenville Clark, Harvard classmate of the new governor, Franklin Delano Roosevelt.

Roosevelt and Moses had long been at odds. When FDR ran for governor, the incumbent vacating the job to run for President was Al Smith, and Al Smith's righthand man and most important intellectual bulwark was Robert Moses. Upon being elected in the midst of a vast defeat for Smith, FDR was faced with the task of either governing in Smith's place by simply continuing his cabinet of Moses, Belle Moskowitz, and assorted others, or of picking his own people for those posts and incurring Smith's lasting wrath and Moses' undying enmity. He had to choose to be his own man, and did. Moses was far from out, though, because he held the presidency of the Long Island State Parks Commission and of the State Parks Council, both positions of no pay and enormous power.

As Robert Caro points out, the battle over the Northern State's routeway had begun even before FDR took office. Clark wrote him a letter at Warm Springs arguing for a detour. Moses countered with his own letter, touching Roosevelt's deep nerve by pointing out that the Wheatley Hills barons were

> people of large wealth who have always been able to buy what they wanted or to get what they wanted by influence and pressure. It is difficult for these people to believe there is anyone they cannot reach in some way.[2]

For a few months it appeared that Moses was winning. FDR went out of his way to keep on his side the brilliant man whom Al Smith had prized so highly. Even if he did not want Moses dominating the state capitol as he had done in Smith's time, Roosevelt appreciated the quality of the man. Moses drove the governor over the two proposed routes and FDR wrote Clark that he saw no reason to change Moses' plans. But then the game got dirtier.

Clark discovered an earlier deal between Moses and his relative Otto Kahn. Kahn had persuaded Moses not to have the route touch *his* private golf course, in exchange for $10,000 with which the highway people could buy the right-of-way from a poor farmer. Clark crowed the mischief to Roosevelt. Moses lamely explained that the gift had had nothing to do with the shifting of the route, but he was losing ground. Clark went to legislators and got them on his side, hinting exposure of the Moses-Kahn deal. Over the summer, various tries at compromise failed, and as the autumn drew on, things got very serious.

Clark and the barons got their forces together and wrote FDR on October 23, 1929, an unmistakable ultimatum. Because of Moses' recalcitrance, they said, they would be forced to launch a major legislative fight over appropriations for the Northern State in the 1930 sessions. No appropriations would be gotten, it was made clear, until the roadway had shifted its route out of Wheatley Hills. Roosevelt was in a bind. Should he pressure Moses to change the route, or should he risk the displeasure and active antagonism of this powerful group in 1930? In FDR's mind, 1930 was a crucial year. He would run for the governorship on his own record, not on Al Smith's. If he won, and if times were to turn bad—as he had long predicted they would—that meant, in his mind, and in the minds of Louis Howe and his other political advisors, that Franklin Delano Roosevelt would be the logical front-runner for the Democratic nomination for the presidency in 1932. And that race would be against Hoover, an incumbent Republican who would stand for bad times. Could FDR risk this surefire scenario on a bitter fight against people with serious money, over a small matter in which the governor was being forced against his will to back a man he personally detested, a man who had deliberately snubbed him at his own inauguration, a man who had laughed at him for years in private Smith circles?

On October 24, 1929, the Clark letter lay waiting in Albany for the governor's return, a time bomb threatening all future plans, a bomb which had to be defused.

In an issue of *The Nation* dated October 23, 1929, which was being read in a few households as the Crash hurried on, Stuart Chase searched for definitions of prosperity against which to measure America's twenties. There were many yardsticks: economic productivity, the distribution of material goods and services, the balance between work and leisure and security in the average home. Chase found an additional one:

> Fourth and last, we might define prosperity as the life more abundant . . . compounding security and leisure with a wide variety of useful and beautiful material things, and above all an atmosphere in which the creative arts flourish, great poets sing, and man climbs one step nearer to his remorseless destiny.[3]

In ancient Greece, perhaps one person out of three had some great contact with the higher things in life, Chase guessed. How was America doing?

The talk among the wealthy men may have been of parkways

and golf courses, but the talk among the wealthy women in the fall of 1929 was of art. True, the wealthy had always been collectors—recently, Francis P. Garvan had bid the absurd price of $5,500 for a tea-strainer that had something vaguely historic to do with early Rhode Island—but for the most part the wealthy had been content to follow whatever the dictates of society seemed to be and simply apply the leverage of their money on the side of the establishment.

A chance meeting which would help even the score had taken place in Egypt the previous winter. Both Mrs. John D. Rockefeller, Jr., and Miss Lizzie P. Bliss had repaired thither to avoid the rigors of the New York winter. They met and exchanged views about starting a museum in New York devoted to what were considered at the moment the outrages of "modern art." Returning on board ship to New York Mrs. Rockefeller discussed this with Mrs. Cornelius J. Sullivan, and a formidable trio was born. Home, the three sat down with A. Conger Goodyear, a former military man who was trustee of the Albright Gallery in Buffalo, and asked him to be chairman of a committee to organize the new Museum of Modern Art.

Modern art was then deplored in America. An article in an art journal worried whether such a museum as the ladies contemplated was really necessary: it was headlined "Albert Sterner Questions/Need for Modern Art Museum/Sees Peculiar Modes and Mannerisms in Art as/ An Invention as Impermanent as the/ Queer Is Unenduring,"[4] and that said it all. The article was illustrated with examples of "unbridled self-expression" to be frowned upon, such as "Early Snow" by Vlaminck, Cézanne's "Olympia," a Maillol sculpture, a Derain, a Ryder, and a Diego Rivera called "Social Chaos."

Goodyear was sent to Europe in the summer of 1929 to gather the first choices for the exhibition of "radical" paintings which would open the fledgling museum. The ladies wanted what they considered the best in the world, even if what they thought to be the best was badly thought of in conventional circles. Goodyear came back with promises of canvases, watercolors, and sketches by Cézanne, Gauguin, Seurat, and Van Gogh.

In the early afternoon of October 24, the first exhibition of the Museum of Modern Art was being installed, with great trepidation, in rented quarters in August Heckscher's building (which also housed that paragon of taste, Jesse L. Livermore). Bliss, Sullivan, and Rockefeller wondered whether anyone except their friends would come to the exhibition when it opened in a week's time. As Frank Crowninshield of *Vanity Fair* was on their board, for instance, the rival *New Yorker* had already sniffed alarmingly at their enterprise.[5] There was so much to do, and the catalog wasn't even ready. When they heard the news of the stock market, they could pay it no heed.

As for the other arts, they were similarly betwixt and between. In a contemporary article, Robert Herrick wondered what was happening to American fiction. "Already," he said,

> the rugged generation of Norris and Mr. Dreiser is fading from the scene. Mr. Upton Sinclair and Mr. Sinclair Lewis are almost *vieux jeu;* while the shapes of Howells, James, and Cable loom out of the mists of a past that seems as far away as the world of Scott or Balzac.[6].

Today, Herrick said, was the day of individualistic abandon, when novelists were amateurs and not dedicated craftsmen. He lamented the passing of certain novelistic taboos and noted that contemporary novels were fixated too much on sex.

> One cannot mention sex today without considering the vagaries of the "new psychology." . . . Writers have lapped up the atrocious jargon of psychological fantasy and plastered it thickly over their fiction, trying to ram life in all its variety into the narrow mold of "complexes." . . . Whatever one may think of the scientific importance of psychoanalysis—I leave that to the medical profession—there is no doubt that its influence in contemporary literature, on the serious as well as the more imaginative aspects, is disastrous both verbally and mentally.[7]

Herrick wondered why novelists of the day, other than Upton Sinclair, did not deal with the protean characters that leaped out of the daily newspapers: Grundy, Senator Bingham, Fall, Doheny, Lindbergh, the Sacco-Vanzetti case. Herrick hoped soon that the creators of the novel—

may become sufficiently devoted to it to stick to their lasts
like good workmen and not take flyers in fiction as in the
stock market when the whim or the pecuniary exigency
moves them.[8]

Nowhere in the article did the critic mention the names of Hemingway, F. Scott Fitzgerald, Lardner, Dos Passos, Faulkner, and
he passed lightly over Edith Wharton, Willa Cather, and Ellen
Glasgow.

If an astute critic like Herrick could miss such writers, what
was happening in America's heartland?

The Lynds, in Middletown, found culture of any sort to be
shallow. The favorite poet of the multitudes was Edgar Guest;
the only book in a great many households was the Bible (and
that, largely unread); literature, painting, the drama, and music
were fit subjects mostly for women of the upper middle class
who discussed and politely pigeonholed their knowledge of
them in club meetings on alternate Thursday afternoons. This
fit nicely with H. L. Mencken's definition of the "Bible Belt" and
the "booboisie," and allowed many artists to secrete themselves
in the more hospitable atmosphere of postwar Europe where culture was supposedly more appreciated.

The life of the mind was in crisis at the moment. The brightest lights of the expatriate generation, as Malcolm Cowley has
pointed out, were at the end of their tether economically and
emotionally. Hemingway was complaining that he got many
postcards and letters from fans, forwarded by his obliging
publisher, but no money, even though *The Sun Also Rises* was
shining out from this year's best-seller list. Scott Fitzgerald was
suffering through Zelda's first real breakdown. Harry Crosby
teetered at the brink of suicide, only a half-year after sending a
cable to his family that said "Please sell $10,000 worth of
stock—we have decided to lead a mad and extravagant life."

"Though they had fled from machinery," Cowley writes,

> they had continued to live on the profits of machine pro-
> duction, or else to live on the demand for luxuries of the
> people who received these profits. . . . The religion of art
> had failed when it tried to become an ideology and an eth-
> ics: as a way of life it was completely bankrupt. During the
> 1920s all the extreme courses of action it suggested had

been tried once again, and all its paths had been retraced—the way of the dream . . . of escape . . . of adventure, contemplation and deliberate futility had all been followed toward the goal they promised of providing a personal refuge from bourgeois society, an individual paradise. . . . The search itself was ending.[9]

Sinclair Lewis's articles on the textile mill troubles were running in the Scripps-Howard papers, and Lewis was trying to write a big novel about the Southern mills. There was something quintessentially American in the strikes, repression, absurdities, profundities, in the murder of Ella May Wiggins and the trials of Fred Beal. Lesser writers in a dozen locations were already grappling with Gastonia—a fistful of books and as many plays, all forgettable, would come out about the subject in a few years—but Lewis, the man who had given the world *Babbitt*, *Arrowsmith*, and *Elmer Gantry*, couldn't feel his grasp on the subject as sure, just yet. The complexity, the necessary complexity which would elude all these other writers, kept getting in his own way. And he was drinking heavily.

Another writer for whom things were not going well was the venerable Lincoln Steffens, now at the twilight of a remarkable career of writing and political influence which had spanned half a century. He was hopelessly stalled, at his home in Carmel, on his autobiography.

The arc of Steffens's career was enough to send any man into difficulties contemplating it. Steffens had been one of the great muckrakers at the turn of the century. From his muckraking had come, in a strange way, money, fame, and access to the pinnacles of American power. Using these, Steffens broadened his horizons, camping with revolutionaries and conservatives in Mexico, in Russia, in Italy. He developed a curious admiration for those who wielded power both for "good" and for "bad." He viewed Mussolini, for instance, in the vein that any great changes wrought by a powerful man necessitate riding roughshod over certain liberties.

As an older man, Steffens's lectures had still been drawing good crowds, but he felt in many ways that his life was over. The paradox came to the surface during the episode of his loving divorce, the summer of 1929. In 1924 Steffens had told his young wife Ella Winter that, after their marriage, what they ought to do was get secretly divorced so that she could stay with him out of love, not out of obligation to an old man with a child as hostage. In the spring of 1929 Ella was finally persuaded to go with Steffens to a lawyer and file papers, including a trumped-up complaint that he objected to her attending dances. This was all to be put through the courts quietly, and then they would be free to go on as they wished.

An alert local reporter, in the best Steffens tradition, smoked out the story. Ella was in England when it broke, and she believed that Steffens now really wanted her to stay there without him, for good. Steffens was equally depressed. They started to exchange letters, trying to break through the obfuscatory barrier of public articles, no-longer-private secrets, the age difference, and everything else. In mid-October they seemed to be coming to a meeting of the minds. Steffens's fondest hope was that once they got back together again he could finally feel free to attack the writing of the autobiography. Ella embarked for America, for Steffens, for better or worse, marriage or divorce, on October 24.

Steffens' two most illustrious protégés were John Reed, the brilliant and flaming revolutionary who rode at the right hand of Lenin, wrote *Ten Days That Shook the World,* and died shortly thereafter; and Walter Lippmann, author of 1929's seminal book of philosophy, *A Preface to Morals.* This book examined the efficacy of faith in a modern, machine-age civilization, and looked for new insights into the human condition to keep the candle of faith burning.

Two other writers, who more than most tried to provide such insights, surfaced with meteorlike alacrity in the fall of 1929. William Faulkner, whose earlier novels had showed promise at best, wrote his first truly great novel, *The Sound and the Fury.* Much of it infuriated critics, though its power and brilliance could not be denied. If Faulkner was, as Maxwell Geismar puts it, "the final and fullest expression of the artistic despair evoked by the American twenties," the other emerging spirit looked to the future. He was Thomas Wolfe, a twenty-nine-year-old who, as he himself said,

> wrote and wrote with that bright flame with which a young man writes who never has been published, and who yet is sure all will be good and must go well.[10]

On October 24, Wolfe was waiting anxiously for the first important critical reviews of *Look Homeward, Angel.* Much would depend on what Margaret Wallace would say in this Sunday's *New York Times.* A week ago he had been an unknown lecturer at New York University, living mostly off Aline Bernstein's benevolence. In another week he would be the literary sensation of the year.

Other art notes of the day: George Gershwin was said to be writing an opera of the classic Yiddish play *The Dybbuk.* Stokowski, conducting the New York Philharmonic earlier in the week, had become upset when the audience had gotten restless and noisy during some incomprehensible modern music and had chastised the audience verbally for its bad behavior. Edna St. Vincent Millay seemed too depressed by Sacco-Vanzetti to resume her lyricism just now. Yeats was publishing a new volume dedicated to Ezra Pound. Robert Frost was chiseling himself into granite. Eugene O'Neill's depth-soundings of Freudian psychology, *Mourning Becomes Electra,* was currently banned in Boston, to the delight of thinking people everywhere and to the especial chagrin of Harvard undergraduates who wanted desperately to see it.

Thousands of playgoers in New York were preparing for afternoons at Thursday matinees in New York City. One could catch George M. Cohan, Gertrude Lawrence, Leslie Howard, Helen Morgan, or Eva LeGallienne in various forgettable plays. *Journey's End,* about the war, and *Street Scene,* Elmer Rice's glimpses of "life, love, and sudden death in a New York tenement" were the highlights of serious drama. The reigning queen of Broadway, Rachel Crothers, had another hit with *Let Us Be Gay.* George S. Kaufman's collaboration with Ring Lardner, *June Moon,* was at the Broadhurst, while his collaboration with Alec Woollcott, *The Channel Road,* had just opened at the Plymouth. Clayton, Jackson, and Jimmy Durante were in a review, and Eddie Cantor was making *Whoopee.*

The Marx Brothers, who had just finished filming *Cocoa-nuts* (by Kaufman and Ryskind) in Astoria while performing in *Animal Crackers* on the stage at night, were in financial hot water because of friend Cantor. "I went to see his act," Groucho recalled, "and he told me what stocks I should buy. It turned out to be the most expensive act I ever saw." The brothers Marx, on tour with *Animal Crackers* in Baltimore, were heading for Pittsburgh today, and were almost ready to close their act at the market news. Cantor would later find it necessary to write a funny book about the Crash, sue his brokerage firm—and win.

At around this time in late October, George S. Kaufman was meeting for the first time with a young man about collaborating on a second draft of a play. The young man was Moss Hart, and the script was *Once in a Lifetime*. Producer Sam Harris liked it—he was losing his shirt in the market at this moment, as well—but had agreed to produce it only if Hart would work with the older man. Hart was ecstatic. The play, which found its way to Broadway and instant success in 1930, was about a time of crisis for the motion picture industry, a crisis going on at that very instant in Hollywood, the shift over from the making of silent movies to the making of talkies.

Out in the dream factory, Jim Reed of Brooklyn was feeling that transition keenly. After a year working as a Wall Street runner and going to law school at night, he had decided to look for adventure and had thumbed his way to Los Angeles with a friend. You couldn't exactly go across the country on paved roads right then; west of St. Louis, traveling was more of a seasonal thing. The trip had been so perilous that Jim had at one time gotten stranded and badly sunburned in the New Mexico desert, barely getting rescued by a Mexican's truck with a load of canteloupe. His face had been so hot that Jim had cracked open one of the fruits and washed his face with the canteloupe to cool it. When he got to Los Angeles, broke, a picture called *Captain of the Guard* was being filmed at Universal, and, right in the middle of it, the studio decided to change it from a silent to a talkie. They put out the call for people who could sing "The Marseillaise" in French, and Jim was in the movies. Five dollars a day as an extra if you wore your own clothes, seven dollars if you had to wear a costume.

Jim wanted to work with Chaplin, but that was a closed shop. Charlie was taking an enormous gamble, staking everything he had on a new picture. Flying in the face of the trend, he was making another silent. He had taken his money out of the stock market after reading Major H. Douglas's *Social Credit*. Last night Charlie had had dinner with Irving Berlin, and had had an argument with him over the market. Today Berlin was losing millions, and Charlie was filming *City Lights.**

Back home, the world was crashing down around the ears of Jim's father in Brooklyn, but Jim knew nothing about that yet. What he was looking for was to play anything—dead bodies, falling soldiers, what have you—to get in on the new picture with Lew Ayres, *All Quiet on the Western Front,* which would start filming in a week.

Already finished that year were the Mary Pickford-Doug Fairbanks' *The Taming of the Shrew,* George Arliss in *Disraeli,* Roland West's *Alibi,* Rouben Mamoulian's *Applause,* and King Vidor's all-black *Hallelujah.* On the planning boards were Howard Hughes' *Hell's Angels* and Howard Hawks' *The Dawn Patrol,* as well as a movie version of the then-popular novel *Little Caesar.*

The revolution from silent to sound had also given birth to Mickey Mouse in 1928. Walt Disney was becoming known for his tremendously imaginative fusing of animation and the new sound techniques. Within a few years, Mickey would be world-famous, drawing raves even from Soviet Russia, where he was thought of as that sterling thing in a decadent and capitalistic society, the symbol of the proletarian spirit.

The transition to talkies—an enormously expensive task—had brought the major studios to the feet of the banks. They needed financing. By October 1929 nearly all the majors were in hot water. The most precarious Hollywood juggling act of them all was entering its final stages on October 24 in the war between Adolph Zukor and William Fox.

Two years before Zukor and Paramount had been caught flatfooted by *The Jazz Singer,* and, though they had ruled Hollywood with an iron hand for years, they then lost the initiative. William Fox found it. A three-way battle was on, with talkies as the money-making soldiers. Warner Brothers and Fox, making money quickly from the novelty, started acquiring theaters, which made more money and more power. The next logical step was to acquire a producing studio. Warner's got First National, and Fox had to look elsewhere.

*Winston Churchill had visited Chaplin on the set a few weeks before. The had charmed each other.

When old Marcus Loew died, his producing subsidiary, MGM, seemed to be available. But Zukor and Loew had been old vaude-villians together and had an understanding whereby Paramount and Loew's theaters would show only their own, or each other's, films. MGM was then under the leadership of Louis B. Mayer and Irving Thalberg and was the highest-ranking studio for stars and successful films. Fox salivated to buy Loew's.

To do so, Robert Sklar reports, Fox had to persuade Nicholas Schenck, then president of Loew's, to assemble a big block of stock for him while keeping the deal secret from MGM executives. Schenck's price for doing so was $10 million. In February of 1929 the deal seemed sure to go through, and Fox thought he was king.

Fox already owned 800 theaters, had 11,000 people on his payroll, and owned Movietone City. Ten thousand theaters a week showed his products, including half of the country's 2,709 houses equipped for sound that subscribed to Fox Movietone News. He had a mansion on Long Island, an apartment on Park Avenue, and a personality described by contemporaries as "megalomania afflicted with elephantiasis." To make the first enormous expansion of his empire earlier in the twenties, Fox had sold shares of his corporation directly to the public, advertising them in his theaters at the end of the newsreels. In doing this he bypassed normal channels, thereby supposedly earning the undying enmity of Wall Street.

.Notwithstanding, Fox got a lot of money from the Street, through Halsey Stuart, with which to outmaneuver Zukor and buy Loew's. The money came from AT&T, Chatham-Phenix Bank, other investors of similar caliber, and from the sale of some of Fox Theaters' shares. Hoover's Attorney General designate, William J. Donovan, had given his verbal approval to the merger, said he wouldn't prosecute under antitrust—but then Donovan's nomination was withdrawn in June. The new man told Fox to sell the stock or he would prosecute. Fox called Hoover. No help. He called Louis B. Mayer, who, as well as being a movie mogul, was also chairman of the California State Republican Committee. A word from Mayer—prompted by Fox's promise of $2 million for him personally—and the Justice department called off its dogs.

Fox thought he was home free. Not quite. In a wonderfully

convoluted way, Fox had found himself suing AT&T over patent infringements while he was taking their money to acquire Loew's, but in the manner of great business dealings everywhere such peccadilloes were forgotten for the nonce while serious money changed hands. Then, ridiculously, Fox continued to press his suit. John E. Otterson of AT&T finally threw up his hands and was not pleased. The suit was still hanging when, on July 17, Fox was in an auto accident on Long Island and had to be hospitalized for some time.

Today, on October 24, Fox was getting out of his sickbed for virtually the first time, to get ready for this evening's dinner for his old friend, Colonel Claudius Huston, new chairman of the Republican National Committee. Earlier in the week Fox's office had announced his proposal for a chain of theaters with low admission rates that would be devoted entirely to newsreels. He was also planning to sell projectors to families on the installment plan, and was putting $9 million of his personal money into a complicated scheme to educate children by use of movies, which he said would promote churchgoing in American homes.

It was a crucial moment for Fox. After a polite hiatus for the accident, the big boys were closing in—AT&T, the bankers, even Halsey Stuart. Perhaps, he worried, he had made a fundamental mistake by not going with a Jewish investment house, but the only one available—Kuhn, Loeb—was backing Zukor! When the fur was flying, as it certainly was right now, would the non-Jews support him or stab him in the back? If only prices would hold out a little longer, he would be able to sell some stock, get enough cash to cover the blasted loans, and be all right. The future of the entire motion-picture industry of the United States depended on it.

As he was being dressed for the drive into New York for the dinner, he received word of the prices of his stocks on the various exchanges. Not good, and getting no better.

Chapter Thirteen

WAITING FOR A HERO
1:15 P.M.

It was 1:15. The day that had shown frost as far south as the Gulf of Mexico was thawing a bit; skies were clearing. At a private aviation strip in New Jersey, Charles A. Lindbergh, with an official of the company which made the German Fokker planes, practiced take-offs and landings with one of the new craft. Marquis Childs had written in the *Herald Tribune* that "Five centuries have been required to make a saint of Joan of Arc, but in two years Colonel Charles A. Lindbergh has become a demi-god." Anne Morrow and Charles Lindbergh had been married five months, and were recently back from a flying trip to the Mayan ruins in the Yucatan, Quintana Roo, and Guatemala. The young couple were looking for a farm with a working cow barn. Anne wrote to her mother,

Of course we are certainly going to have trouble with publicity. It will all have to be done under someone else's name and the publicity run on a *false* place—the *second* break won't be as great. Then if necessary we can keep a policeman there. . . . Oh, Mother—It is so wearing. I wonder if it will ever slacken. Think of the people—any person, any two people who can be alone on four square feet of beach in Miami, or on a park bench anywhere, alone and independent, and we can't get it where there is *anyone* around. . . . We can never catch people or life unawares. It

is always looking at us. . . . It is like being born with no
nose, or deformed—everyone on the street looks at you
once, and then *again*; always looks *back*—the second look,
the *leer*. No one else gets that. President Hoover doesn't get
it; Daddy doesn't get it; they get a dignified curiosity. But
that look, as though we were a public amusement, monkeys
in a cage.[1]

Going anywhere with Charles was difficult, so Anne looked for a
farm mostly alone with trusted real-estate agents, or, more often, with decoys.

It was a critical time in the Lindberghs' life. Anne had been to
a doctor, and they were waiting for the confirmation of their
hopes. Anne was sure she was pregnant, and happy of it, because

After a year of peripatetic living, constantly travelling, always on guard, avoiding all personal questions, speaking in
discreet banalities, I longed for privacy, a home, an ordinary
home. Everyone else, I thought with envy, has a home, a
family life, privacy, a baby.[2]

The demigod's status was wavering. Every single day the papers
still printed some item about him, but Charles had noticed that
there were now occasional references to his "mania" for privacy,
or to his annoyance at crowds which tore off his clothing at ai-
rfields. At this moment, Dixon Wecter suggests, Lindbergh was
"between crowd adoration and its only possible sequel, crowd
hate."[3] As a consultant to Pan American Airways (which just
yesterday had completed the first airmail flight from South
America) and to Transcontinental Air Transport, Lindbergh was
at the core of American aviation at the moment and knew much
about, for example, aviation stocks. This knowledge was para-
doxical. Upon his return from Mexico, he had been advised to
sell his aviation stocks because the market was going to go down
badly. After due consideration, he decided not to sell, reasoning
that if the public found out he had sold aviation, they would do
so as well, and this might seriously dampen the future of aviation which was of paramount importance to him personally.

So in the midst of the decline of October 24, Lindbergh was
testing Fokker planes. Holding tight to his stocks, he took his
losses: it was part of the price he had to bear.

Aviation had been an ascendant star. Pan American and Transcontinental were relative giants, but hundreds of tiny companies crowded the new field: American Eagle, Sky Specialties, Crescent Aircraft, Swallow Aircraft, Cessna. Most of their stocks were traded over-the-counter or on the Curb. They weren't considered solid enough for the NYSE yet. Yet on this day, one small New Jersey aviation company—perhaps Lindbergh could see it as he circled—was having a large effect on the NYSE through the circuitous agency of a brokerage firm in Providence, Rhode Island.

In the Rhode Island capital, the firm of Mandeville, Brooks, and Chaffee was doing an awfully good business. Of the partners, Mandeville was a smooth, aristocratic man, a wheeler-dealer; Brooks was a dynamic go-getter, a great salesman; and Chaffee, who actually owned the seat on the NYSE (for which he had recently paid $420,000 loaned to him by a woman friend) was a very tall Texan who liked to gad about. One of the firm's largest accounts was that of New England Ford dealer Dutee W. Flint. Flint had a mansion south of Providence, and an agreement with Henry Ford that gave him a personal cut of $75 on each Ford sold in all of New England—which made him wealthy. When Ford was in the area, he'd park his yacht at Flint's dock. They were friends.

By means unknown, Flint had become interested in a small aviation company in New Jersey. He bought heavily. And he convinced his brokerage firm of Mandeville, Brooks, and Chaffee to do likewise. Most brokerage firms usually convinced their customers to buy something; here, it was the other way around. No matter, because the stock went up. One day, however, Chaffee, being in New York with nothing to do, decided to go over to New Jersey and have a look at the company which was making them all rich. What he found was an unoccupied office in a field, with no planes, no hangars, and no equipment. Chaffee worried. Next day the partners called Flint in, told him the bad news, and demanded that he put up some security for the aviation stock. Reluctantly, Flint pledged 400 shares of Ford stock, with the request that it never be shown on his account because he had promised friend Henry that he would never pledge that stock. It was implied that Ford would never allow friend Flint to go down the drain.

MB&C had various loans: a million with the Industrial Trust Company, $750,000 with the Rhode Island Hospital Trust, $600,000 with the Providence National Bank, $260,000 with the Union Trust Company, and ten more loans of $50,000 each spread around various small banks in Massachusetts. The net of money interested in MB&C was spread wide. But it was not enough, so when the partners discovered the aviation hoax and found there was no way for them to unload their stock or Flint's stock quickly without taking losses, smooth Mandeville brought in five new "partners" for $90,000 to bolster the firm's capital. He didn't bother telling the new men about the field in New Jersey.

Now, a bit after one o'clock on the twenty-forth, aviation stocks were plunging like falling stars, and the banks and institutions which held the MB&C loans were getting nervous. Unlike banks in New York, these out-of-town fellows were not used to heady ups and downs, nor to throwing good money after questionable money. So the MB&C loan-holders started to call their money, and the brokerage firm of Mandeville, Brooks, and Chaffee teetered on the brink of insolvency.

On the floor of the Exchange, the ticker was 92 minutes late, that is, printing the prices of 11:28 A.M., that time of horrendous slippages, of air pockets like hollows beneath the earth's surface. Today an hour was not an hour, at least not on the tape: the trough had been showing its ugly self since eleven that morning and was hardly done: in boardrooms all over America those bad prices had been staring customers in the face for two hours and would stare at them yet another hour. Nine million shares had been traded in three hours, approximately three million an hour. This was already more shares than had ever changed hands in a single day, and the trading day had two more hours to go.

Brokers had not dared to take a moment off for lunch. They were on the floor, clothes sopped in perspiration, collars awry, gardenias wilting—and they were making mistakes. Stuffing sell orders in wastebaskets because there were too many of them for the usual holders. Forgetting executions. Mis-hearing prices. They were besieged with requests for information: in the last hour Post 8, where AT&T and American and Foreign Power were traded, had received over 1,300 inquiries for price quotations. Already more than 35,000 quotes had been given out today by a beleaguered staff working constantly at a rate of more than two quotes a minute per person. One small saving grace concerning the volume: New York State, by its charge on floor transactions, had made over $200,000 in taxes in four hours.

There was so much work that brokers were resorting far more than was usual to "two-dollar brokers" to take care of surplus orders. These brokers received a commission of two dollars for every 100 shares traded, which sum came out of the broker's normal commission.

Usually discounted in stories of stock trading, commissions were important this day. On a one-dollar stock, the commission was 7.5 cents; on a $50 stock it was 17.5 cents; on a $100 stock, 25 cents. Above $200 it was 5 cents additional for each $50 in valuation of the stock. However, a minimum commission of one dollar was charged on all transactions involving $15 or more, and most firms made it a practice to charge a minimum of $3–$5 per transaction "because the work on small transactions is as great as on large transactions and relatively more burdensome."[4]

One might argue that commissions were quite small. On a $10,000 order, say a $50 stock in a block of 200 shares, the commission was 17.5 cents a share, or a modest $35. However, each broker in the transaction—one for the buyer and one for the sell-er—made $35. At one o'clock, 9 million shares had changed hands on this day. Figuring an average price of under $100 a share, brokers' commissions were in the neighborhood of $1,800,000 for the sellers, and another equal amount for the buy-ers, or about $3.6 million total.

Even though so much money was changing hands, many of the brokers were self-admittedly "uninformed" as to what precisely they were buying and selling. A report to the Investment Bankers Association by its Business Conduct Committee noted that in 1927, with 1,450 issues traded on the NYSE floor,

it is obviously impossible for any ordinary house to give even superficial information [to its clients]....Even the houses which pretend to supply good information are apt to have only a general idea on a large part of the market and to specialize in their detailed knowledge of a few compa-nies....The average house has none too much money to spend on statistical departments.[5]

In the same report, there were some confessions. One member said that

> We here, and our customers, are groping around to find what our securities are worth.... There is no yardstick at all for us to go by.... [Another member said] we are all quite densely ignorant of our own business...we have been "chasing rainbows" and looking for Santa Claus instead of for facts.[6]

In the light of such statements, Mandeville, Brooks, and Chaffee seems to be rather typical. The attitude of unconcern was fostered by the Investment Bankers Association and the New York Stock Exchange itself.

During the twenties, the IBA, as Michael Parrish points out, lobbied successfully in state capitals against all forms of regulation except those which would eliminate bucket shops, which drained money from regular exchanges anyhow. The IBA insisted it could regulate its own members better than any governmental body could or should. "This responsibility," said Parrish,

> did not exceed their pretensions, but it was incommensurate with their organizational development and with their fund of economic intelligence.... The internal weakness of these private groups contributed to the speculative boom and retarded [the government's] capacity to govern a vital area of the economy. During the course of the decade, conservative members of the financial elite, in addition to the more radical critics of investment banking, had perceived the breakdown of self-regulation. It was both an institutional and an intellectual crisis; the IBA and the New York Stock Exchange were at the center of the crisis.[7]

For instance, E. H. H. Simmons, president of the Exchange, did not like the idea of regulation. If mischievous state legislatures wrote statutes and then expected the Exchange to enforce or control companies set up under these statutes—that was an impossible task. It was not, he thought, the Exchange's function to impose national standards of financial disclosure through its listing requirements. In 1929, most companies reported only annually, some reported semiannually, and only a third or so showed regular quarterly earnings in some public way. Simmons thought it would be impossible for the Exchange

> to verify ... the accuracy of the statements made to it in the listing application.... The NYSE is a private organization, and as such is not suitable means for the performance of an obviously public function.... It is by no means equipped to undertake any policy of controlling American corporate practice.[8]

Eight members who worked part-time after business hours for no pay made up the Exchange's sorely taxed listing committee, which had to pass on 300 new stock applications in 1926, 571 in 1928, and 759 in the first nine months of 1929. Nevertheless, all of these were approved, as listing requirements were relatively easy to satisfy. Real listing control? Simmons suggested it be handled by the local Better Business Bureau.

At shortly after one o'clock on October 24, then, this admittedly imperfect machinery, in the hands of men who similarly admitted their inability to keep up with the stocks in which they were trading, was having a chaotic day. Trading was going on in staggering volume. Prices, when they could be determined, were sluggish, inching slightly upwards on the good news of the bankers' meeting. But where and when were the representatives of the bankers' pool going to materialize on the floor? The brokers waited impatiently, or as impatiently as they could, while they executed orders madly. Most of the orders had originated in the trough of the day; many had just reached the floor from out-of-town.

Who were the men who handled these orders? Most of those on the floor worked for medium-sized concerns which processed a fair volume of business, say 20,000 shares a day, say a commission of $4,000 a day, out of which expenses took quite a bit. These brokers made no great waves and carried no great weight. Others, however, were generally acknowledged as bigger fish who dealt in larger amounts of money and power. These were the specialists and their opinions were consulted regularly. And then there were the dozen or two top movers and shakers, the brokers who "led" the market, either because they handled large volumes of shares, or because they had large followings of smaller brokers who plunged, turned, and twisted when they did. Frank Bliss, "the silver fox," was known to be close to Livermore and handled several hundred thousand shares on large-volume days. Benjamin Block, another big fish, sometimes made an appearance buying or selling for Durant and the Fisher brothers; this morning he had done over 250,000 shares. By all lights, though, the most influential broker on the Street was thirty-seven-year-old ex-Broadway-ticket-salesman Michael J. Meehan.

While hawking spots on the aisle for the downtown branch of McBride's agency during the war years, Meehan became friendly with many brokers. In 1918 he bought a membership on the Curb, but kept selling theater tickets to stay alive. By 1921 he was able to buy as well a $90,000 seat on the New York Exchange. Within eight years his firm had a large office at 61 Broadway, held eight seats on the Exchange (an investment value, alone, of $3.5 million),* and Meehan was acknowledged as a major shark. To talk of Meehan was to tell fabulous stories, and the biggest story of all was Radio.

Meehan's most spectacular move had been in the stock of the Radio Corporation of America, known familiarly as Radio, in which he "held the book" as specialist. In 1928 the stock had been at 85, a reasonable price for a stock which had never paid a dividend in its several years of existence but whose future was obviously bright. A syndicate of sixty-three participants was formed, including Nicholas F. Brady, William F. Kenny, and John J. Raskob, each down for 50,000 shares and a deposit of $1 million; and Percy Rockefeller, Durant, Walter P. Chrysler, the Fisher brothers, Herbert Bayard Swope, and others, including comedian Eddie Dowling and Meehan's friend John J. Riordan, for smaller amounts. The rules of the Exchange precluded the specialist himself from participating, but Mrs. Meehan was in for a million bucks and 65,000 shares.

When rumors told of the pool's formation, the stock was at 74, but by the time Meehan got to buy it, the price had risen to 91¾. On the first day when Meehan, Brad Ellsworth, and Thomas Bragg bought 392,000 shares, they also managed to sell 246,000 and pushed the price up to $109.25 a share. This tremendous ac-

---

*Seats on the NYSE were selling in October of 1929 for $420,000 each.

tivity brought the rest of the public in, and during the next two days the pool purchased 210,000 shares, and Meehan concurrently sold 449,000. Small traders, scrambling to get in on what they thought surely was an ever-rising stock, bought everything in sight. On an investment of $13 million the pool made $5 million in three days.

After Meehan got out of Radio, it dropped instantly to 101, and five days later was back to 87. Those who sold out then were losers. But those who held on could take advantage of other Radio pools which Meehan managed during the latter part of 1928 and the early part of 1929, which pushed the stock (taking into account several splits) all the way to a high of 549. It was the most spectacular rise of any stock in the era.

In the view of many smaller brokers, the tactics of Meehan were, to put it mildly, buccaneering. Earlier in the year, a young man who had just bought a seat on the Exchange, and whose telephone was near Meehan's, overheard the following shouted conversation between Meehan and well-known operator Ben Smith:

Smith: "How's Radio?"
Meehan: "2,000 at 47."
Smith: "Not good enough."
Meehan: "10,000 at 47."
Smith: "Not good enough."
Meehan: "50,000 at 47."
Smith: "I'll take it."

So Smith bought 50,000 shares of Radio at 47, and ten minutes after the order hit the tape Radio was up to 52. In dribs and drabs, Meehan then sold Smith's 50,000 shares at that price or better all during the rest of the afternoon. Smith realized a ten percent profit in a few hours.

Another young broker had watched part of a Radio operation in which the players were Meehan and Richard Whitney, brother of Morgan partner George Whitney. Dick Whitney, generally known to be the floor broker for the Morgan interests, arrived on the floor and bought 20,000 shares of Radio; word spread quickly that "the Corner" was buying Radio; if Morgan interests were in, it must be a sure thing, so people rushed to buy—and then, quietly, Meehan sold all that Whitney had just bought and much more, to liquidate some other client's position at a substantial profit.

That was another day. Today, at 1:20 P.M., everyone was waiting for Whitney to appear. The Dow-Jones wire quoted the leading prices as Steel, 203; GM, 52; AT&T, 261; Radio, 61; Bethlehem, 98, and so on. The tape was 102 minutes late, or registering the prices of 11:38.

At 1:30 P.M., finally, with many rumors having preceded his actual arrival and thus creating a grandly theatrical entrance, Richard Whitney strode onto the trading floor, dressed as was his custom in formal attire. A large, handsome man, Whitney had an impeccable background at Groton and Harvard, was the son of a bank president, the nephew of a former Morgan partner, and the brother of a present Morgan partner. Richard's own firm, which he started in 1916, was today quite successful, as evidenced by his New York town house and his five-hundred-acre farm in New Jersey, where he often rode to hounds. The Morgan partners having made it a habit never to sully themselves with actual transactions on the Stock Exchange, many of their dealings on the floor had been made these past ten years by Richard Whitney. Yesterday Richard had helped to preside over the races associated with a prestigious hunt in New Jersey. Today, in E. H. H. Simmons's absence, he was acting president of the Exchange. His appearance now, however, was in order to fulfill his primary function. And everyone knew it.

Whitney went over to the crowd of fifty to seventy-five brokers hovering about Post 2 and, in a loud clear voice, bid 205 for 25,000 shares of U. S. Steel—or in dollar terms, $5,125,000. The share-price was quite as important as the amount of shares. The bid of 205 was above the present market quotation, and substantially the same as that price at which Steel had started its precipitous decline that morning. An offer of 200 would have bought him the stock in the context of the shaky market. By bidding 205, Whitney signaled that Steel was actively being supported. The gesture was so sudden, though long awaited, that Whitney was able to buy only a few hundred shares at this price immediately. Within moments he went on, leaving the vast bulk of his order with one of the specialists.

From Number 2—the wood of which he would later purchase

for a trophy in his office—Whitney went to other posts, where he bought generous chunks of General Motors, AT&T, and the several other stocks agreed to at the noon meeting. It went virtually unnoticed at the time that the prices he paid for these stocks were at or below the market quotations. The talk was of the Steel buy and of the magnitude of all his orders, which totaled $20 to $30 million. Everyone came to the same logical and justified conclusions: such orders were not placed by an individual nor even by a pool, they could only have come from a bankers' consortium spearheaded by the Corner.

It had been done with what the other brokers defined as characteristic class, a gesture fully as grand as the elder Morgan's giving away of tea at Christmas anonymously, a gesture as magnificently defiant as not removing the bomb scars in the cement at 23 Wall. A most successful broker, in a classic tradition, had, as expected, come in on a white horse to save the day.

A happy, seismic shock went through the Exchange. Brokers started buying for their own accounts, a sure sign that confidence and cupidity, those two intertwined motives had been regained. Word spread in ripples that the bankers' pool had bought, and prices began to rise in a steady, orderly fashion. A few people made a few dollars buying and then reselling quickly. The bond ticker and the Dow-Jones wire printed the good news, and the idea began to take hold that the market had been saved. A rally had begun. When Richard Whitney walked off the floor, his work done, he was on his way to becoming an overnight national hero, the symbol of the entrenched and benevolent powers-that-be who had once again saved America from financial ruin in a single, wonderful, grandiloquent moment.

Chapter Fourteen

HIGH ROLLERS AND LOW DEALS
2:00 P.M.

It was two o'clock.

Jesse Livermore had sold short all day. Prices were rising slowly this afternoon. Should he cover while they were still comparatively low and take the risk that the rally would wipe out his profits, or should he wait it out, hoping that tomorrow and the next day prices would plummet still further and that he would make even more money? Livermore's nerves of steel and antennae of quicksilver told him to hold on, not to cover just yet. So he didn't.

Arthur W. Cutten, away on a hunting trip, was taking an incredible licking, though he knew nothing of it. His losses could be measured in terms of millions of dollars per hour. Still, Cutten held all of his stocks outright, not on margin, so his losses were, he might well have argued, only on paper.

Other big rollers had a mixed day. William Crapo Durant was happy that he was out. But the Fisher brothers were losing tens of millions of dollars. It was hard, however, to feel sorry for a family whose fortune of hundreds of millions was being reduced by mere percentage points. John J. Raskob was out for the most part, but not happy. His pet project, the Empire State Building, was in trouble. He put the heat on Metropolitan Life's new president, Frederick H. Ecker, to come through with the loan he had promised. After some agonizing, Ecker agreed: the insurance company would put $27 million up to guarantee the financing of the world's largest skyscraper.*

A friend of Raskob's was in deep trouble. This afternoon a $200,000 margin call went to James J. Riordan, a successful realtor with extensive holdings in Greenwich Village. Riordan was president of the County Trust Company bank, whose officers also included former Governor Al Smith. Riordan knew all the Irish bigwigs—Mike Meehan, for example, and District Attorney Edward Swann, from whom he had bought his brownstone on Eleventh Street. This afternoon Riordan met the call, but was soon reported among friends as suffering from nervous exhaustion and was put under a doctor's care, though he continued to live at home. His financial affairs were confused: some said he had lost a great deal of money, others said that, no, his investments and especially his bank were financially sound—that he had, for instance, gotten out of Radio entirely by this time. Everybody was worried about him.

Other high rollers were in trouble, too. The Van Sweringens had been buying all day, trying to reinforce the idea that their stock was sound. Marcus and Singer of Bank of U.S. were doing the same. So was Samuel Insull: from his tower in Chicago, the one-time Edison office boy tried to keep his multimillion-dollar electric utility empire in the Midwest under firm control.

Utility stocks had suffered less than many other groups so far during the day; perhaps they felt immunity from the flood. They had some reason to believe so. Utility empires, including Insull's, were just on the verge of a terrific comeback from a public onslaught that had hit them in 1928. As Senator Raushenbush was writing in *The Nation,*

> The legislatures of 1929 have met and adjourned. With a few minor exceptions the power men have beaten every bill intended to make regulation more effective or intended to relieve the municipal ownership of power plants from the handicaps put upon it in earlier days. [For the power industry] it has been a year of triumph.[1]

The power companies' stranglehold over electricity derived

---

*Metropolitan Life was known to be beholden to the Morgan interests.

from the free rivers of the country came from a tangle of public and private malfeasance that typified the excesses of the pre-Crash period.

Abuses followed a pattern. A company would ask for rates based on its investments and earnings capacity, and, once obtained, the rates were virtually unchallengeable. But the companies routinely lied about their investments. Indianapolis actually put in $10 million, got a rate base of $19 million. In New York State, for four years, the state power commission let private companies get rate bases $202 million over what they had put in. In San Francisco, where the city tried to take over power production and claimed the cost of the private companies' plants plus severance damages were to be $31 million, the power companies wanted triple that, or $90 million, for their investments.

The abuses arose, in the first place, out of a sort of primitive American fear, exploited by the companies, of state-run enterprises which smacked of socialism. In Ontario, Canada, a publicly run utility provided power for two cents a unit. Just this side of the border, as supplied by a private utility, the cost was six cents a unit. Despite the evidence that several thousand small cities could run power plants efficiently themselves, most power generators were reserved to private purveyors. Much of the reason for this was that there were severe restraints on municipalities' abilities to raise money. All money for power generation is raised on the strength of expected earnings. In most states, regulations forbade raising money above debt limits which were between 5 and 10 percent of assessed valuation. Private companies had no such limits.

Power operations were also wonderful arenas in which to employ the most elegant devices of financial manipulation, such as holding companies. Having a holding company, for example, enabled an operator to escape state regulation, vapid though it might be, by letting one company wholesale power to another, across state lines. The Federal Power Commission in Washington, which might have been expected to step into this gap, was laughable as a regulator. Successive Secretaries of the Interior— Albert Bacon Fall, Roy O. West, and now Ray Lyman Wilbur— left the running of the commission to the executive staff, which was mostly in the pockets of the companies it was supposed to be regulating. O. C. Merrill occupied the position of executive secretary for nine years, then took a job with the power trust when Hoover entered office. Looking for a replacement, Wilbur was given the name of Frank E. Bonner. Not knowing anything about the field, Wilbur phoned his friend, president of Pacific Gas and Electric Paul Downing, to see if Bonner was acceptable. He was, quite so. Nonregulation continued as before. Indeed, it was pointed out that Hoover, an engineer, had long held that engineers did their best work for nongovernmental employers who could reward them handsomely and that therefore power companies were the correct providers of power. Although Hoover was supporting some regulatory legislation, the power companies' hold on power generation remained unbroken by his administration.

The problem was exacerbated by the fact that power companies were, basically, made out of money and little else. Guy Tripp, chairman of the board of directors of Westinghouse, told an investigating committee that 80 percent of the cost of producing electricity from water power consisted of fixed-cost charges, principally dividends on stock and interest on bonds. Alvin C. Reis commented that this fact

> is not true of any other productive business. In the ordinary manufacturing business the elements which go to make up the cost are mainly labor and material. In the mining business it is practically all labor and transportation. Go into any ordinary manufacturing place and you will find swarms of workingmen and piles of material. Go into a power plant and you will find nothing sitting there but an investments.[2]

At the moment, United (the Morgan company) in conjunction with the Insull utilities and Electric Bond and Share together controlled and generated over 44 percent of the nation's power. All of them were high-flying stocks, and none more so than Electric Bond, which had as a subsidiary the even-more-high-flying American and Foreign Power. Investors gobbled up these stocks, and, as the afternoon of October 24 wore on, many of them began to be revealed as little more than hot air, holding companies piled on top of holding companies piled on top of excessive rates. In the *Congressional Record* for October 24 was mention of the fact that Electric Bond and Share had refused to answer Federal

Trade Commission questions about its operation, that it had refused to let investigators look at its books, and also that it was
asking consumers in the West to pay the cost of powwows—
which gatherings were held to woo the Flathead Indians away
from a valuable power site which Rocky Mountain Power Company, an EB&S subsidiary, was trying to buy for peanuts.

It was a regular practice for power companies such as EB&S to
vastly inflate their capital accounts by means of write-ups in the
valuation of their properties, changing them from year to year.

Suppose a holding company owned an operating company
which supplied power in the South, and that company's worth
was $10 million. If it wanted higher rates, the holding company
could simply reevaluate its property, carry it on the books as
worth $20 million, and apply to the requisite power commission
for rates based on that $20 million valuation. Another trick was
to have the holding company "manage" the operating company
for a fee. EB&S got $18,513,300.85 by this practice in 1927. By
means of such practices power holding companies made wonderful returns on their investments. EB&S was making something like 42.95 percent on the original cost of its holdings on
the average, an average that included one case of a 3,102.62 percent markup and another of 2,191 percent. No wonder its stock
flew high! Electric Bond and Share was not alone in this practice.
It was industry-wide. American Power and Light was getting
over a 50 percent return on its investment in its operating companies, American Gas and Electric somewhere between 46 and
65 percent. Cities Service had written up $12 million in invest-
ments as $100 million. But Electric Bond and Share was still
champion at this, having written up in excess of valuation, in
1927, some $399,201,827. Chairman of the Board S. Z. Mitchell
should perhaps have received an award for boosting the gross national product by an amount equal to about $3 a person in the
year 1929—spuriously.

It is the false nature of this that is of concern; an overinflation
of values atop an already inflated pyramid of stocks. Would
EB&S and its subsidiary, American and Foreign Power, have
flown so high with honest valuation? Impossible to tell. Of
course, such overinflation was not completely known on October 24, 1929, though the practices by which the companies in
the utility field were operating had been under public scrutiny

for some time. What these practices meant was that as the stocks came crashing down in price, the companies had little to fall back on. Their stock prices were based on being able to maintain these unreal earnings ratios. Once these were revalued to more accurate levels, there were no more reasons to hold these stocks. One would be much better off, it was obvious, putting one's money (such as there was of it), into a stock like U. S. Steel, backed by so many obvious millions in physical plant, production capacity, manufacturing strength, hundreds of thousands of workers.

On the surface on October 24, though, all of this was not apparent. Insull, S. Z. Mitchell, and Doherty were throwing money into Insull Utilities, EB&S, and Cities Service respectively, buying nearly everything that was offered in attempts to keep up prices. A man in the South, hearing from a friend at work that the market was collapsing, tried a call to his broker in New York—which, against all odds, went right through—and sold his several thousand dollars' worth of Cities Service at about this time in the afternoon, practically without losing a cent. Cities Service, then, had a recovery, while other stocks, fundamentally sound, were being compromised right and left as the afternoon progressed.

Even so, the brokers on the floor of the Exchange felt that things were looking up at 2:10, because they had buy orders, and prices had started to climb ever so slowly with Whitney's bid.

But was there really a recovery, as newspapers, commentators, brokers, touts, and everyone else so valiantly looked for at this time? Certainly *some* people who had money tried and got in on slowly rising prices, but not many. Only those in the immediate vicinity of the marketplace, who had prices that were not 131 minutes behind, could do this.

Prices were deceiving. What did you believe? The Dow which told of Whitney and a recovery, or the ticker which told of disaster? In the hinterlands, there was no real choice—the ticker had to be believed, though late. Small investors continued to sell, could not take advantage of small price breaks upward.

Evidence of this could be seen in the volume indicators. At 2:10 P.M. the indicators showed 11,416,500 shares total so far for the day, about 1.2 million more than at 1:30 when Whitney had arrived. If we consider most orders at 2:10 buys, this still didn't mean a great recovery: a million shares going up slowly as against 8 million going down quickly that morning. By 2:30 the ticker had fallen even further behind, 147 minutes late, losing 16 minutes while real time had raced ahead 20. And the hinterland was still selling.

People who were buying at that moment were not holding on very long. There were many quick turnovers, people who got in at 1:30 and out again by 2:30—including, some said later, part of the bankers' pool. In any event, those who were in and out, just then, were not playing for big stakes. The high-fliers were taking things a bit more closely to the vest, now. Having taken a beating in the morning, they perhaps did not wish to come back in the same old wildly swinging way in the afternoon.

Was this justified? It was certainly easy to rationalize: the dozen leading stocks were not very rosy when compared to their prices a month ago, two months ago, six months ago, which time was equivalent to today's worst prices. Six months of gains gone in less than a day, made for investors who could be happy with a point or two net. It had become a different game. And there was not much time left in the day to recoup very much.

There was no rally, and the insiders—in their hearts—knew it.

So as 2:30 came and there was only a half-hour left of trading for the day, pressure mounted. People wanted to be able to show some gain, or some stoppage of their losses. Action heated up once more. A broker's false teeth flew out of his mouth and were trampled. So were a dozen pairs of glasses. Wing collars were lost, trodden to pulp.

Why the sudden surge? The evening was coming—the night, the time when people would find out how much they had lost, the time when they would become most disheartened and decide to sell out the next morning.

Everybody knew that regardless of how prices might inch up in the last half-hour, there would be plenty of margin calls tonight. Brokerage houses would not want to risk another potentially disastrous day; a few people might be spared, but the majority of small investors would be asked to cough up some more dough, because the net trend of the day would obviously be down, and down seriously. In past months a great deal of trading had come each day in the half-hour before closing. Yesterday there was a torrent at this hour, and today the pressure was no less apparent.

Everyone, though exhausted, put on a last burst of activity, knowing the day to be finite, feeling the close coming soon. The human heat of several thousand bodies rose to the emptied gallery above. Outside on the streets the crowds had grown, swollen with people who had taken the afternoon off, aware that in the Exchange's great hall their money was escaping from them. They waited. For what? Some sign, some indication that all was not lost. They could hear the combined voices of the brokers and helpers, blocks away. There seemed to be a race going on, but why? And where to? The strain coming from the floor was a palpable thing to those who stood as if sentenced to the spot and waited behind concrete walls just yards away from the trading.

There is an old story of the Japanese executioner who dreamed of the perfect beheading. His blade would be so swift, so sharp, that the victim would feel virtually nothing. The day for an execution came, he swung his sword, the man was cut through—yet the head remained on the neck, the victim was still alive. He jeered at the executioner as if nothing had happened. The swordsman bowed low to him and requested, "Please nod."

The stock market had said "Please nod" to America by this drizzly midafternoon hour of October 24, 1929, but those who stood in the street and waited, and those who watched with disbelieving eyes in the boardrooms, and those who sniffed with rational disdain in the corridors of power did not know it, would not know it, refused to accept the fact. But everything in the life of the country had changed. It would henceforth never be quite the same.

Those who should have known this, somehow did not. Or if they knew, they did some curious things.

Consider the meeting, in the early afternoon and still going on at this time, of the directors of the Federal Reserve Bank of New York, under the direction of Governor George Leslie Harrison, and including some of the men from the noon bankers' meeting.

During the past ten weeks, member banks of the Federal Reserve Bank of New York, such as the Chase, the National City, and so on, had taken an important step which had a definite hand in precipitating the crisis of the moment. They had cut back all collateral loans as well as loans to brokers. Their action 1) reduced the amount of money available to buy stocks during the September-October slide, and 2) reduced the member banks' indebtedness to the Federal Reserve system.

The effects of (1) were chaotic. Banks called loans from brokers. If brokers wanted to keep up their customer loans, they had to borrow from inexperienced, nonbanking sources. If they didn't want to borrow more from these sources, they had to *increase* their own indebtedness while paying off their bank loans—a difficult task. If they didn't want to do either, they could put out margin calls and take money in from their own customers. All of these things happened: nonbanking sources went up; brokers (in some cases) took up the slack to clients while themselves paying off their banks; and lots of margin calls went out.

What this meant could be seen as meeting directors considered a report that in the week up to Tuesday night (the twenty-second) brokers' loans had been reduced $167 million in a single week! That much money, taken out of the market as if by a vacuum cleaner! The result of all the contracting actions meant that in the period since September 3 when stocks had been dropping steadily but (in light of later events) slowly, customers had been putting up cash and depleting ready reserves (cleaning out their rainy-day funds) to the exhaustion point.

While this had been going on, so had (2), the reduction of the banks' indebtedness to the central system. This had meant, in effect, calling in loans in order to retire the banks' *own* loans from the Fed. In other words, clearing the decks of unwanted sail and deadwood, battening down the hatches. Why would a bank do this? For the same reason any sailor battens down: because of the clear feeling that some sort of battle was about to begin, that you'd be in better fighting shape for it if the decks were clear.

Just as clearly, the banks had been doing this because the Federal Reserve Bank requested them to, saying that if a member was overextended, that member bank would no longer be the recipient of any further credit.

If the Federal Reserve Bank of New York was encouraging this stance, it was doing so on express orders from the Board in Washington. That morning Dr. Goldenweisser, director of the Division of Research and Statistics for the Board, had pointed out to that body—as he had been doing for some time—that member banks ought *not* to be in debt to the central system for the amounts that had been prevailing for the past several years. He pointed out that the credit structure of the country had been built up on the basis of enormous additions to the gold supply, and that

> a large volume of indebtedness for a long period works against the valuable tradition against continuous borrowing by banks and exerts a permanent pressure on credit conditions.[3]

Therefore, borrowing must be curbed by member banks—which was what had been happening, gratifyingly, in the past ten weeks in New York. However, while that was happening, something else was also happening. With the consent of the Federal Reserve Board's Open Market Investment Committee, Harrison had recently started to buy $25 millions' worth of "governments" a week from the member banks, an operation which might allow member banks to retire loans to the Federal Reserve Bank, or else use the money to *expand* their loans because it gave them more cash on hand. In fact, Harrison had complained bitterly to whoever would listen that the $25-million-a-week amount was too low, that he had sought more latitude, but that the request had been disapproved by Washington.

Now the fat was in the fire of October 24. Every Thursday the officers of the Federal Reserve Bank submitted to the directors for approval a list of loans made to member banks since the previous meeting. In prior weeks banks had been asking, we have seen, for less money. Today, suddenly, the trend was hugely reversed: requests were made for borrowing large amounts to take over out-of-town loans, and to loan money to brokers for shoring up accounts in the rapidly sinking market. What did the Federal Reserve Bank of New York do in the face of such a request?

It decided by a vote of 4 to 3 to establish a rediscount rate of 5.5 percent, pending approval by Washington. This meant slightly easier money. But it was a hedged bet, and a compromised one, because Harrison would shortly report not only the outcome but his strong dissent to the Board, which would consider his dissent as important as the vote. Harrison wanted not only the rate changed, but the entire thinking on what was necessary for the system; he wanted to buy governments virtually without restraint, to maintain an easy money position—

lest any evidence of a shortage in funds or an increase in money rates lead to some sort of a money panic. If we should have added to the panicky state of mind relating to security values any fear of a money shortage, we might indeed have faced the most serious calamity.[4]

Harrison had determined, in other words, to open his coffers. He was afraid of a run on the banks, so he wanted to make sure the banks had enough money to prevent one. In the process, though, he also made sure that banks had enough money to make those loans he had been trying, with wonderful success, to curtail in the past ten weeks.

In those weeks, though money had been coming out of the market, it had not been "lost." That is, there had been buyers at prices that were not behind air holes, which meant sellers could get out with modest losses, not enormous ones. True, they might be unhappy, but they were not destitute.

Now, however, the Federal Reserve Bank, the Board, the member banks in New York, and all were getting into a position of supreme paradox. For the loosening of credit at this important moment *did* make money available, and that money was poured without hesitation into supporting stocks. But instead of going up, as they were supposed to do after such infusions, stocks went down—down for three weeks, down for four years. In other words, in a very short time those going-down stocks took with them *all the new money that was unsparingly poured into the market with the active participation of the banks following the opening of the floodgates on the twenty-fourth of October.*

What the Federal Reserve Bank's actions meant was that a man who was in debt $10,000 to his brokerage house, and who might have had much of that debt wiped away by being sold out—that man was given an additional loan to support his stocks and ended up further in debt, with no greater resources with which to pay off that debt. Which meant that the brokerage house's own debt was increased. Which meant that the debt of the bank was similarly increased, that the bank was in even deeper to the Federal Reserve system. It was a chain of events calculated to help turn Crash into Depression.

Could the Federal Reserve Bank have said no? Would it have made any difference if it had? Possibly so. The Crash itself would have been far worse if the Bank had shut the spigot rather than turned it on, but it is possible that it would have been cleaner, that the potential debt of people who lost money would have been less. It was the difference between a bankruptcy—clean, complete, and a chance to start over—and a slower, more crushing necessity to pay charges on a debt for a long time.

The ancillary question—Would there have been a run on the banks?—is unanswerable, but during a previous crisis of this sort in 1914 at the outbreak of the European war the newly wrought Federal Reserve System had easily prevented such a run, though the Exchange closed its doors for many months.

The Federal Reserve Bank's meeting broke up at 2:45, and the directors from the banks walked quietly to their nearby offices. They had no wish to be recognized, now. While they had been meeting, Lamont had managed to have the Dow print a correction of his earlier statement which had "misquoted" him as saying the Fed would "take action"—because the action had not yet been settled, and he didn't want to appear to be unduly trying to influence that action.

After the Federal Reserve Bank's meeting, and that correction, the bankers agreed to meet again when the events of the day were done, when the Reserve Board in Washington had met and decided on the rate, when the Exchange was safely closed. Brokers' loans had fallen $167 million in a week, mostly from out-of-town and nonbanking sources pulling in their horns. Today they were falling by as much as that in a day—maybe even in an hour—but nobody could know, because such facts weren't easily ascertainable. Much waited on the close of the Exchange's business day.

On the trading floor, the last minutes were total bedlam. Prices had crept up—the major ones. Steel, for example, was back where it had started the day, and there were last-minute buyers. There were also hundreds and hundreds of orders which wouldn't get executed and would have to wait for tomorrow. The noise was deafening, shouts rising from every corner. Young Mr. Crawford mounted to the balcony, watched the time, leaned over the edge, and rang the gong.

There was a second of shocked silence, and then the roar resumed again, this time full of groans, sighs of relief, moans of exhaustion—what the *Times* reporter called a "primitive requiem." Inexplicably, some of the people on the floor laughed and jumped about, threw scraps of paper into the air. They were long past their breaking points and were simply glad that, for good or ill, this immense day of trading was over.

Shortly, the brokers and employees melted away from the floor with its carpeting of paper scraps, collars, pencils, false teeth, eyeglasses, wishes, and dreams. Much more work awaited, but this was the work of paper shuffling, not of trading. Shares and transactions had to be recorded and readied for physical transfer. The ticker was still back in nightmare land and churned onward now somewhat slower, as the necessity for up-to-the-moment prices fell into the past. Here, too, the operators were tired. At closing time the ticker was about three hours late. It would get four hours late before it was done.

On the street, a now-silent crowd waited for news. People approached the few hardy souls who ventured out of the Exchange's building, looking for news. They were given the inspired but inadequate platitudes about prices being up at the bell. Indeed, some of them had been. Montgomery Ward had recovered nicely, so had AT&T, and Steel had actually closed a fraction of a point higher than it had opened, but few knew anything for a fact. Closing prices would have to wait until the ticker printed the last transactions of the day, which would be hours from now. But the Dow-Jones averages showed a final of 299.47 for its dozen stocks, off only 6.38 points on the day as a whole. Who bothered thinking that the Dow was composed of only a relative handful of stocks and that the vast bulk of the issues had suffered incredible losses?

Reporters rushed to print the story of the terrible day and the afternoon's "recovery," unable to believe in their hearts the depth and breadth of what had happened. The establishment line was readily accepted by these men even if their eyes told them differently: no one in the newspaper world wanted to be accused of contributing to panic by making things out to be worse than they were.

High above the construction on the Bank of Manhattan building, engineer Walter Peterson could see the crowds below. Neither he nor his colleagues could tell what was going on, but they noted, as they exited the elevator at street level as the shift drew to a close, the incredible sadness on many of the faces in the crowd. People seemed thunderstruck. Yet some went about their ordinary lives. Mike Kelley, floor clerk at the Curb Exchange, with some of his buddies, changed clothes quickly and got on the subway to go up to the Paramount Theater at Times Square. If you got there on Thursday afternoons before five, you got to see not only the last performance of this week's show but the first one of next week's, for the price of one ticket, 55 cents. Today the attraction was *The Return of Sherlock Holmes*, with Clive Brook. With all the great Holmes stories to choose from, Paramount had gone ahead and made up a silly story of its own—but the movie was still fun. Back in the Wall Street area, young Afton B., a secretary from the Midwest, proceeded on her first day ever in New York, by taxi, on the way to her first interview for her new job. Looking about at the crowds, she thought that pandemonium was natural for Wall Street. In the office to which the taxi took her, the law firm headed by Charles Evans Hughes (who within months would become Chief Justice of the Supreme Court), the talk was entirely of the Street. It was there that Afton learned of the Crash, which meant nothing to her. Wasn't New York exciting?

Milton Genecin, head margin clerk for a brokerage house, took a break. The tape being many hours late, he would have to wait until it caught up for the closing prices he needed. Then he could begin his work, which would undoubtedly last far into the night, as it had many times in the past few weeks. At his house, as at most others, margin was coming in satisfactorily, but more calls would have to go out, he was sure. The head of his firm, along with the heads of 34 other wire houses which together did 70 percent of the business on the New York Stock Exchange, were meeting at Hornblower and Weeks, under the direction there of Colonel John W. Prentiss, to compose a reassuring message that all of them would send out to their customers that evening, telling them that the market was in good shape despite the heavy trading of the day.

Milton wondered about this. As head of the margin department, he knew that, in addition to reassuring messages, there would be margin telegrams going out tonight; and he knew that decisions would have to be made about what stocks from impaired accounts would have to be earmarked to be sold next morning at 10:00 A.M. if those margin calls were not satisfactorily answered. He was worried about some of the clients. One garment manufacturer, whom he'd never met, had a collection of "cats and dogs" amounting to several hundred thousand dollars but shrinking rapidly. Already the man had met margin calls several times in past weeks, but could he do so again? Perhaps he should be advised to sell all of those lousy stocks now, and get out with what remaining money he had.

Behind the garment manufacturer were hundreds and hundreds of other clients, all of whose affairs were thrown into cocked hats by the events of the day. Margin clerks took a lot of vituperation, sometimes; few clients understood that when the firm sold them out because things were going bad, they were actually doing the clients a favor. Oh, well. It would be a long evening. Milton walked towards the oasis of Battery Park, at the tip of the island of Manhattan, and sat down on a park bench. Here, all was calm. The Statue of Liberty stood bold in the harbor; beyond, in the gray afternoon's mists, were Staten Island and the New Jersey coastline. Ferries passed each other on the way to and from the distant shores. Milton tried to let his mind drift from the events of the day, but he could not rid himself of the notion that the back of the fabulous 1920s stock market rise had been irretrievably broken.

Chapter Fifteen

WASHINGTON REVISITED
3:45 P.M.

The presidential party returned to Washington at 3:45 P.M. on the afternoon of October 24, and Hoover hurried to the White House amidst reports from aides of the horrendous day at the Stock Exchange. No reporter asked him what he thought at that moment. In the office he was busy. Although the appointments calendar and other records show nothing of what occupied him this important afternoon, we can hazard a few guesses, based on other contemporary records, at what happened at the White House.

Hoover possibly talked with Lamont, whose memorandum he had just read; Lamont would have been reassuring, saying that the bankers had taken action and that the market had "recovered." Hoover almost certainly talked with Harry Robinson, still in New York, who had been interviewing bankers and other important financial people for a series of memoranda he was writing for Hoover's attention. Hoover probably asked him to finish those memoranda right away (they arrived on the twenty-sixth) and asked about the stock market and the Lamont paper (which Robinson had prompted in the first place). Robinson probably gave him a few quick impressions and promised to call his sources and get back to the President. Possibly he said more, if his memoranda are any guide:

From my viewpoint, there are greater dangers and greater troubles in the situation than the [Lamont] memorandum would indicate and I am inclined to think that most of the bankers and industrialists would feel that this is true.[1]

Yet, in contradiction to the above:

The immediate speculative situation has taken care of itself for the present in a natural way and the best information I can obtain is to the effect that there is not on the immediate horizon a prospect of any serious failures.[2]

Prophetically, he observed

There will doubtless be great bitterness against "Wall Street" (so-called) and when each individual is explaining to his wife how he lost the family funds or to partners the disappearance of the concern's assets, the blame, of course, must be placed on someone and, as Will Rogers said "It might be on Hoover's Fedora Hat."[3]

Cold comfort for a president who had been agonizing over the market situation for months.

Hoover had Mellon called, and was told that the Secretary was in the Federal Reserve Board's second meeting of the day, along with the Comptroller of the Currency. The President left word that Mellon should come and see him when the meeting broke up. No sense interrupting Mellon when he was about the very business at hand.

Secretary Mellon did not ordinarily attend the Federal Reserve Board meetings, though of course he was nominal head of the Board, and, when present, presided. As he took the chair at 3:45, Governor Young informed the group that he had spoken with Harrison in New York, that the vote was 4 to 3 to establish a 5.5 percent rate of rediscount, that two nonpresent members had no opinion on the matter, but that Harrison was recommending no action since the vote was not unanimous. Mellon and the group debated this for a bit, and then Young was called to the phone to take a call from McGarrah in New York. McGarrah said it was his feeling that the whole credit structure needed a reduction in rate, and that the present was an opportune time to take action along that line. The Board flatly disagreed. Young introduced a motion to keep the rate at 6 percent, and it was passed unanimously. The discount windows would be kept open, but at a larger cost than the New York bankers wanted. It was a slap in the face, and it was the only action of any importance taken by the Board on the matter of the stock market this day.

Reporters were gathering in the congressional halls to seek comment from senators and representatives on the stock market "situation." During the course of the day, the people's emissaries had been turning away steadily from the business at hand—the lobbying, the debate on the tariff—to get reports of market activity. By the time the trading ceased for the day, few of them were left on the job.

Some senators said they would ask for an investigation. Some expressed the view that everything was all right, that whatever happened up there in New York was a temporary readjustment. Nobody said they had lost any money, at least not for publication. Senator King said the Federal Reserve Board was at fault, and that it was "a day of reckoning." Senator Carter Glass, who had criticized Mitchell, the Board, and everyone else for a long time, felt vindicated. The chickens were coming home to roost.

Another inkling of chickens roosting could be seen in the deliberations and decisions this day of the Supreme Court. The Court was divided into two philosophically opposed camps, one headed by the Chief Justice and former President of the United States William Howard Taft, and the other chaired by Oliver Wendell Holmes. Taft was pro-business and conservative, Holmes was the quintessential liberal. The most famous case of the year, that of pacifist Rosíka Schwimmer who refused to swear that she would bear arms to support the Constitution in every instance, brought out the deep division in the Court. The majority held, 6 to 3, that Schwimmer was to be denied citizenship for her views. Holmes, for the minority, dissented:

So far as the adequacy of her oath is concerned, I hardly can see how that is affected by the statement [of pacifism], inasmuch as she is a woman over fifty years of age, and would not be allowed to bear arms if she wanted to. And as to the opinion the whole examination of the applicant shows that she holds none of the now-dreaded creeds [Communism] but thoroughly believes in organized government and prefers that of the United States to any other in the world. Surely it cannot show lack of attachment to the principles of the Constitution that she thinks it can be improved.[4]

Holmes's moral force held nearly as much sway as the majority's decision. This galled Taft.

Taft wanted the eighty-eight-year-old Holmes to retire. Holmes said he would see Taft dead before he resigned, and held on. The two giants in black robes would hardly speak to each other, in Court or out. Holmes had lost his wife Fanny in the spring, but his strength had recently been somewhat reinvigorated by his relationship to a new law clerk, Alger Hiss, who was becoming like a son to him.

The cases of the day were all about business matters. In one, the issue was whether the Federal Farm Loan Board could force stockholders to ante up and make good a bank's bad debts. The Court said it couldn't—limiting government power. In a second case, a Virginia man had set up a trust for his sons in Maryland; when he died, Virginia wanted to tax the inheritance. The ruling? The conservative majority held that Virginia was overstepping her bounds. Holmes interpreted this (in the later, similar case of Baldwin versus Missouri) as an instance of trying to suppress the power of the states to try out economic innovation. He later wrote that "taxes should be on persons, not on property."

Then there was Chesapeake and Ohio versus Mikas. A long-term employee of the railroad who lived by the yards, Mikas was crossing a switch track and attempted to climb over several cars in his way, thinking they were not hooked up. Suddenly, without warning signals, the cars were shunted into reverse. Mikas fell off, broke his back, and was made a permanent cripple. He wanted compensation. The C&O argued that since he had had no real business being where he had been at that moment, and since nobody had known he was there, no warning had been called for, and they wouldn't pay him a cent. The Court agreed with the railroad. A crippled man had no right to sue an enormous company for negligence? Holmes was incensed. Progressivism was impotent, government was hamstrung: in the face of such inequities, he must hang on. With a little luck, Taft would die before him, and perhaps a new day would have time to dawn before he, too, passed on.

Other wars of import were being fought on the Washington scene this moment, and none was more colorful than the war for social supremacy. The leading ladies had more or less retired from the field. Lou Hoover, wife of the President, was not given to parties; Dolly Curtis Gann, half-sister to the Vice-President, was a laughable figure. When Dolly, her husband, and the Veep went out together

A shadow seems to darken an otherwise scintillating party whenever the vice-presidential trio heaves into sight, and the result is that those who crack the whip with greatest success look to livelier pastures for their dinner guests.[5]

In October of 1929, the main social arbiters and the archenemies in Washington society were Alice Longworth and Cissie Patterson.

Alice Roosevelt Longworth was the daughter of former President Theodore Roosevelt and the wife of Speaker of the House Nicholas Longworth who was this day just returning from the President's Midwestern river trip. The Longworths had lots of money, and each was rumored to go his and her separate way at partying times. According to a contemporary account, Alice was "brilliant if not gifted" and dominated the social scene through the prestige of her position and the vitriol of her tongue.

Cissie, more properly called Eleanor Medill Patterson, was the former Mrs. Elmer Schlesinger, and even more formerly was the Countess Gizycka. She was "brilliant and gifted" but had "dissipated her gifts." Their war had started eons ago.

During debutante days, both competed for the same eligible young Washington society men. Then Cissie had married. After that was finished, there was a dinner party at Alice's, which, next morning, produced an exchange of letters.

Dear Cissie:
Upon sweeping up the library this morning, the maid found several hair pins which I thought you might need and which I am returning.

Alice.

Dear Alice:
Many thanks for the hair-pins. If you had looked on the

chandelier you might also have sent back my shoes and
chewing gum.

Love,
Cissie.[6]

Skirmishes like these soon escalated into full-scale battle. A major engagement was fought during the Republican National Convention of 1920, held in Chicago. Cissie had taken a house and
invited the influential and interesting Senator William E. Borah
to stay with her. He did, for the nonce. Then she wrote for the
Hearst papers (owned by her brother-in-law) a laudatory sketch
of said senator. Borah pleaded with her: this was embarrassing
and should not be repeated. A few days later the Hearst *Chicago
Tribune* editorialized, with definite Cissie earmarks, "Borah and
Blah." Alice and Borah consoled each other, and neither forgave
Cissie.

In 1925, with her marriage to Elmer Schlesinger, Cissie published a novel *Glass Houses,* with thinly disguised portraits of
Borah and Alice. Tempers mounted. But then Nick Longworth
became more and more powerful, and people had to pay attention to Alice or be cut out of important doings. It seemed Cissie
was surpassed once and for all, as being the wife of the speaker
meant a lot of clout in a political town. However, a new aristocracy was on the rise, one which had been discounted for a long
time but was now reaching a position from which it would influence politics greatly—the press. Widowed once again, Cissie
took over the position of editor in chief of Hearst's *Washington
Herald*—and socialites hardly knew which faction to favor, or
when.

One group of Washington denizens who shunned the party cir-
cuit and yet knew which way to turn, were greatly affected by
the events of today. Independent and cantankerous for years,
they would in two weeks become dubbed with a name that
fitted them perfectly: the "Sons of the Wild Jackass."[7] These
were the irregular senators, some without national party iden-
tification, who had fought the good fight through the earlier
years of the century, and who would in years to come uncover
many of the abuses cited in these pages. In 1924 a clutch of them
had rallied around Robert La Follette the elder, in his drive for
the presidency: Burt Wheeler was the foremost of these. Among

the brighter lights were Bronson Cutting of New Mexico (a Harvard classmate of Franklin Delano Roosevelt), Blaine of Wisconsin, and others. The redoubtable Senator Borah was one of their number: simple, slow-moving, shaggy-haired, he would walk to the Senate every morning from the stables after cantering his horse Governor through Rock Creek Park. Once there, he would spend a great many hours in the small chamber behind the Foreign Relations Committee room, reading, conducting a voluminous correspondence, and consuming quarts of mineral water.

With Senators Hiram Johnson and George Norris, Borah had worked to block Wilson's internationalism in the wake of the war. They were all considered isolationists at the time, and obstructionists. But their cantankerousness helped to clear the air in the probing of the Teapot Dome and other scandals of the Harding era, in later investigations of the public utilities, of Wall Street, of the attempts of Hoover to place inadequately prepared judges on the Supreme Court. If Senator Borah was the patriarch, Senator George Norris of Nebraska was, according to Borah, "a platform in himself." His integrity was axiomatic. An orphaned, self-educated farm boy who had been a vagabond grade-school teacher, district judge, and daring member of the House before being elected to the Senate, he was one of the only men to have voted against entering the war.

Early in 1931 he would characterize himself as "almost too old to be useful," but in the next session the Congress passed his bill abolishing lame-duck sessions, his bill freeing labor from the threat of last-minute injunctions, and, finally, his bill for the government operation of Muscle Shoals. Congress didn't manage, however, to pass his bill abolishing the Electoral College so that the president might be chosen by a "more representative and constitutional method."

In the context of the twenties these men had been looked on as party poopers, those who, through their iconoclasm or even wrongheadedness, were somehow impeding progress and the great forward thrust of business and prosperity. The events of Crash and Depression would bring their intellects, their anger, their conception of a more responsible government at last to the fore.

On October 24 they were not yet there. Rather, the spotlight was focused on a group of Republicans entraining, in the midafternoon, for a great party to be held in New York that evening, a party that was ostensibly to honor Claudius Huston, the new chairman of the Republican National Committee.

The three senators in the group included George Moses—the very man who would, in two weeks, characterize the independents as Sons of the Wild Jackass—as well as James Watson (Republican floor leader) and Senator Hastings of Delaware. It was, however, a traveling group highlighted by people from the executive branch—the Vice-President, Cabinet members Good (War), Brown (Postmaster General), Hyde (Agriculture), Robert Lamont (Interior), Under-Secretary of the Treasury Ogden Mills, as well as two of the President's secretaries, Richey and Newton. The train left Washington's Union Station not long after Secretary Good had arrived there on Hoover's train, and in time to get to New York City for the celebration at eight o'clock in the evening.

Some yards away, west of the White House in the Treasury building, the Federal Reserve Board was concluding its meeting. Secretary Mellon was hounded by reporters as he tried to get out the door and to Hoover's offices. Mellon gruffly said that what had happened in New York was "the very salutary and inevitable deflation of a highly unhealthy situation," and that the country's underlying business security remained unshaken. It was difficult for reporters to stomach this, because the latest quotations on the ticker were still printing the lows for the day, but Mellon hurried away, and reporters were left with Governor Young. Young told them that the situation had not been deemed serious enough by the Board to issue a formal statement; he also told them there had been no action except that the Board had discussed some minor matters bearing on acceptance rates. How about the New York Federal Reserve Bank's rate? Would it be lowered? The rate was 6 percent, Mr. Young said, and further than that he would have no comment. Reporters pleaded. Off the record, he told them quite forcibly that the market break was solely the result of speculation. Then he, too, managed to get away.

Mellon arrived at the White House for his meeting with Hoover. No records of this meeting, which lasted for only a few minutes, exist, but undoubtedly the market was discussed. Hoover was probably not very happy to have Mellon alone to rely on, but his own man at the Treasury, Ogden Mills, was on his way to the dinner in New York, so there was only the Secretary. Hoover was always uncomfortable in Mellon's presence, and today he might well have been angry except that the two were in virtual accord on what had happened and what there was to be done or not done. Hoover had put off saying anything to reporters who were pressing him, telling them he would have a statement for them in the morning's scheduled press conference. What he would say then more than likely anchored his discussion with Mellon. Certainly the line he took at that press conference— that the business of the country was essentially sound—echoed Mellon's feelings precisely. They may have bruited about the Lamont memorandum, Robinson's verbal reports and memoranda to come, the phone calls the Secretary had had with bankers in New York, the Federal Reserve's actions and nonactions. Whatever they discussed, the tone was unmistakable. What had happened, they agreed, was a natural occurrence, a purgative bloodletting that would soon result in the patient's speedy recovery. Above all, there was no cause for alarm—or action. At 5:20, the President returned to his private quarters. In the evening, the family had dinner alone and retired early.

Chapter Sixteen

OF PARTIES AND PERILS
Evening

It was six o'clock in New York; dusk had fallen and the evening was hurrying in. On the floor of the New York Stock Exchange all was quiet; even the janitors had finished sweeping away the mass of paper and other debris. In the center of the great hall a few employees worked, grinding out the prices and transactions onto the ticker tape, which had still not reached the end of the trading day.

All over the country hundreds of thousands of people did not know where they were financially, whether they had been wiped out, whether the recovery had meant anything, whether the course of their future lives had been altered irrevocably. Men and women stood silently in brokerage offices, unable to tear themselves away, watching the relentless numbers being put up, erased with chamois, replaced by others. An upward trend could be discerned in several dozen leading stocks, but others stayed down, and, indeed, there were indications of heavy selling waves in many of them which assaulted price barriers and would undoubtedly turn them weak on the morrow. Few went home now; they would wait until the last quotation had come across to be chalked up, whenever that would be. No one cried, no one ran screaming into the street: they were all transfixed to the spot. Already they had been standing and watching many hours, but it didn't seem to matter. For them, time had stopped.

In the Wall Street area, squadrons of back-office people were working away at top speed. Some brokerage houses were partially closed down—those who did not "clear" their own stocks—but others, which cleared transactions for small houses, were open now for the first time. Stock certificates had to be physically transferred on all of today's transactions by 2:30 P.M. tomorrow: that was the rule. The clearing houses were dealing with the largest volume of shares they had ever seen in one day, more than an ordinary week's worth at a single time, and not all of the day's transactions had been recorded yet on the tape. Undoubtedly, employees knew, they would be here working straight through until 2:30 tomorrow to get it all done.

Margin clerks waited impatiently for the official closing prices, and started sorting through groups of accounts to get many ready to be tabulated for possible margin calls to go out that evening. This procedure was being repeated in banks all over the country, as well. Restaurants in Wall Street were overloaded with people taking a quick dinner break, and with calls for food to be delivered to those offices which decided not to allow their people to go out for dinner. Many places ordinarily open only for lunch had stayed open for dinner. Food wholesalers had been deluged with last-minute orders which they were now trying valiantly to fill. Every available hotel room from Brooklyn to Hoboken had been booked. Brokers and clerks called their wives and mothers and girl friends and told them they wouldn't be home tonight. It would actually be ten days before most of them were able to go home, except to get a suitcase and come back to work.

Uptown, bootlegger Matty Harris sat contemplating the ruin of his nice little business. The $42,000 he had invested in the stock market was now all gone. All gone. Which meant he had no capital left with which to buy booze, which in turn meant that he was effectively out of the bootlegging business, because—unlike the stock market—it was not the sort of operation where people cheerfully extended you credit. Matty wondered how long it would take him to find a job. At least he still had the big car, though he wasn't sure what good it would do him now.

Harold Dehn was on his way to the D.L.&W. ferry when he heard a paper boy crying "Big Crash on Wall Street." He bought the paper and was surprised to find that the closing prices were not even listed yet. He worried about his margin account, which contained all the dreams of his small family for the future, to the tune of $5,000. What would he do if, as it undoubtedly would, the brokerage house he used called him for more margin? That would be a tough one to talk over with his wife tonight. He noticed many people on the ferry studying the newspaper.

At the convention of *Cosmopolitan* salesmen at Yanna Farms in the Adirondacks, there was a frantic unease. Late in the afternoon a supplier for the kitchen had broken the splendid isolation of the place with the news that "something had happened" on the stock market in New York. After this first news, people had searched until they found a radio, and others had actually gone into the nearest town to make phone calls, to find out the extent of the disaster on the market. It seemed that three-quarters of the men had been playing it on margin. Now, when they were supposed to be enjoying the homemade sparkling burgundy and the delicious dinner, few could bring themselves to eat. Charlie Anderson was the youngest man in the group, and the only one who—admittedly on a whim, not on hard information—had managed to sell his stocks just the day before. Waiting for him at home would be a check, he figured, for $57,000. But he couldn't gloat over that at all when the men around him were staring blankly at their plates, wondering if their homes and their careers were safe. They had been solidly middle class when they arrived a day ago. Where were they now? After dinner, they all decided that the convention could not continue; nobody could keep his mind on business when his fortune was disappearing into the whirlwind. Tomorrow morning they would all go home. Tonight all they could do was worry.

In Providence, at the headquarters of the brokerage firm of Mandeville, Brooks, and Chaffee, people still stood mute watching the ticker at 6:30, and even at 7:00, long after the offices normally closed, long after the sun had gone down and the city's lights were blazing through the gray evening. The business district was closed and shuttered, but the brokerage office was packed. In the partners' room the officers of the concern were no longer watching the board, for there was a more urgent matter. Technically, the firm was already insolvent. Phone calls were being made to the various lending institutions who had loaned them money, pleading for more time to repay the notes that those nervous institutions unused to the vagaries of the stock market had decided must now be called. Each one was refusing to wait much longer. Nobody knew how many days the firm would be able to keep its doors open. If there were a serious rally in the next few days, everything might be all right, but you couldn't tell. It was touch and go. A boy came in from the outer office to announce that the ticker had stopped at 7:08½, after recording a volume of nearly 13 million shares, not counting odd lots which hadn't appeared on the ticker. Final prices were now available for the margin department. There would be many margin calls emanating from this office tonight.

Outside, in the customers' room, everybody was turning to go home, quietly. Few spoke to one another, as they usually did at closing time. They all seemed in shock, walking with small steps, their minds racing. It was a time to be alone.

In Boston, Postal Telegraph messenger boy Bob Austin had been working steadily since he had gotten out of school at 3:00 P.M. Normally his day ended at 6:00, but tonight was something special. All the messengers were going like crazy, and the 'grams were coming in bunches of 25 to 30 at a clip, instead of the usual one or two. The brokers' offices had signal boxes with handles that turned like timers on a stove. These registered in the PT office, and when one of them was on, a messenger would go to that office to fetch whatever they had. As he went to answer one of these calls, Bob, walking along State Street, was struck by the fact that the street was a blaze of light. You could read a newspaper in the middle of the street with no difficulty, because all the offices were completely lit up.

In the brokerage house to which he went, Bob found men on the floor shooting craps, money piled high on the rugs. In an inner office they had cleared off a desk and put a green drape across it to facilitate the action. The men had taken their suit coats and ties off, wrenched open their collars, and they were playing for money, wristwatches, rings, anything of value. It didn't seem to matter to them whether they lost, because they had already lost everything in the market that day. Bob felt as if someone had said to them that the end of the world had arrived, so you should get what you could to take with you wherever you were going to go. Too young to have any money in the market, Bob merely wondered if he'd be finished tonight in time to get the last trolley to his home on the outskirts of town.

In West Baden Springs, near Louisville, the plush resort hotel was in a state of near-nervous collapse. All day long the guests had jammed the stock-market room and caused utter confusion among the hotel's few long-distance operators as they tried to get brokers in Chicago, New York, and many cities around the nation. Not a few guests had boarded trains to go back home already, and as for the rest, many were saying their vacations were thoroughly ruined. Within a week the hotel would be practically vacant; in another year or so the management would give up and deed the place to a religious order.

On board the ships in mid-Atlantic, the news cast a similar pall. Many passengers made plans to book return passages as soon as they landed on the other side of the Big Ditch. It wouldn't be so easy, because every berth on every ship was already booked with people trying to get home. On the *Berengaria*, the woman who had lost $160,000 during the morning managed, by being daring, to retrieve all but $40,000 of it in the afternoon. The other passengers were not so daring or so lucky. In a few years the *Berengaria* would become known as the "Bargain-Area" because there were no takers for its elegant rooms.

In Florida, firing notices were typed out in several real-estate offices. In Seattle, a woman heard the market news and decided to conceal from her employer the fact that she was married and pregnant so the firm wouldn't dump her. In Oklahoma, the superintendent of schools in a rural district gathered what he had left of the funds he had purloined from the school district's coffers and slipped over the Mexican border. In a hundred towns, employers thought about who and what was expendable. In a thousand towns, people drank bootleg whiskey and tried to forget what could not be forgotten.

At a small gathering of forty in the New York residence of Bernard Baruch, people chatted about the Crash, politely. Winston Churchill, lately so entwined in the British economic scene, thought it not so bad. Next morning he would see, right in front of his eyes, a man jump out of a building. The guests proceeded to the well-laden table, attended by servants. Baruch had got all his money out months before. A glass was raised. "Dear friends and former millionaires," began the park-bench statesman. Laughter cut off the rest of the toast.

It was eight o'clock. Over the Red network the sound of a familiar tune floated, then dipped down as the mellow voice of Graham McNamee floated out over the airwaves, introducing the Fleishman's Yeast *Sunshine Hour:*

> Tonight we want you to picture a quiet luxurious supper club where soft mellow blue lights cast their shadows over white linen and sparkling glass and silver . . . waiters hurrying to and fro . . . palms all around . . . clear-eyed, clean-cut men dancing with beautiful girls in lovely gowns. Everybody is looking and feeling his best tonight. For here on the stage are Rudy Vallee and his Connecticut Yankees![1]

Rudy's numbers during the hour included his famous "Vagabond Lover," "The Pagan Love Song," and "Little By Little." It was a scene out of F. Scott Fitzgerald. At this moment, in the vaults of CFI in Hollywood, the entire negative of Rudy's first film, *The Vagabond Lover*, was heating up towards a flash point which would destroy it and $2 million's worth of other negatives before the night was over, and, in the process kill film custodian Albert Lund as he struggled to bring out many cans of precious artistic endeavor. From a clubroom of palms in New York, though, the band played on.

Across town, motorcycles noisily announced the arrival at the University Club of the Vice-President of the United States and his star-studded entourage, for the dinner honoring Claudius Huston and the Republican party. Among the guests were William Fox, W.W. Atterbury of the Pennsy (and other railroaders from the meeting of executives earlier in the day), and many others. Albert H. Wiggin had persuaded his wife to attend the Metropolitan Opera without him while he went to the testimonial. Otto Kahn, president of the Opera (and a Kuhn, Loeb senior partner) was also at the dinner. Percy Rockefeller, in whose "flat" Churchill was staying, had come here rather than to Baruch's. Hayden of Hayden, Stone; Schwab of U.S. Steel; Winthrop Aldrich: one hundred and thirty guests in all. Senator Moses and Senator Watson both made brief speeches about the necessity for the Republicans to maintain control of the Senate in the off-year elections of 1930, and suggested that the heavy contributors to Hoover's campaign who were among the guests tonight keep that necessity uppermost in their minds. James Nutt, treasurer of the Republican National Committee, was on hand in case anybody wanted to ante up on the spot.

The featured speaker, other than the Vice-President who had to be obliged to say a few words even though no one really listened to him, was Jeremiah Milbank, the actual organizer of the dinner. Milbank had been chief fund raiser for Hoover in the East, the man who in the past had put the touch on nearly everyone here. His words bore on the day's events, where no one else's would. And the message that Milbank gave out was loud and clear and would be echoed in a broadcast of the Halsey, Stuart *Old Counselor* over the ten o'clock airwaves: it said that the speculative and investment situation had recently changed and that what serious investors should do right now—was buy bonds.

At 8:30, a group of young messengers was let out of one of the great buildings on Broad Street and, full of beans from their incredible day, began to skylark through the near-empty streets, tossing a ball made of ticker tape back and forth. Someone in another office building thought them anarchists or worse, perhaps even rioters moved south from the Union Square Gastonia rally that had drawn several thousand in the late afternoon, and called the police. The boys were soon rounded up and sent on their way home, and the people who shuffled paper in the canyons of steel went back to work.

Down in North Carolina, Governor O. Max Gardner contemplated the fiasco of the trial of the killers of Ella May Wiggins and started procedures which would lead to a new trial, though one which would never lead to a conviction. The torrent of passion had come and gone, and things remained the same.

Mayor Walker was arguing for his reelection to a full hall at the Odd Fellows and over the airwaves of WOR; at Madison Square Garden the rodeo was in full swing; downtown, Brooks Atkinson was not liking the premiere of Sean O'Casey's *The Silver Tassie* very much. In New York City, at the epicenter of a disaster, life was going on fairly much as usual. No ships had crashed with thousands on board; no earthquakes had opened chasms to swallow lives; there were no guns being fired in anger; indeed, many of the leaders of the nation were not in hushed conference behind closed doors, but in an open, gala party well attended by the press. For that matter, reassuring announcements had been placed for next morning's newspapers, saying that this was the time to buy; and messages had been sent to the customers of the thirty-five largest wire houses who did 80 percent of the New York Stock Exchange's business, counseling calm. If ten thousand people still toiled in the Wall Street area, it was only an avalanche of paperwork that was annoying but not terribly detrimental. The reporter from the British papers who had telegraphed London that bodies were strewn all over lower Broadway had been thoroughly discredited. The explanation of the day, even now gathering force through being repeated from mouth to mouth, was that some paper profits had disappeared, and that was all. Easy come, easy go. A necessary deflation. A technical situation. Nothing to worry about.

But in Chicago, young bank clerk Ed Zellar went into a one-arm joint for his dinner before attending night classes and was asked by the very ordinary guy who dished out his meal, "Jeez! Have you heard what American and Foreign did? I'm goin' nuts 'til I find out!" Making his way with his tray to the one-arm chair, Ed wondered about the guy. Being a hashslinger at Pixley and Ehlers in the Loop was surely at the low end of the economic spectrum as far as jobs went. What the hell business had a counterman here got playing the stock market?

And, in the basement of a bungalow a few miles away on the corner of Eighty-second and Chappel, there was a small party that wasn't very gay, even though it was a masquerade. The guests, all white members of a Baptist church which had recently turned over its old building to its colored members, were celebrating their recent purchase of a lot for the site of a new church, farther out. These were ordinary people: a clerk in the employment department of the Elevated; a man with Commonwealth Edison; several with the steel mills and the railroads; a tire salesman; a floor supervisor at Marshall Field. They and their wives played parlor games and had a good time and each kept up a brave facade. None of them had the heart to tell the others that they had lost every cent they had saved for the future, all their hopes and wishes and middle-class dreams, in the curious events of October 24, 1929.

Chapter Seventeen

FIVE WEEKS OF DOWNS

Friday the twenty-fifth was better. Stocks were steady for the most part, though there were some losses. Levels remained virtually the same, and fewer than 6 million shares changed hands, a big day compared to the average, but only a trickle when measured against 13 million of the day before. In the morning it was generally acknowledged that a crash had taken place, and it was pronounced more or less officially over, to be perceived as a past event, dubbed Black Thursday, one for the history books. The bankers' consortium quietly disposed of $10 to $20 millions' worth of the stocks it had bought on Thursday, without much difficulty, and, in some instances, at a reasonable profit. Bank stocks continued to drop, as they were not listed on the NYSE. A message, based on a conversation with Lamont, went out over the Dow-Jones wire suggesting that the object of the group had not been to place a stop on the market's decline, *as no person or group could do that,* but rather to assure "an orderly market" for trading.

There is some evidence that Lamont or another group spokesman communicated with Hoover to get the President to issue a reassuring statement about the market in his morning's press conference. Hoover, on this occasion and others, refused flatly to tell people they should buy stocks. He did say that "the fundamental business of the country, that is, production and distribution of commodities, is on a sound and prosperous basis." The President's sentiments were echoed by a chorus of nearly all business and governmental leaders in the country, regardless of party. Only fanatics like Senator Carter Glass grumped that the whole thing was Charlie Mitchell's fault.

Some other things happened Friday, too, though they were little noticed at the time and have to be deduced from later statistics. Manufacturers, despite the reassuring statements and the firmer market, began pulling in their horns. Approximately two hundred thousand people were given pink slips. Production quotas for November and December were revised downward; here and there, a man would decide to cut back on producing his commodity and coast on his inventory for a while. Too many inventories were too high, at that moment, throughout the country. Banks kept coming up with more money in their coffers from called-in or sold-out loans, but, aside from those in New York City, fewer banks were *making* loans. There were a few suicides, but not many, though the newspapers reveled in the ones they could find.

Saturday the market had a short session, and it was not a good one. Prices were off again, and only the brief nature of the trading day saved the market from a truly disastrous decline. Over the rest of the weekend many people brooded, made decisions, awaited anxiously the events of Monday morning.

Monday the twenty-eighth was, as expected, horrendous. From the moment the bell sounded the opening of trading, stocks tumbled and took with them all the money that had been poured in during the afternoon of Thursday and in Friday's gracious pause. Steel burst through the Whitney barrier and went down 18 points. General Electric plummeted 48, AT&T 34, Westinghouse another 34; *The New York Times* average of leading industrials was off 49 points. Bank stocks gyrated wildly. In the early afternoon crowds spotted Charlie Mitchell going into the Morgan office, and a slight rally occurred on the strength of this. It was a false hope: Mitchell was going in this time to float a multimillion dollar loan for himself. In the weeks to come, NCB upper-echelon employees such as Mitchell would be allowed great grace and extra loans from the bank itself to pay off what they owed on their stock purchases (of NCB); regular employees who had also bought NCB received no such special dispensation: Julian Sherrod and thousands of others paid off for years or went into bankruptcy, while the officers did no such thing. Monday's loss on the market was a larger cumulative decline than that of the entire preceding week, though the volume was *only* 9.25 million shares. In the boardrooms all over the country, something noticeable had taken place: a thinning-out. There were only a few real small-fry left. Now the middle class and the wealthy were the ones standing mute in front of the lagging ticker. In the last hour of trading, on Monday 3 million shares were tossed into the whirlwind, while prices accelerated downward at such a rapid pace that all were grateful for the sound of the closing bell. People who had met margin calls on Friday, Saturday, and Monday morning and whose stocks had continued to drop were now deeper in debt than they had been right after Black Thursday.

At 4:30 the bankers' group met again, this time augmented by George F. Baker, Jr., whose assistance had been limited to phoned promises before this time. Baker's father, ninety and in a sickbed, had lost an estimated $20 million *personally* in the last five days. The story goes that in the days to come he argued with his doctors and his family, and got up and went to his office, telling them that this was his ninth panic and he had made money in all of them and wasn't going to lose any in this one. He didn't. He got it all back and more. The bankers' group was worried. Resources were dwindling. Though Lamont would tell the press after the meeting that their purpose had been to maintain that orderly market (which seemed now a virtual impossibility), it appears that what they were actually doing was organizing ways to get out of their monetary commitments at the least loss to themselves.

Prices were to be allowed to fall: this, read between the lines of Lamont's veribage, was the message of Monday evening, and many took it to heart.

Tuesday, the twenty-ninth of October, was the worst day ever experienced on the New York Stock Exchange. It was not the first, immediate, world-upsetting shock that October 24 had been, but it was in many senses a far worse crash. There was to the day, however, a sense of *déjà vu,* a feeling of inevitability, a sense of retreat and despair. There were, for example, the early-morning huge lots being dumped, the midday hopes, the late-afternoon rally. It felt like going through the motions when the script was already well known.

By October 29 most of the naive and the credulous had been washed away, and there were only those who were in the market because they could not get out in time, or because their stocks were paid up and they had decided to see if they could outlast the storm. It was bears, all the way. (The term "bear market" came about when one old speculator had sold a bearskin before having caught the bear.) In the first half-hour of October 29 nearly 3 million shares changed hands; had this rate kept up, it would have meant a 33-million-share day. The final tally was half of that, 16.5 million shares, far in excess of Black Thursday's volume and ferocity, though the ticker did not lag so much. There were many large blocks, evidence of big operators finally giving up and getting out. The bankers' pool threw some millions into the fray, but they were quickly washed away in the downward tide, and the rest were held carefully in reserve. People remembered Black Thursday, saw a pattern emerging, and it scared them. Nobody would hazard a guess on how far down things would go. In the five trading hours between 10:00 A.M. and 3:00 P.M., 8 billion dollars vanished, an amount equivalent to half the Federal government's debt expenditures for the entire fiscal year.

At noon, members of the governing committee slipped away from the trading floor in twos and threes to meet surreptitiously underneath it in the unaccustomed offices of the president of the Stock Clearing Company. "The office they met in," wrote Richard Whitney,

> was never designed for large meetings of this sort, with the result that most of the Governors were compelled to stand, or to sit on tables. As the meeting proceeded, panic was raging overhead on the floor. Every few minutes the latest prices were announced, with quotations moving swiftly and irresistibly downwards. The feeling of those present was revealed by their habit of continually lighting cigarettes, taking a puff or two, putting them out and lighting new ones—a practice which soon made the narrow room blue with smoke and extremely stuffy.[1]

But they decided not to close the Exchange, in the face of some strong feeling that it should close, and even stronger feelings that if it did, it would never open again.

The bankers' group met, as well. Twice. This time, however, there were rumors that the banks were not buying, but selling! On a bear raid themselves! Lamont hastily denied this, but stocks continued to fall in a fashion that had become horrendously predictable. Steel went down to 167 before a brief rally to 174. Westinghouse dropped 30 points to an even 100. Goldman, Sachs Trading Corporation went from 60 to 35, Blue Ridge from 10 down to 3. The volume was so overwhelmingly large that wastebaskets full of orders were lost and not discovered until after trading had ended for the day. Mayor Walker appealed to movie houses not to show newsreels of Thursday's crash, but "to show pictures which will reinstate courage and hope in the hearts of the people."

That evening, a young man who was the only floor broker for the small brokerage firm of Merrill Lynch, was called into the head office by the venerable Charlie Merrill. He was handed a list of ten stocks. Twenty thousand shares of each had been mishandled. Not executed. Hadn't been sold when customers had ordered them to be sold. If these orders were executed first thing next morning, Merrill told the young man, the firm stood to lose $500,000 and would very possibly have to go under. Neither man knew exactly what to do to prevent that loss, but the young man agreed to wait for his best opportunity and then sell.

In half a dozen days, including a Sunday, brokers' loans had fallen a billion dollars. Out-of-town banks and nonbanking sources of money had pulled $2 billion out of the market. But the New York banks, with the aid of the Federal Reserve Bank of New York, had taken up the slack in the city, providing money to investors so that every single share of margined stock would not have to be thrown onto the Exchange for what it might bring.

Dr. Julius Klein, Assistant Secretary of Commerce, said once again, in a nationally broadcast address that evening, that the fundamental business of the country was sound. And U.S. Steel and American Can announced they were declaring extra dividends, just to back him up!

On the strength of these portents, the market opened a bit firmer on Wednesday, October 30th. Then came the biggest boost, a statement from John D. Rockefeller, who had not uttered a word in public for a decade. Press man Ivy Lee had been urging Rockefeller's son to have the old man make a statement for nearly a week, since Black Thursday, but it was only now forthcoming. In a quavering voice, Rockefeller said:

> these are the days when many are discouraged. . . . In the ninety years of my life, depressions have come and gone. Prosperity has always returned, and will come again. . . . Believing that the fundamental conditions of the country are sound, my son and I have been purchasing sound common stocks for some days.[2]

Though comedian Eddie Cantor retorted, "Sure—who else had any money left," it was very good news. The market moved upward. The floor broker for Merrill Lynch took the opportunity to sell those 200,000 shares and gave the company a profit of $500,000 rather than a loss of the same magnitude. Richard Whitney announced at 1:40 that the Exchange would close early on Thursday, and stay closed Friday and Saturday so that the brokerage firms could catch up on their book- and record-keeping. The bottom was pronounced as having been hit by various parties. Only a few sour notes emanated from the Democratic National Committee, suggesting that the whole thing had been Hoover's fault. Even John J. Raskob—head of the ONC—told *The New York Times* that now was the time for people to buy stocks. Quietly, without anyone noticing, another one- to two-hundred thousand people were laid off around the country.

Confidence was increased over the weekend by the revelation that enormous purchases of governments by the Federal Reserve Bank of New York (over $100 million in two days) had made it possible for New York City banks to take over out-of-town loans, thus further preventing a money panic and making money available for "investors." Everything pointed to the idea that the twenty-ninth had been the nadir and the thirtieth the beginning of the upward trend. With a nice rest of several days, the market ought to be steady and confident at the opening of trading on Monday, November 5.

Exactly the reverse happened. It was another Niagara of liquidation right through to the end of the week. By Saturday, November 10, the papers were reporting not only the sad figures but also the story of the suicide of James J. Riordan, friend of Al Smith and John J. Raskob—a story which was withheld from the press for just enough time so that the bank which Riordan headed would be able to close Friday night without having a run on it.

The nadir—for the moment—was reached on November 13, precisely when Jesse Livermore was saying that the down side had run its course and that he expected the market to right itself again. In the period since Labor Day, $30 billion had gone out of stock valuations, vanished into thin air, never to be seen again. The figures told it all:

	High price, Sept. 3, 1929	Low price, Nov. 13, 1929
American Can	181	86
AT&T	304	197
Anaconda Copper	131	70
GE	396	168
GM	72	36
Montgomery Ward	137	49
NY Central	256	160
Radio Corporation of America	101	28
Union Carbide	137	59
U. S. Steel	261	150
Westinghouse	289	102
Electric Bond & Share	186	50

The New York Times average of 50 leading stocks had gone from 311.90 in September to 164.43 on November 13; and their averages for 25 industrials had sunk from 469.49 to 220.95. Brokers' loans had shrunk from over $8 billion to $3.5 billion. Bank debits to individual accounts in 141 cities across the nation decreased from $95 billion to $60 billion, and loans did not increase at all. The discount rate which Harrison and others had sought to have lowered for so long went to 5 percent on November 1 after long pleading, and by November 13 it seemed certain to be again reduced to 4.5 percent as an inducement for investments in anything but the market. The stock crash created panic conditions in the markets for farm products. The sudden drop in prices and the calling of loans forced vast quantities of commodities onto the market through liquidation to pay the loans. Wheat fell 17 cents a bushel and cotton $7.50 a bale. Federal Farm Board loans kept the prices and supplies from going even further afield. It was estimated unofficially that 500,000 people had lost their jobs in three weeks.

In Europe, reaction to the Crash was mixed. British and Continental stock exchanges scrambled for some time and suffered deflation. The most pronounced reaction was in Germany.

Just around the time of the Crash, ten years after Versailles, the Germans were being asked to decide, in a referendum, if they would continue to knuckle under to the reparations payments set up after the war or if they would reject them. This referendum was spearheaded by press lord Alfred Hugenberg, who employed as his front man, rabble-rouser Adolf Hitler. In a 1929 book, a former British ambassador to Germany had had to explain the Nazi in a footnote, as everyone had "forgotten" him by this time. The Hugenberg-Hitler referendum against the Young Plan was voted down overwhelmingly two weeks after the Crash, but, through the publicity given to the campaign, Hitler came out of obscurity.

He had long said to his friends that all he needed to rise to power was bad times. The Crash provided them. American loans had long been Germany's source of revenue. When they started to be unavailable in 1928, unemployment had begun to soar. Now, after the Crash, it rose 2 million in two months! The Berlin papers worried about the inordinate number of suicides, and Nazi party membership began to double every six months. Before another year was out, Hitler would be knocking at Hindenburg's door, backed by the power of millions of unemployed as well as by his small band of fanatics.

In the days just following October 24, the United States Army was reaching the climax of a long-term study on what to do for the next several years. Two plans were presented. Plan I, for an expanded army with new equipment, was widely supported by the military. Secretary of War James Good died just after the Crash, and his successor had no wish to push this bolder plan in the post-Crash atmosphere. Plan II, cheaper, but which many criticized as inadequate, was adopted. Few new weapons or even replacements for older ones were built in the next half-dozen years under the austerity budgets of this plan, and preparations for active participation in World War II were hampered thereby.

In the weeks following Black Thursday, President Hoover had been energetic in coping with the Crash and the Depression which seemed already to have begun. He was in constant touch with "experts" on the market, the monetary situation, the economy as a whole. The Lamont memorandum had been digested. So had the Robinson papers which covered banking, the currency system, balance of payments, and other aspects of high and international finance. Mellon, Ogden Mills, and Julius Klein had had their say. Roy O. Young of the Federal Reserve Board, who had long predicted an inevitable collapse, had begun to have increasing weight with the President for his correct prognostications. A confidential report that he sent to Hoover pulled no punches:

> The situation is far from liquidated . . . it is honeycombed with weak spots . . . it will take perhaps months before readjustment is accomplished.[3]

Hoover was thoroughly convinced that he had to do something. He said:

> Words are not of any great importance in times of economic disturbance. It is action that counts.[4]

So on November 15, he proceeded into action. He was no novice at depressions. As Secretary of Commerce under Harding, he had been chairman of the 1922 Unemployment Conference, and had argued vociferously then for expanded public works as a means to get people back on the job and stimulate the economy. Now, he did the same from a position of command. As soon as Congress met, he told Mellon, the Federal Buildings program should be increased by $423 million. All such building was at that time in the Treasury bailiwick.

He also called a conference of railroad presidents, to persuade them not to slack off on any maintenance or construction work. He summoned a wide array of business, labor, and governmental leaders to White House conferences in the second half of November: Henry Ford was there, and so were the bigwigs from

General Motors. The discussions were confidential, says a book friendly to Hoover,

> in order that those present could express themselves freely without danger of sensational or partial reports disturbing the public mind.[5]

Hoover's prepared note says that he would not have called the conferees here had he not regarded the crisis more seriously than as a mere stock market crash. The depression must last for some time, Hoover said, and *2 or 3 million were unemployed by the sudden suspension of many activities (as of November 21; six weeks* earlier the estimate had been under 1.5 million).* Hoover painted in the direst terms the prospects for the future: it would be bad, very bad, "much liquidation of inflated values, debts and prices with heavy penalties on the nation." In the words of the official chroniclers of his administration,

> The President further proceeded to point out that our immediate duty was to consider the human problem of unemployment and distress; that our second problem was to maintain social order and industrial peace; the third was orderly liquidation and the prevention of panic, and the final readjustment of new concepts of living. He explained that the immediate "liquidation" of labor had been the industrial policy of previous depressions; that his every instinct was opposed to both the term and the policy, for labor was not a commodity.[6]

Hoover was convinced that letting labor go down the unemployment drain would deepen the depression by suddenly reducing purchasing power, and that it would possibly bring violence. He believed cost of living would fall even if wages were temporarily maintained. The first shock, he was convinced, must fall on *profits*, not on wages. Labor leaders agreed with the President, and in some instances agreed to withdraw demands for wage increases already made. The employers were similarly responsive, authorizing the President to make a public state-

---

*Another, earlier estimate put the precrash unemployed figure at 2.5 million and guessed that in the six weeks that followed unemployment had jumped to between 3.5 and 4 million.

ment on their behalf that they would "not initiate any movement for wage reduction." Ford and GM went further: they reduced the price of new cars by several hundred dollars each.

Every day for a week the President met with important groups. Building and construction leaders were next. They were exhorted to build whatever they could. On November 23 telegrams went to all governors and mayors requesting them not to decrease public works, but to expand them "in every practical direction" to take up the slack in unemployment. On the twenty-fourth answering telegrams came back and were made public: they all pledged support and told of programs they would be recommending to legislatures at their next sessions. November 25 it was farm people. The twenty-seventh it was the public utility people. Construction was the theme of all these meetings: build, the President urged them, don't stop, but go ahead at full steam as if nothing had happened. As a further inducement to keep going, Hoover had Mellon ready to propose an across-the-board tax cut for individuals and businesses, especially beneficial for those with small or moderate incomes. Federal programs were pushed to a great degree as well: postal service work was expanded, and new contracts for overseas mail were discussed to stimulate additional shipbuilding.

There was one thing Hoover did not do in all of this: consult Congress. Why? Because he believed that what was necessary was not new legislation, but force and fervor in the private sector. Two years later he would outline his philosophy about actions during this period:

> For the first time in history the Federal Government has taken an extensive and positive part in mitigating the effects of depression and expediting recovery. I have conceived that if we would preserve our democracy this leadership must take the part not of an attempted dictatorship, but of organizing cooperation in the constructive forces of the community and of stimulating every element of initiative and self-reliance in the country. There is no sudden stroke of either governmental or private action which can dissolve these world difficulties: patient constructive action in a multitude of directions is the strategy of success. This battle is upon a thousand fronts. Some . . . have indomitable confidence that by some legerdemain we can leg-

islate ourselves out of a world-wide depression. Such views are as accurate as the belief we can exorcise a Caribbean hurricane by statutory law.[7]

By the end of November, high government officials and private businessmen were estimating sixty to ninety days before the country recovered its full economic steam again.

It didn't take sixty or ninety days. By the most modest of estimates it took four years; by more hardheaded guesses and figures, it took ten to twelve years, or until the full fury of the Second World War had engulfed the United States and the world.

Epilogue

The Children of 1929

When the Lynds, who had painted a detailed and accurate picture of pre-Crash America in *Middletown,* went back to the city of their studies in the midthirties, they found:

A city exultantly preoccupied with the question, "How fast can we make even more money?" was startled by being forced to shift its central concern for a period of years to the stark question, "Can we manage to keep alive?"

A city living excitedly *at* a future which all signs promised would be golden, lived for a while *in* the present with its exigent demands.

A city living by the faith that everyone can and should support himself lived through a period of years in which it had to confess that at least temporarily a quarter of its population could not get work. . . .

A city built around the theory of local autonomy has lived in a world experiencing rapid centralization of administrative authority and marked innovations in the interference by these centralized agencies in local affairs. . . .

A city still accustomed to having its young assume largely the values of their parents has had to listen to an increasing number of its young speak of the world of their parents as a botched mess.

A city in which the "future" has always been painted in

terms of its gayer-hued hopes has been forced to add to its pigments the somber dark tones of its fears.[1]

These are changes in the American psyche; changes which, one can well argue, are permanent, cruel, and yet evidence of a more realistic attitude towards life. What had happened to America that this great a change should have been made and so deeply ingrained? Some answers are to be found in the study, ongoing since 1931, of the Oakland Growth Study division of the Institute of Child Welfare at the University of California at Berkeley. This remarkable study summarizes in sociological terms many of the personal catastrophic consequences of the Crash and Depression. The following passages are condensed from Glenn H. Elder, Jr.'s book about the project, *Children of the Great Depression.*

The originators of this study began it because they believed that parents who experienced extreme social change would seek to raise their children differently from the ways in which they themselves had been raised, adapting their methods to train their children so they would be better suited to meet life in a changed world. Oakland was an ideal place to study the change: in 1929 it was a rapidly growing metropolis of 284,000, and the median income of its families was a healthy $3,179 a year, well above the national average and poverty line. In 1933 it was $1,911 a year. Though the study looked at the children—indeed, it has followed them for over forty years—it revealed much about the parents as well.

Those parents were mostly born before the turn of the century, and entered the Depression as mature adults. In many senses, a great proportion of them were seriously destroyed by the events of Crash and Depression. Middle-class parents fought desperately against the loss of status, withdrew into themselves, alcohol, apathy. Lower-class families, more used to economic deprivation, suffered in different ways: here the consequences were often physical as well as mental, with many becoming debilitated and dying early.

As for the children, things were more complicated. What happened to them depended in large measure on how old they were at the time of the Crash and the onset of the Depression. An early psychoanalytic prognosis said that the children of the Depres-

sion would experience fear, loss of confidence, continued sub-
mission, masochism, and discouragement as a result of seeing at
firsthand the devastating effects of breakdown of morale in their
parents. The Oakland Study found this to be only partially so. It
was bad, but in different ways from what had been expected.

The study's main focus was on children born from 1916 to
1925, a "cohort" which has tremendous historical significance
as a major source of World War II soldiers, the postwar baby
boom, and the parents of the children who entered colleges in
the 1960s. This generation, in a major sense, were never teen-
agers: the protected, nonresponsible experience of adolescence
was denied them, because adult tasks were extended downwards
into adolescence. However, most of these young people were in
school during the worst years of the Depression, graduating only
in the latter thirties. "All of the evidence," says Glenn H. Elder,
Jr.,

> suggests that economic loss and work roles tended to free
> boys from the traditional restraints of parental control.
> While most girls responded to family hardship by assuming
> household responsibilities, this adaptation had little conse-
> quence for their dependence on the family or parental con-
> trol, with the possible exception of girls from working-class
> homes. . . . For the Oakland children, economic depriva-
> tion in the 30s increased the common involvement of
> mother and daughter in household operations, and en-
> couraged economic activity which often placed boys in a re-
> sponsible position to nonfamily employers. . . . In an im-
> portant sense, the transference of attachment from parents
> to nonfamily adults represents a step towards adulthood, a
> movement away from the particularistic world of family
> and kin.[2]

Some families split apart, others were rendered closer by hard
times. Another study says that unemployed fathers maintained
their power and esteem among family members most satisfactorily when love and understanding were prominent in marital relations. Fathers who lost heavily in the Depression were generally perceived as less powerful in family affairs than mothers, with
all the consequences for "modeling" behavior in the children.
There were very few cases where fathers were favored in family

conflicts during the Depression years—a finding the Oakland investigators found striking.

It is not surprising that male victims of the Depression were frequently blamed for setbacks over which they had little or no control, given a value system that extols individual responsibility and self-sufficiency. More important, however, is the generalized acceptance of this utilitarian self-evaluation among husbands and fathers who were deprived of the means to adequately support their families. Instead of attributing the cause to deprivational conditions in society, to a force beyond the individual actor and his understanding, the record, such as it is, shows that the unemployed or hard-pressed workers were inclined to direct hostile feelings and frustrations toward the self, punishing themselves for the consequences of an economic system.[3]

The Oakland study managed to compare three age groups: (1) those born in 1910–1911, (2) those born 1920 and 1921, the heart of their sample, and (3) those born in 1928–1929. The older the child at the time of the Crash, the lower the probability of adverse psychological damage. Which means that the younger the child, the more marked the psychological damage—that infants who had not reached puberty before, say, the onset of WW II, bore a great deal of the weight of their parents' disintegration.

Reaching the age of majority in 1932–1933, the oldest group had, nevertheless, great burdens to bear. They were more vulnerable to deprivational factors in establishing a life course than the others.

Consider: to be twenty-one in 1931: a chilling prospect; the full brunt of lack of opportunity in jobs and education lay heavy on the back; they watched fathers and mothers submerge in the flood tide of despair, and were permanently affected. Young Jim Reed returned from an idyllic existence as a Hollywood extra to watch his father get thrown out of his Brooklyn house with all of his family and furniture; he has never been able to banish the scene from his mind.

"I worry," said one woman to the authors of the Oakland study, "about the shadow of my mother and its effects on me and my children. You think your life is your own, but each life affects the next, and each generation affects the next." The author comments that in family after family,

> Mother consciously defined her labor or effort for the family as an extreme sacrifice, a contribution which could not be adequately repaid by the children without the sacrifice of their independence and integrity. . . . When offspring reach adult status, the sacrificial investment of parents may be used to ensure some consideration in important decisions—on where to live, what job to take, where to spend a vacation or holiday. Sacrifices generate power and a sense of obligation when they are interpreted as such by the recipient, but this response is at least problematic. Indebtedness fosters resentment, which erodes the sense of obligation, especially when it is used to excess as a means of control.[4]

Economic hardships and family adjustments spurred many of the middle group, born in 1920, to high achievement. But overall, the effects were, if not bad, then terribly fixed.

Today the children of the Oakland study are characterized by an amazingly cohesive and widespread adherence to bureaucratic styles, language, culture, and personality. They are white-collar employees, managers, professionals, junior executives, service workers in higher-status services such as education, recreation, leisure, social work, psychiatry. In contrast to their fathers, who were mostly small entrepreneurs, businessmen and independent craftsmen, self-employment is largely foreign to them. Seventy percent have never experienced it at all. In the parents' group there had been quite a few engineers of the freelance sort; today, typically, the sons of such fathers occupy positions of managerial responsibility in a large corporation or firm.

But these were middle-class children. Those from the lower class fared badly. They left school earlier, and this single factor has been pinpointed as the major reason for less attainment in later years. In a Boston study similar to the Oakland one, Stephen Thernstrom concluded that the unskilled and semiskilled who found manual labor jobs in the thirties were those who spent the remainder of their productive lives without ever gaining access to the white-collar stratum. More than three-quarters of the men who held semiskilled first jobs in the Depression were still in this stratum at the time of their last job, while of those born much before or much after, only half remained in the lower portion of the economic ladder by the time they reached retirement age. For those on the low end, the Depression was, then, a permanent damper on aspirations for a better life.

* * * *

After the German defeat at El Alamein in 1942, Winston Churchill commented that this was not the end of the war, not even the beginning of the end, but that it was, perhaps, "the end of the beginning." October 24, 1929, was the end of the beginning, the beginning of the Depression, the beginning of a new kind of necessary consciousness, the beginning of a modernity unalloyed by both the wonderful simplicity and the obvious imperfections of an older and earlier American civilization. The Crash was a time of instant change—not the cause of the change, but simply the moment when it happened.

What follows here is an attempt to bring into focus again certain of the stories told earlier in this book. This is not the place to tell the story of the Depression—that has been accomplished, many times—but there remains a need to gather together certain loose ends, to satisfy the need for conclusions. That this is a task difficult of accomplishment in an event whose start, finish, and results are still loudly debated, is clear. Yet there exists the need, and the following list is an attempt to satisfy it. The list has been alphabetized for the unexpected pleasures which derive from such contiguity.

Dottie Alber, the secretary who tried to conceal both her marriage and her pregnancy because her employer, Traveler's Insurance, frowned on women working for them who were in either of those conditions, finally had to quit. She had her baby, then two more. Her engineer husband dug ditches when the phone company couldn't find anything else for him to do. They used the bathtub to age "green" beer, and had modest parties in their home with friends in similar circumstances through the Depression years. Years later she went back to high school and graduated the same day as her eldest son. "Guess what I'm trying to say," she writes, "is we lived through it, and I think in some ways we had more then than now. I feel extremely sorry for young people starting out today because most of them have learned to live high and have so much when at home that it must be tough on both of them when they first get married. . . . Maybe we need to get back to basics and basic needs—personal and material."

Anaconda Cooper, left to float by the bankers' pool after a small fling, sank and became one of the first large casualties of the Depression years. Its stock certificates are now collectors' items.

Charles Anderson, the *Cosmopolitan* magazine advertising salesman, returned home to find a check for $57,000 waiting for him because he had sold his stocks the day before Black Thursday. "It was a fortune in those days," he writes, "but a year later when President Hoover was telling us that we would all have two cars and all kinds of things, I once again went back into the market and lost what had come so easy."

Harry B., who worked for a major oil company and who had bought its stock, held on to his shares through the Crash and Depression, and today they're worth quite a bit. Fellow employees who had bought on margin were not so fortunate. Harry's boss, who lost big, started using alcohol to drown his sorrows, lost his good job, his wife, everything. Something similar happened in the house of nine-year-old Mary B., the daughter of Polish immigrants. Pop got stock crazy, mortgaged the house, lost it all. They went from riches to rags. Mary recalls resenting her mother taking the ten dollars which Mary had saved for school and using it to buy food for the family. Pop went to pieces and never recovered, but the rest of the family was all right after the war started.

Eugene B., a Safeway store manager in San Diego, watched the Depression settle in on Southern California within weeks after the Crash. Older folks would come into the store with their market baskets and mill about as if in a daze; some would mumble incoherently; many would not be able to buy anything and would wander back out again. William H. ran a small grocery store in Costa Mesa. He'd carry people on credit because he couldn't bear to see his neighbors go hungry. Years later, some would come and pay him off, while others simply disappeared.

When the local bank closed, the manager allowed Mr. H. to secretly draw out a few thousand, because he knew how the man had helped the community. Competition from the chains, though, soon forced Mr. H. out of business.

Fred Beal, the Communist organizer from New England who had been convicted in the murder of Chief Aderholt in Gastonia, fled to Russia, where he remained for some years until he became bitterly disillusioned about communism and returned to the United States to face arrest and jail. He served some years, but clamors for pardon and commutation fell on deaf ears: the governor who could have helped him was the former prosecutor at the Gastonia trial. Beal eventually got out, but died in poverty and obscurity.

The Binga Bank of Chicago was one of the early victims of the wave of bank closings in the wake of the Crash. Mortgages on black homes were thoroughly compromised when black men and women were thrown out of work quickly under a policy of last hired, first fired. Many authorities believed at the time that if the bank—and Jesse Binga—had been more attuned to the white majority, this important economic pillar of Chicago's black community would have weathered the storm. Blacks in general fared terribly in the Depression. Whatever economic and social gains they had made in the prosperity years were ruthlessly wiped out. Hard times made many things bitter, and hard times reinforced the color line.

Monroe Bloom, San Francisco banker, recalls times, often as long as half an hour, when, despite midday crowds in the streets, not a soul would enter his bank, so depressed was business and so great was unemployment. Loans were being paid off, dollar by dollar over long periods—some as long as twenty years. "Many people were ruined morally as well as financially, and never recovered," he writes. "When the veterans of adversity are gone, there will be left only those who have experienced nothing but never-ending price and wage increases and easy credit, and are conditioned to accept them as a way of life regardless of their ultimate consequences."

Hazel Cardozo, farmer's daughter and high-school student in Oklahoma, was working after classes in Woolworth's when it was learned that the superintendent of the district had put school money into the market, had lost it, and had skipped to Mexico. Christmas came along, and Hazel worked hard at the store. Then it was time for the next semester at school, and she was faced with a decision: whether to take the full-time job offered by Woolworth's or return to school. The family was in dire need; Mother cooked and cleaned house for other people— father was long gone—and got paid in eggs or a chicken for a full day's work. The school district now had no operating money and was forced to charge $6 per month per student for the privilege of going to a state-run school. It was too much for Hazel; she took the job at $8 a week. One day Hazel's Latin teacher came into the store and begged her not to quit school. If it had been anyone else, the woman said, she wouldn't have been concerned, but Hazel was the brightest, most promising student of them all. Hazel cried so hard she had to leave the floor until the teacher was gone. Every night for ten years Hazel dreamed about school, about going back, reading books, reveling in the wonders of education. After a while the dreams subsided; life had to be lived as it was, and besides, she was embarrassed now because she didn't have very much education. "I had heard so many people say," she writes, "that anyone who wanted an education bad enough could find some way. But I could never find that way. Tied down raising the family, and then tied to meager jobs in department stores, I didn't find time or opportunity." Hazel retired recently with no pension, only a Social Security check of $240 a month.

Winston Churchill returned to Great Britain shortly after October 24. The prize that had so far eluded him had to wait another ten years. He became Prime Minister of Great Britain in 1940.

Berta and Phil Cooley were teachers in Hawaii. Outside of Honolulu, there were no real towns then, mostly plantations. The paper gave weekly stock reports, and a Dean Witter man gave margin accounts. They were worth, Mrs. Cooley remembers, $150,000 on paper before the Crash. "Looking back," she writes, "if we had cashed in, it would have been bad for both of us to have that much money, so young."

Arthur W. Cutten's fortune was reduced in the Crash from $150 million to $100 million—as near as could be determined. People in his home town of Guelph, Ontario, complained that by following him they had lost all their savings. He built them a golf course.

Harold Dehn, who answered a margin call on the morning of October 25, saw that money go down the same drain as his earlier investment. If he had not answered the call, he would have owed less. It took him years to work back to his financial position before the Crash.

Marie E., whose father had been a motorman on the trolleys in Chicago, managed to find work as a waitress at age seventeen and married in 1931. By this time her husband had been cut back to two days a week at the steel mill. They moved in with his parents, along with other relatives, fourteen of them at times in a three-room house. Only a pregnant sister-in-law and a brother-in-law with pneumonia got an egg and an orange each per day; the rest subsisted on bread and milk gravy and an occasional wild rabbit. Because he knew the owner's son, the husband was able to get a job temporarily at a canning factory at ten cents an hour; a gift of a case of tomatoes and one of corn fed them for three weeks until the bookkeeping machinery got him paid. Still, it was better than the welfare Marie had been on as a child. At least during the Depression everyone was poor, and you didn't notice it so much.

Thomas Alva Edison's health failed swiftly after the ceremonies marking the fiftieth anniversary of the first electric light: that was, for better or worse, the end of his career.

The Empire State Building was completed on schedule and opened in 1931. There were virtually no takers for its many offices at that time. But it was the tallest building in the world.

Albert Bacon Fall, the only government official to take the weight of the Harding administration scandals, was convicted and sentenced on October 25, 1929. Edward Doheny, who had bribed him, threw one of the most lavish parties ever for his daughter's debut in the winter of 1930, while around the block a breadline stretched in wait for largesse from a Washington charity.

Carl Fisher's plans for Montauk never got going again after the Crash. In the summers of 1930 and 1931 he tried desperately to make Montauk attractive, with tennis matches, auto races, and even maneuvers of the Navy's Atlantic fleet as an enticement to visitors. The Secretary of the Navy got bounced over that last one. A lot of people lost money on Montauk, Fisher among them. One skyscraper of seven stories remains, and despite Fisher's departure Montauk is worth today every bit as much as he once said it would be.

William Fox's fortunes did not survive the Crash well, though he heeded the admonition to buy bonds and its corollary, sell stocks, starting October 25. Unfortunately, the stocks he held as collateral behind his takeover push in Hollywood were such things as National City Bank, whose health was debatable at best. He lost control of Fox Studios to the much smaller Twentieth Century and never again gained a position of prominence in the industry. His arch-rival Adolph Zukor, who landed in France on the day of the Crash, returned shortly to a grand career in films, celebrating his hundredth birthday a few years ago with a gala attended by seemingly all the stars in the dream factory's firmament.

Navy veteran Fred Galvin, in Boston, was laid off from his job in a milk factory within weeks of the Crash. He walked the streets trying to find work until he had to put cardboard in his shoes to cover the holes. At home he punched the wall in frustration. Welfare got him four dollars a week but insisted that he sweep gutters two days a week for it. One day he came home to find the electricity had been turned off for nonpayment. Fred walked down to Edison Electric and offered to work off the bill doing whatever the company wanted, cleaning toilets, anything. The company said it couldn't do that, because they'd been laying off people, too, but it was the last he heard from them about the bill. Fred had two kids at home. "Hunger is a terrible thing," he writes. "It finally got to where you just didn't care what did happen anymore, you might just as well be in jail, at least you'd have something to eat, and they'd have to provide for your family somehow." One morning he was so desperate that he took a paper bag, left the house at 5:30 A.M., and stole some doughnuts, bread, and milk from the doorway of a store. He trembled all the way home and was sick when he got there, but at least the kids had food. When he found a federal job, he held on to it for the rest of his working life.

Pharmacist Art Garson, who bought shares of Inspiration Copper while the market was plunging, made a modest profit and got out. It was lucky he did: in a short while Inspiration was selling for half of one percent of what he'd paid for it.

Margin department head clerk Milton Genecin sold out many people during the Crash days, and most of them were later grateful: at least they hadn't thrown good money after bad, as had many others. As he began to see the effects of depression he did some reading, and turned to socialism and the writings of Leon Trotsky.

The Gold Coasters of Long Island, as with most of the rich, fared generally well through the Crash and Depression. But the time of gaudy opulence was firmly over. Few estates were built in the coming years: too expensive to maintain in the necessary style. Ferdinand Lundberg, in *America's Sixty Families*, contended that the rich grew richer and the poor grew poorer in the aftermath of the Crash. This was most importantly true of those whose wealth was more than a generation old in 1929. The Crash wiped out the recently elevated, not the entrenched wealthy.

Uncle Joe Grundy's lobbying efforts continued unabated after the Crash. The tariff bill for which he worked so hard was passed by both houses of Congress and signed into law in 1930, over the objections of one thousand professional economists who signed a petition against it. The tariff helped deepen the Depression by starting a wave of recriminatory barriers across the world, which effectively shut off markets for American products abroad for many years.

In a farm community in the Midwest, the H. family, as well as most of their neighbors, were deeply religious people. Faith helped them through the Depression years, especially after the town's bank closed within weeks of the Crash. The H. family traded their own work repairing automobiles for food, wristwatches, whatever was of value. Farmers had bought machinery and land on credit, and insurance companies and banks took over many holdings. But faith prevailed. One farmer who had been losing chickens regularly tracked the culprit through a new-fallen snow: when he saw that it was a man with a family of five, he refused to vent his anger. One family of Christian Scientists "worked out" their troubles through prayer and "knowing nothing but good." That family had an idea: turn their corn into popcorn. Summers saw them at ballgames selling sacks for five cents each; later, they made carmel corn, all to pay off the farm's mortgage. "We rejoiced with the community over victories," Mrs. H. writes, "and what hurt one family hurt us all for miles around." Mrs. H's recipe for "Karmel Korn":

2 c. white sugar	Boil until crackles and breaks
1 c. brown sugar	brittle-y when held between
1 c. white Karo	teeth after being cooled in
1 c. water	cold water. (Drop small amounts in water.)

Then
add 2 tbsp. butter, pinch salt, 1 tsp. maple flavor,
½ tsp. vanilla. Pour over about one gallon of
popped corn, and stir until coated. Store in a
sealed container. Leave by the popped grain, or
make into balls.

Bootlegger Matty Harris was ruined financially by the Crash, which wiped out his $42,000 and thus his capital for buying booze. In weeks he was reduced to an apartment that rented for $3 a month and had one light; the bulb in it was a small one, but when he asked the landlady to change it she refused, saying that was all he got. He flirted with suicide but was talked out of it.

Nobody would buy the big car from him. One day a date stood up telegrapher Gloria Heller, and she started walking downtown towards her cousin's restaurant for a free meal. It started pouring, and then she was wet as well as angry. A man with a big car came along and offered her a ride; she had never accepted rides from strangers, but made an exception; she and Matty were married within the year.

George Leslie Harrison, governor of the Federal Reserve Bank of New York, had a long career of public service, including a stint with the Manhattan Project and the Atomic Energy Commission. He later married wealthy Altrude Gordon Grayson, widow of the Navy physician Gary Grayson who had befriended and treated President Woodrow Wilson.

Arch Hettman, now in his nineties, recalls that in California after the Crash companies would not hire men over forty years of age: the reason usually given was that when a man reached that age he would be unable to meet the requirements of the insurance and pension plans before mandatory retirement would force him from the company. Therefore, companies hired only younger men. In some instances, as Ed Zellar reports, younger men like himself were given great promotions and responsibilities regularly right after the Crash in order that the companies could give older, better-paid workers, who were costing more to keep, pink slips.

Oliver Wendell Holmes outlasted Chief Justice Taft: on Holmes's 89th birthday, the former President stepped down, to be later replaced by Charles Evans Hughes. Clerk Alger Hiss, who went on to more celebrated doings, treasures to this day the Queen Anne mirror bequeathed to him by Holmes at his death.

President Herbert Hoover was defeated in a try for reelection in 1932 by Franklin Delano Roosevelt. WPA and other federal agencies in the thirties completed much of the work on the river-and-waterways system Hoover had envisioned on the eve of the Crash.

Wall Street brokerage house clerk Frank Howell, who worked under the frosty, aristocratic female margin-department head, thrived in the immense amount of work that came with the stock market Crash:

> I took to eating an extra meal at the end of each night's work, then walked it off going to my apartment further uptown. There was little time for the ordinary frolics of a 20-year-old. . . . I found a dollar stock that was being offered at 25¢ a share, with no takers. So I put in a bid at 6¢ a share, and got thousands of shares which I immediately offered at 18¢ each. Soon people began buying those bargains, and from the middle of November until the middle of January of 1930, anybody who wanted to sell Kerr Lake Mines sold it to me, and anybody who wanted to buy it had to buy it from me, at 200% profit. Then it went back to being a dollar stock again.
>
> At Christmas 1929 there was a juicy bonus for all concerned. What the firm gave its margin department head I do not know, but I have since realized that she earned every penny of it, and ten times more. . . . The office boy, whose Radio frolics had cost the firm three thousand dollars in the Crash, expected to be fired. But he was kept on to pay that loss back out of his salary, then $20 per week.
>
> I did what any normal 20-year-old would do. I took my extra eight pounds and my more-or-less ill-gotten wealth, and went to Paris. When I came back minus both, men were selling apples on the streets of New York.

Leon Khalaf, who ran a battery store in New Jersey, did all right for a while, but he watched his customers suffer. Two committed suicide. Lumber dealers and real-estate people were wiped out almost overnight, as all building stopped at once. A man with a chain of theaters lost very heavily. Chevy dealer. Restaurant owner—who was going to eat out, when there was no money? Leon was all right for several years because people would not give up their radios. Many times friends would come to his place, and he could see they were broke and wouldn't admit it. "How about lunch?" he'd say. "Not hungry," they'd reply. He'd tell them to come along for a cup of coffee; then, when they were in the diner, Leon would whisper to the waitress to "make it two." The friends would eat everything on the plate. Later, the plug-in, all-electric radios finally closed Leon's shop.

Baltimore tailor Max Klitenic had an entrepreneur's problem.

With fewer customers after the Crash, he had less money, and with less money he couldn't buy cloth and other supplies, and without these he couldn't make suits—so the whole business went steadily down the drain until it was gone. He hadn't invested in his cousin's schemes and so hadn't lost money, but he was a casualty of the Crash nonetheless. Unable to pay rent, one day he was evicted from the shop, had a violent argument with his wife, and left home. Lillian, her five brothers, and their mother begged and borrowed and wondered about him. After a while a letter came: Max had found a job in another city, sent money, wanted to come back as soon as he could but didn't know when that would be. During that winter of near-starvation a miracle happened: a farmer stopped by the house, selling eggs, and Mrs. Klitenic persuaded him to let her sell them in exchange for keeping two dozen a week for the family. A close relationship developed between the farmer's family and that of the immigrant tailor's and carried them through the terrible years. Being a family man, Max returned. Seeing a competing tailor still in business, he sent one of the kids to find out why. The answer: renting tuxedoes. No matter how down and out people were, if they needed to go formal to an affair, they managed. He bought one suit secondhand, and, being a whiz of a tailor, somehow made it fit every man who needed to wear it. In time he bought another, and the family was on its way to recovery. Max bartered tailoring for violin lessons for the boys. Everybody helped out, even young Lillian, working in a Five and Ten. Today the family boasts musicians, doctors, a federal judge, a writer (Lillian), and a chain of formal-wear stores.

Ruth L. was a pre-med major in college. Prior to the Crash her life was well ordered and secure. The descent was cushioned for her and others in school in that the big dances in New York hotels and other large affairs, having already been arranged, were held as scheduled. But medical school was out of the question: too expensive. Ruth took a job teaching home economics with the electric company. "I guess I was really one of the lucky casualties of the Crash," she writes. "If nothing else it taught many of us to reconcile ourselves to conditions we would never choose, and make the best of things." After a lifetime of teaching, some recognition and satisfaction, Ruth still feels much of her potential was wasted. Her life dream never materialized.

Thomas W. Lamont of J. P. Morgan held the bankers' group together through February of 1930, when he issued a public statement that the group had liquidated its holdings at no profit. In the Pecora hearings of the thirties, he was grilled unmercifully but stated the Morgan position with dignity and eloquence. In later years he resumed the diplomatic work he had carried out before the stock market boom and crash. Morgan partners lost heavily in the early years of the Depression, and by the end of it their dominance of the New York financial industry was gone.

In Melrose, Massachusetts, Ernest and Marjorie Leger made do. The construction industry shut down tighter than a drum, but Ernest managed to find some small jobs. Marjorie went out with the baby in the carriage and sold maid's uniforms and novelties to her richer friends. It wasn't door-to-door—people called ahead—and she didn't feel it was exactly charity. Ernest got one job working on the construction of a local high school, objected to the fact that he had to pay a kickback to the contractor on it, and got fired. He took other jobs, anything he could find. "I learned to be kinder to those in need," Mrs. Leger writes, "and if it had not been I had an industrious fine man, life might have been worse." All over the Boston area, women were looking for lost husbands, sons, brothers, who couldn't take unemployment or failure, and who had disappeared. An estimated half-million men and boys were riding the rails.

Sinclair Lewis received the Nobel Prize for literature for 1930. He never completed his novel about the textile mill troubles.

Life insurance companies, always among the most conservative elements in our society, were for the most part out of the stock market when it crashed or had stock holdings of not more than 5 percent of their total investments. During the lean years, many insurance companies took over title to farms, houses, and much property; in many cases, the companies allowed mortgagees to remain in possession and eventually to buy back the properties; in just as many, the companies sold the properties for what they might bring. Statistics show a large number of people borrowed on their insurance, but that contrary to popular opinion few policies were allowed to lapse: people felt that if they paid one bill it would be that insurance bill, to allow their families something if they died. Life insurance companies emerged from the Depression in an even stronger position in American business than they enjoyed before the Crash.

Jesse L. Livermore made a few millions in the Crash period, but, in the following years, could not believe the market would go as low as it did and lost all that he had won—a bear fleeced by those more bearish than he. His estate was auctioned off at a fraction of what it cost; his wife became an alcoholic, and he kept turning to younger and younger women. The irrevocable trust he had set up after World War I saved him from having no income, but he was never again a big roller. He became increasingly superstitious, placing his stock market orders on whether or not a cat had a litter of kittens. One night in 1940 he had his picture taken at the Stork Club, a strange, bitterly eloquent photograph; next day he blew his brains out in the men's room of a New York hotel.

Vic McClain, the maintenance man in Pittsburgh, who could not prevent a speculator's suicide, felt the Crash within his own family as well. His father had been working for the Pennsy for twenty-four years and through penny-pinching had amassed the grand sum of $700 which he kept in the Railroad Brotherhood Bank. This bank, along with hundreds of others, closed in 1933 and never reopened. Its assets were bought by the Mellon Bank of Pittsburgh, which picked up many other such bargains—and paid off depositors at 10 cents on the dollar. Vic's father had $70 to show for a lifetime of saving. "The poor and under-privileged then, were exploited to the fullest extent," he writes. "Nothing affects the destiny of human lives as does the economic upheaval of the environment in which those lives are lived."

Mandeville, Brooks, and Chaffee were in trouble on October 24, but not yet totally insolvent. It was discovered that Dutee W. Flint's Ford stock was pledged to a bank at the same time it was pledged to MB&C, and the trouble got worse. The airplane stock dropped out of sight. Flint went to visit his friend Henry Ford at the Wayside Inn in Concord, and it was not a pleasant meeting. Ford would not help a man who had pledged Ford stock when he had promised not to. MB&C closed its doors forever on November 18, 1929, tying up several million dollars' worth of assets. It was the first firm to fold in the wake of the Crash, and it was a closing regarded by the Exchange's official report as "insignificant." Many people disagreed. Years of entanglement followed the closing. Receivers got huge fees which ate up most of the receivables; then came banks with their loans; finally the customers whose money had been used. The average recovery was thirty cents on the dollar. Those who had been unfortunate enough to sell their stocks during the hectic days of the Crash, and who did not collect right away what meager cash was due them, saw very little of it ever again. Many questionable practices were used; after the final report was made to the Federal Court, all the records were burned. The partners disappeared, some to surface in later years in other schemes. Flint, washed up, became a yacht salesman in New York. His magnificent mansion in Rhode Island is now a Masonic temple.

Bernie Marcus and Saul Singer's Bank of U.S., in dire trouble on October 24, 1929, got into worse straits. The stock kept going down; the examiners kept closing in. It looked like real-estate investments such as the Beresford and San Remo apartments, then under construction, would never get rented because there were fewer rich people around. Nevertheless, the boys declared a dividend of $1.5 million in December, instead of reducing debts, in order to keep up the market price of the stock. In 1930, in order to gain back what they had lost, they gambled even more of their stockholders' and depositors' money. In October of 1930 a meeting took place at Governor Roosevelt's house in New York City. Lieutenant governor Lehman chaired it, and attending were Charlie Mitchell, Seward Prosser, Davidson of Central Hanover, and Leffingwell of Morgan's. The object was to save Bank of U.S. by merger of Hanover, Public National, and International Trust with it. State Banking Superintendent Broderick got down on his knees and begged those there—who were later accompanied by Thomas W. Lamont and Albert Wiggin—to save the bank, because it had the largest number of depositors in the city, and a great many of them were poor. They refused. Bank of

U.S. closed on December 11, 1930. But that was not the end. Depositors who had been stockholders got letters telling them they *owed* money up to the amount of stock they owned. Broderick went to jail. Marcus went to jail. And a half-million people in New York waited for years to get back their life savings.

Broker Mike Meehan was upset over the suicide of his friend Riordan, and overworked by the frantic weeks of work during and after the Crash. In later years he was committed to a posh mental institution.

Secretary of the Treasury Andrew W. Mellon said baldly to Herbert Hoover that he should order the liquidation of labor, farms, inventories, stocks—everything. This the President could not, would not do. Mellon was soon eased out of his Cabinet post in time to take the full brunt of recriminations for the plummeting economy. As with most extremely wealthy people in the country, he came out of the Depression wealthier than ever.

Charlie Mitchell's frantic manipulations were for naught. His personal fortune melted away in the failure of National City Bank stock. Hopelessly in debt to Morgan's, he tried desperately to pay it all back, but his heyday as a wheeler-dealer was over, and it was to no avail. Some questionable transferrals of his stock to his wife, and back, eventually resulted in his conviction for income tax fraud. He paid the government every cent demanded, with interest. He was the only big fish who had to suffer such penalties.

Seward Prosser and W. C. Potter, rival bank presidents, lived very quiet lives after the Crash. Making no waves, they attracted no attention. And they died wealthy.

Auto road man Earl P. and his wife, Bea, had a difficult time together after Earl lost all their money in the market. His self-esteem never returned, and neither did his health. Bea watched and tried to help, as she continued her practice as a podiatrist, but it seemed there was nothing she could do. Earl sank into habit-forming drugs to ease the pain, then mental instability. Finally they were divorced and Bea went on to a different sort of life. That day in October so long ago, that had been his thirty-fifth birthday, had turned into a nightmare from which Earl never fully regained consciousness.

Brokerage clerk Alton Plunkett could not save his brother's NCB stock, but he did manage to stay on and work through the Crash and into the Depression years. There were many mistakes that had to be rectified. Some clients who bought at high prices never paid up as the market receded. In one stock, Curtiss-Wright, there were two shoe boxes filled with wrongly executed orders. The difference was $175,000, which the firm had to bear. Some wealthy young men would come in and ask for any stocks selling at badly depressed prices and buy them for a lark. Every once in a while Plunkett would be asked to work a "Scotch week," that is, without salary. You didn't refuse that when there were people lined up outside waiting for any job. One night, as he was walking towards the Hudson Tubes with his brother, a jumper narrowly missed them by inches.

Dr. Lynn Rumbold, who had missed investing in the market only by a hair, found medical practice after the Crash much changed. People bartered goods and services for medical care; he even got a pedigreed dog from one patient. To supplement their incomes, doctors began joining local health boards on a part-time basis. At that time, emergency rooms were virtually non-existent, and most care was done in doctors' offices or in homes. But "finally the hospitals felt the need to do something and formed Blue Cross, the insurance to pay hospital bills. Physicians followed by forming Medical Care Insurance, for payment of surgical procedure charges (now Blue Shield). . . . Few people were denied medical care in the Depression. They received medical attention regardless of their circumstances, and I believe with dignity and understanding. Medical know-how and technological advance give perhaps more knowledgeable care today. But with the understanding and humane treatment of then? I doubt it."

John J. Raskob was eased out of his job as chairman of the Democratic National Committee soon after the onset of the Depression. His major legacy there was Charlie Michelson, the vituperative-tongued writer who worked hard writing speeches for Democrats which hung the Depression around Hoover's neck. Raskob's fortunes declined in the thirties, but his faith and investment in the Empire State Building did not. His stock in that enterprise constituted the bulk of his estate. Side by side with his fellow Lower-East-Sider Al Smith, united in death as in life, Raskob's name appears on a commemorative panel at St. Vincent's Hospital in Greenwich Village. He awaits his biographer.

Franklin Delano Roosevelt's first reactions to the Crash were bifurcated. Publicly, he remonstrated against the "orgy of speculation" that had caused it. Privately, he inquired as to whether or not his own stocks had been badly hurt. In the early years of the Depression, Roosevelt watched carefully the flounderings of the Federal government's attempts to let private charities heal the wounds and learned from these what not to do. Early New York State attempts to deal with the problems of unemployment and welfare were spearheaded by Frances Perkins, and Roosevelt championed and actively pursued them in the legislature and by executive fiat. Bowing to pressure, he let Moses' Northern State take a ludicrous turn around Wheatley Hills, in return for a promise of nonopposition on the allocations in the 1930 legislative session. Commuters today go more than ten miles out of their way each round trip, because of this squabble. Winning election easily in 1930, FDR became, as predicted, the front-runner for the Democratic presidential nomination in 1932. There were two undying hatreds born of these maneuvers. The first was Robert Moses; he and FDR never forgave each other. Later, they were bitter enemies, FDR in a petty way trying to force Moses from positions of power, Moses going to the public to suggest how the Federal government was hampering the building of the Triborough Bridge—that project which began with a ceremony the morning after the Crash. The other casualty was Al Smith, who resented deeply FDR's surpassing him as the Democratic spokesman. This bitterness later turned to active, public dissent. In the terrible times between 1930 and the election of 1932, Roosevelt put together what was later known as the "brain trust," which helped shape New Deal philosophy and policy. Much was taken from Smith's innovative programs, some of which had been actively influenced by Moses. And each

Hoover failure pointed to a dead end that need not be pursued, while each Hoover success pointed to a program to be taken over, augmented, re-knighted as part of the New Deal. Winning election handily in November 1932, at the height of the Depression, FDR consistently and maddeningly refused to say what he would do when he took office, and, as later accounts document, let things get as bad as they possibly could in the "interregnum of despair." Banks closed in fear of what FDR would do, and he had a bank holiday declared to vitiate the impact of those closings. Many never reopened. The first hundred days of the New Deal saw an incredible flurry of legislation and motion to attempt to turn the country around. Eventually, it responded.

Engineer Ray Schroeder in Cleveland married his sweetheart with the same last name, but never did get to Russia. Hard times came. So did a baby. Ray had to hock his drafting instruments to buy milk for the child. He watched helplessly as his parents were evicted from their home, then separated in order to survive at different relatives' houses, and never got back together again. His own family made do, using kerosene lamps, making jokes about the fact that nothing would go bad in the electricity-less and now-defunct refrigerator because there was no food in the house anyway! It took a dozen years to pay off the debts, but he, as with hundreds of thousands of individuals, paid off every cent they owed—while banks paid off only ten cents or thirty cents on the dollar. Ray worked to get Congress to pass the Townsend plan for old-age insurance and realized a victory when Roosevelt adopted this idea for Social Security. "It was a Godsend," he writes, "to help the wrecks of 1929."

Julian Sherrod, NCB salesman, wrote a book about his experiences in order to make money to pay off the stock he had bought on credit. Unlike the higher-tier executives in the company, he was forced to the wall to try and pay off this stock. His creditors even went so far as to try to attach the earnings of the book. He declared bankruptcy, but kept his humor and wrote another book about that part of his humiliation.

The Sons of the Wild Jackass, who had earned so much disapproval from the conservative majority of the Congress in earlier boom years, came to the fore in the Depression as the leaders investigating what had happened and the proposers of legislation to remedy it.

Lincoln Steffens was reunited with his young wife just after the Crash. Reinvigorated, divorced but living in harmony, he managed to finish his *Autobiography* in short order. Published in 1931, a monument to the adventures of a restless mind, it brought him money and fame again in his last years.

Contrary to popular opinion, government figures indicate there were not many suicides during the time of the Crash and for months thereafter. New York City's figures for October 1928 to January 1929 compared to the same time period the following year (October 1929 to January 1930) show a slight *decrease* for the latter period. What did happen, however, was that stock-related suicides were played up by the papers when they could be found. Many investors and speculators who had lost heavily also committed suicide in less conspicuous ways than defenestration, in order to enable their families to collect on life insurance. Many women and children, fearful that husbands would try to take their own lives, dismantled family guns and took other precautions, and prevented not a few suicides. A conspiracy of silence surrounded many deaths: a number reported to me in letters did not appear in newspaper accounts. In one that did, there was a bitter but humorous note: A Chicago man willed his body to science, his soul to Andrew Mellon, and his sympathy to his creditors.

The Van Sweringen brothers' financial empire collapsed soon after the Crash, but few knew about it because the Morgan firm took pains to see that the collapse did not become public. They carried the brothers, giving them $100,000 salaries each, while stripping them of any control over their vast empire. One of the brothers actually married, leaving the other one very much alone. After five years, the Van Sweringens were let down gently, and everything was sold. The losses were absorbed by operating companies which passed them on to train users for the next thirty-five years.

Jimmy Walker won reelection as New York's mayor in 1929, defeating LaGuardia and Norman Thomas handily. Governor Roosevelt ignored the scandals of Walker's administration until the 1930 gubernatorial election was safely over, then cracked down. LaGuardia won the next mayoral election handily. Norman Thomas continued to run for various offices, including the presidency, until near the time of his death.

Richard Whitney was elevated to president of the Stock Exchange after E. H. H. Simmons's retirement. Several years later he was convicted of larceny and sentenced to Sing Sing, where he was a model prisoner, clerking in an office for 15 cents a day. With his eclipse, an era of veneration for a well-brought-up and dandified way of life vanished. It was a disillusionment for those who believed in the high principles and standards of a certain class of people. Today, the real power in the stock exchange rests not with the floor brokers, but with those in brokerage offices who may never set foot on the trading floor. There are no more gardenias.

Albert H. Wiggin, "the most loved banker on Wall Street," made $4 million in the weeks of the Crash by selling short. Though this was later questioned, along with his income-tax dodges, he was never convicted of a crime against anyone. He served with distinction on a team of American bankers attempting to ease Germany's burden of postwar reparations, where he argued the case for compassion with great eloquence. Control of his bank, the Chase, was soon after the Crash acquired by the Rockefeller interests, who viewed Wiggin's genteel rapacity with utmost disdain and eased him out of his job.

Ella May Wiggins's murder has never been solved. Those brought to trial a second time were acquitted. The troubles in Gastonia passed without changing anything.

Werner Willke, the ten-year-old in Indiana, hardly ever felt the silken noose of the Crash as it cut into and through his life. The bank where he had his money closed within six months. The farm of his grandfather went the way of the Dust Bowl; the railroad for which his father worked shuttered its cabooses; the small town vanished into the canyons of the nearest big cities. Odd jobs, minimum wage, furnished rooms, a family blasted to a hundred corners have been his lot all his adult life. We see him, still, at age ten, on October 24, 1929, as he stands at the edge of a chasm in time, with his new long-pants suit and oaken chest of drawers patiently purchased from chore money, his past bright and uncomplicated, his future forever compromised.

Notes

Chapter One

Impressions of Gaston County and the Gastonia troubles are from *The Lean Years*, by Irving Bernstein (Houghton Mifflin, 1960); *Millhands and Preachers*, by Liston Pope (Yale University Press, 1942); *Some Southern Cotton Mill Workers and Their Villages*, by Jennings J. Rhyne (University of North Carolina Press, 1930); *Cheap and Contented Labor*, a pamphlet by Sinclair Lewis (Women's Trade Union League, 1929); *Proletarian Journey: New England, Gastonia, Moscow*, by Fred Beal (Hillman-Curl, 1937); and Mary Heaton Vorse's article in *Harper's Monthly*, for October 1929.

The vignette of the Leger family and other people unknown to the newspapers of the day are compiled from letters written to the author, and interviews conducted by the author in 1977 –1978. In some cases similar stories have been combined. In some instances where correspondents have requested anonymity, names and locations have been changed.

Material on President Hoover comes from the *State Papers*, as edited by W. S. Myers (Doubleday, Doran, 1934); Myers and W. H. Newton's *The Hoover Administration* (Scribner's, 1936); Gene Smith's *The Shattered Dream* (Morrow, 1970); newspapers of the day; and the October 5, November 2, and November

9, 1929, issues of *The Literary Digest*. Additional material on Hoover's retinue comes from day-sheets in the collection of the Herbert Hoover Presidential Library.

The Edison material is from *The Literary Digest*'s issue of November 2, 1929, and from *Edison, the Man Who Made the Future*, by Ronald W. Clark (Putnam's, 1977). Most of the Churchill material is from Martin Gilbert's *Winston S. Churchill, The Prophet of Truth, 1922-1939* (Houghton Mifflin, 1977). Material on the West Baden Hotel has been supplied by the Northwood Institute of Indiana. The entire book is informed by a reading of Arthur M. Schlesinger, Jr.'s *The Crisis of the Old Order* (Houghton Mifflin, 1957).

1. *Middletown,* Robert S. and Helen M. Lynd (Harcourt, Brace & World, 1929).
2. "Everybody Ought to Be Rich," by John J. Raskob with Samuel Crowther, *Ladies' Home Journal,* August 1929.
3. Ibid.
4. Quoted in *The Literary Digest,* November 2, 1929.
5. Ibid.
6. Letter from Martin Egan to Thomas W. Lamont, in collection of Herbert Hoover Presidential Library.
7. President Hoover's speeches quoted in *The Literary Digest,* November 9, 1929.
8. RCA Central Records Library, programs of October 24, 1929.
9. *Herald Tribune,* October 25, 1929.
10. Alfred North Whitehead's introduction to *Business Adrift,* Wallace Donham (Harvard University, privately printed, 1931).
11. *The Living Age,* April 29, 1929.
12. *The Nation,* April 24, 1929.
13. Quoted in *The Prophet of Truth,* op. cit.
14. "The Dole," by Winston S. Churchill, *Saturday Evening Post,* March 29, 1930.

Chapter Two

Material on the Waldorf Astoria and the Empire State Building comes chiefly from Theodore James, Jr., *The Empire State Building* (Harper & Row, 1975), from various issues of *The New York Times* for 1929, and from *The New Yorker*'s issue of February 20, 1954. Prosperity vistas are compiled from Frederick Lewis Allen's *Only Yesterday* (Harper, 1931); Daniel Boorstin's *The Americans, The Democratic Experience* (Random House, 1973); Paul Carter's *The Twenties in America* (Routledge & Kegan Paul, Ltd., 1969); Malcolm Cowley's *Exile's Return* (Morton, 1934); William E. Leuchtenberg's *The Perils of Prosperity, 1914–1932* (Chicago University Press, 1958); the *Life Magazine's History of the United States;* Stuart Chase's *Men and Machines* (Macmillan, 1929); Gilman M. Ostrander's *American Civilization in the First Machine Age* (Harper & Row, 1970), and volume XII of *A History of American Life,* by Preston W. Slosson (Macmillan, 1930).

Material on the stock market comes from these above sources, and more especially from Frederick Lewis Allen's *The Lords of Creation* (Harper, 1935); John Brooks' *Once in Golconda* (Harper & Row, 1969); *A Monetary History of the United States, 1867-1960,* by Milton J. Friedman and Anna J. Schwartz (Princeton University Press, 1963); John Kenneth Galbraith's *The Great Crash: 1929* (Houghton Mifflin, 1955), Matthew Josephson's *The Money Lords* (Weybright & Talley, 1972); Ferdinand Pecora's *Wall Street Under Oath* (Simon & Schuster, 1939); Earl Sparling's *Mystery Men of Wall Street* (Greenberg, 1930); Dana L. Thomas's *The Peacocks and the Plungers* (Putnam's, 1957); a series of articles by Edwin Lefèvre in the *Saturday Evening Post* during the spring of 1930; and Howard Florance's "What Really Happened," in the *Review of Reviews,* January 1930.

1. *Review of Reviews,* September, 1929.

2. Quoted in *The Empire State Building,* op. cit.

3. *Movie-Made America,* Robert Sklar (Random House, 1975).

4. *America Comes of Age,* Andre Siegfried (Harcourt, Brace, 1927).

5. Quoted in *The Twenties in America,* op. cit.

6. *The New York Times,* October 24, 1929.

7. Discussion follows that in *The Modern Corporation and Private Property,* Adolph A. Berle and Gardiner C. Means, (Macmillan, 1933; reprinted 1968).

8. *Mystery Men of Wall Street,* op. cit.

9. *Atlantic Monthly,* July 1929.

10. *Atlantic Monthly,* June 1929.

11. *The New York Times,* November 4, 1929.

12. *A History of American Life,* vol. XII, op. cit.

13. Advertisement in *Atlantic Monthly,* October 1929.

14. *The Autobiography of a Bankrupt,* by Julian Sherrod (Brewer & Putnam, 1932).

15. *The Great Crash: 1929,* op. cit.

16. "Benjamin Strong," by O. Ernest Moore, *The Banker's Magazine,* 1973.

17. George L. Harrison papers, Columbia University. "Conversation of March 26, 1929," memo dated March 29, 1929.

Chapter Three

1. *Atlantic Monthly,* June, 1929.

2. *Atlantic Monthly,* July, 1929.

3. *Jesse Livermore, Speculator-King,* by Paul Sarnoff (Investors Press, 1967).

4. *Mystery Men of Wall Street,* op. cit.

5. *The New York Times,* October 21, 1929.

6. Ibid.

7. Ibid.

8. *The Great Crash: 1929,* op. cit.

9. *Wall Street Under Oath,* op. cit.

10. *The Saga of American Society,* by Dixon Wecter (Scribner's, 1937).

11. Quoted in *Once in Golconda,* op. cit.

12. Quoted in *Wall Street Under Oath,* op. cit.

13. Thomas W. Lamont papers, Baker Library, Harvard University.

14. Ibid.

15. Quoted in *The Perils of Prosperity,* op. cit.

Chapter Four

Material in this chapter is from correspondence and interviews conducted by the author, 1977–1978.

Chapter Five

Discussion about the Stock Exchange at this time owes much to my conversations with members of long standing, as well as to E. H. H. Simmons's article in *North American Review,* March 1929, and Richard Whitney's speech, "The Work of the New York Stock Exchange During the Panic of 1929," which has been widely reprinted. Additional information has been based on calculations in "Who Owns The Stocks Everyone Sold?" by George Putnam, in *World's Work,* August 1930, which I have refigured for October 1929. The New York Stock Exchange's *Yearbook* for 1929–1930 is the source for all statistical data about the Exchange. Carleton A. Shively's articles about Hatry and Boston Edison in the *Atlantic Monthly*'s issues of October 23 and 30, 1929, are the basis for my discussions of these incidents.

1. *North American Review,* March 1929.
2. Described in *The Great American Stock Swindle,* by A. Newton Plummer, privately printed, 1932.
3. Advertisement in *The New York Times,* October 25, 1929.
4. *Saturday Evening Post,* October 26, 1929.
5. RCA Central Files, programs of October 24, 1929.
6. Quoted in *The Great Crash: 1929,* op. cit.
7. *A Preface to Morals,* Walter Lippmann (Macmillan, 1929).
8. Ibid.

Chapter Six

1. *Harper's Monthly,* July 1929.
2. *America As a Civilization,* Max Lerner (Simon & Schuster, 1957).

3. *A Preface to Morals,* op. cit.

4. Steffens, quoted in *The Perils of Prosperity,* op. cit.

5. Leo Lowenthal study summarized in *The Twenties in America,* op. cit.

6. Bernard Baruch, *My Own Story* (Holt, 1957).

7. *Autobiography of a Bankrupt,* op. cit.

8. "A Trip on the Magic Carpet," by Edwin Lefèvre, *The Saturday Evening Post,* February 1, 1930.

9. Ibid.

10. *New York Journal of Commerce,* March 1929.

11. Lefèvre, op. cit.

12. *Children of the Great Depression,* by Glenn H. Elder, Jr., (University of Chicago Press, 1974).

Chapter Seven

The Washington material in this chapter owes much to the sources cited above for Hoover material, and to R. S. Allen's *Washington Merry-Go-Round* and *More Washington Merry-Go-Round* (1930 and 1933); Eugene Lyons' *Herbert Hoover, A Biography* (Doubleday, 1964); Mr Hoover's *Memoirs,* volume II (Macmillan, 1952); Albert U. Romasco's *The Poverty of Abundance* (Oxford University Press, 1965); *This Was Normalcy* by Karl Schriftgreisser (Little, Brown, 1948); and Jordan A. Schwarz's *The Interregnum of Despair* (University of Illinois Press, 1970).

The workings of the Congress are, of course, from the *Congressional Record* for October 24, 1929. Much material on the tariff, Albert Bacon Fall, and such comes from the November 9 and November 16 issues of *The Literary Digest.* Discussion of the errors of Versailles follows that of Andreas Dorpalen's *Europe in the Twentieth Century* (Macmillan, 1968) and *Before the Deluge,* by Otto Friedrich (Harper & Row, 1972). The "Lamont memorandum" is from the Hoover Library; earlier versions are in the Lamont Papers at the Baker Library of Harvard Business School. The critique of Andrew Mellon is culled from contemporary newspaper accounts and from *Mellon's Millions* by Harvey O'Connor (John Day, 1933). Discussion of the Federal Reserve Board's work comes from the minutes of the Board's October 24,

1929, meetings, and from an article about the Board in *World's Work,* June 1930.

1. *Congressional Record,* October 24, 1929.
2. Ibid.
3. *The Wall Street Journal,* October 28, 1977.
4. Quoted in *The Literary Digest,* November 16, 1929.
5. Ibid.
6. Quoted in Rexford Tugwell's pamphlet (1932), *Mr. Hoover's Economic Policy.*
7. Quoted in *Herbert Hoover, A Biography,* op. cit.
8. *Outlook and Independent,* September 18, 1929.
9. Quoted in *More Washington Merry-Go-Round,* op. cit.
10. Quoted in *Herbert Hoover, A Biography,* op. cit.
11. Ibid.
12. Note in Hoover handwriting, on Hoover Library copy of Lamont letter.
13. Lamont letter, op. cit.
14. Ibid.
15. Earlier draft of Lamont letter (Lamont Papers, Harvard).
16. Lamont letter, op. cit.
17. Quoted in *Mellon's Millions,* op. cit.
18. Ibid.
19. Quoted in *Mellon's Millions,* op. cit.
20. *World's Work,* June 1930.
21. Ibid.
22. Federal Reserve Board minutes, meetings of October 24, 1929.

Chapter Eight

This chapter relies more heavily than most on newspaper accounts, notably those of *The New York Times,* the *Herald Tribune, Daily News,* and *New York Post* issues of October 25, 1929.

1. Edwin Lefèvre, op. cit.
2. Whitney speech, op. cit.

3. Quoted in *The Prophet of Truth,* op. cit.
4. Ibid.
5. Biographies of all the bankers from *The New York Times,* November 4, 1929.

Chapter Nine

This chapter has been largely constructed from newspaper accounts, and from material in the Thomas W. Lamont papers and the George Leslie Harrison papers, and utilizes Pecora's *Wall Street Under Oath,* Richard Whitney's speech, oral history interviews with George Whitney and James Paul Warburg, as well as references cited above for stock market stories.

1. *Wall Street Under Oath,* op. cit.
2. *Once in Golconda,* op. cit.
3. *New England Son,* by Marjorie Wiggin Prescott (Dodd, Mead, 1949).
4. *The Lords of Creation,* op. cit.
5. *Wall Street Under Oath,* op. cit.

Chapter Ten

Stories of food, pajamas, and movie pioneers are from the pages of *The Nation,* in various fall 1929 issues. The three-way mayoral race account comes from contemporary newspapers, and from *Beau James,* by Gene Fowler (Viking, 1949), *LaGuardia, A Fighter Against His Times 1883–1933,* by Arthur Mann (Lippincott, 1959), and *Norman Thomas, The Last Idealist,* by W. A. Swanberg (Scribner's, 1976). Bank of United States material is drawn from *Little Napoleons and Dummy Directors,* by M. R. Werner (Harper, 1933). Welfare discussion is from the pages of the social workers' magazine, *The Survey,* issues of 1929 and 1930, and from Josephine Chapin Brown's *Public Relief, 1929–1939* (1940). References for Gastonia were cited in Chapter One.

1. *The Nation,* August 7, 1929.
2. Quoted in *LaGuardia, A Fighter,* op. cit.

3. *The New York Times,* October 20, 1929.

4. *Little Napoleons and Dummy Directors,* op. cit.

5. *American Foreign Service Journal,* October 1929.

6. *Harper's Monthly,* October 1929.

7. *Cheap and Contented Labor,* op. cit.

8. Quoted in *Harper's Monthly,* October 1929.

9. Quoted in *Proletarian Journey,* op. cit.

10. "Ella May's Songs," by Margaret Larkin, *The Nation,* October 9, 1929.

11. Ibid.

12. *Millhands and Preachers,* op. cit.

13. Quoted in *Millhands and Preachers,* op. cit.

14. Ibid.

15. *The Nation,* September 25, 1929.

Chapter Eleven

Material on black Americans and their institutions and problems is drawn from a remarkable series of articles in the March 1929 issue of *Opportunity.* Much thought on prosperity comes from Stuart Chase's series of articles on that subject in issues of *The Nation,* later published as *Prosperity: Fact or Myth* in 1930. Farm problems are culled from *Agricultural Discontent in the Middle West, 1900–1939,* by Theodore Salutos and John D. Hicks (University of Wisconsin Press, 1951); *Seeds of Revolt* by Mauritz A. Hallgren (Knopf, 1933). Jack Simpson's memoir of October 24, unpublished, was supplied to me by the author.

1. *Opportunity,* March 1929.

2. Ibid.

3. Ibid.

4. Ibid.

5. Ibid.

6. *Current History,* January 1929.

7. "Laid Off at Forty," by Stuart Chase, *Harper's Monthly,* 1929.

8. Ibid.

9. Quoted in Chase, *Prosperity,* op. cit.

10. Ibid.

11. *Mind and Money,* James T. MacCurdy, 1933.

12. *Middletown,* op. cit.

13. *Statistics in these paragraphs from History of Labor in the United States,* vol. III, by Don D. Lescohier (Macmillan, 1935).

14. *The Nation,* July 10, 1929.

15. "Iowa Banking in the 1920s," by H. Mac Bohlman, pamphlet, privately printed, 1977.

16. *Agricultural Discontent in the Middle West,* op. cit.

17. Simpson memoir, op. cit.

Chapter Twelve

The discussion of the very rich is compiled from Cleveland Amory's *The Last Resorts* (Harper, 1952), Stephen Birmingham's *"Our Crowd"* (Harper & Row, 1967), Ferdinand Lundberg's *America's Sixty Families* (1936), Robert Caro's *The Power Broker* (Knopf, 1974), and various entries in *The National Cyclopedia of American Biography,* 1940 edition. Material on Carl Fisher comes from Southampton *Summer Day,* issue of July 27, 1976, and from Jane Fisher's *Fabulous Hoosier* (McBride, 1947). The art scene is reported on by Russel Lynes's *Good Old Modern* (Atheneum, 1973), and R. H. Rush, *Art as an Investment* (Prentice-Hall, 1961). Malcolm Cowley's *Exile's Return* reports on writers, and there is additional material culled from *Lincoln Steffens, A Biography* by Justin Kaplan (Simon & Schuster, 1974), *Thomas Wolfe, A Biography* by Elizabeth Nowell (Doubleday, 1960), and the *Collected Letters of Sinclair Lewis.*

Motion-picture industry material has been gathered from *Movie-Made America,* by Robert Sklar, op. cit., from Charlie Chaplin's *My Autobiography* (Simon & Schuster, 1964), from *The Marx Brothers Scrapbook,* by Groucho Marx and R. J. Anobile; special material on William Fox is found in *Upton Sinclair Presents William Fox,* privately printed, 1933, and *Outlook* for July 31, 1929, as well as in *Movie-Made America.*

1. Quoted in *The Last Resorts,* op. cit.

2. Quoted in *The Power Broker,* op. cit.

3. *The Nation,* October 23, 1929.

4. *Good Old Modern,* op. cit.

5. September 21, 1929.

6. "What Is Happening To Our Fiction?" by Robert Herrick, *The Nation,* December 4, 1929.

7. Ibid.

8. Ibid.

9. *Exile's Return,* op. cit.

10. Quoted in *Thomas Wolfe, A Biography,* op. cit.

Chapter Thirteen

This chapter has relied heavily on interviews with Stock Exchange members of long standing, and on contemporary newspaper accounts. The Mandeville, Brooks, and Chaffee saga comes from NYSE records and an interview with David Donnelly, former MB&C employee. Also see sources listed above for stock market information.

1. *Hour of Gold, Hour of Lead,* Anne Morrow Lindbergh (Harcourt, Brace, 1973)

2. Ibid.

3. *The Hero in America,* Dixon Wecter (Scribner's, 1941).

4. *Introduction to Wall Street,* John Francis Fowler, Jr. (Harper & Brothers, 1930).

5. Quoted in *Securities Regulation and the New Deal,* by Michael E. Parrish (Yale University Press, 1970).

6. Ibid.

7. Ibid.

8. Simmons article, op. cit.

Chapter Fourteen

Utility company material comes from a series of articles in the September 18, 1929, issue of *The Nation,* and from Ernest W. Gruening's *The Public Pays* (Vanguard, 1931) and P. W. Hansl's *Years of Plunder* (Smith & Haas, 1935). For Federal Reserve matters, I have used the sources cited above as well as the Federal Reserve Bank of New York's *Annual Report* for 1929.

1. *The Nation,* September 18, 1929.
2. Ibid.
3. Federal Reserve Board minutes, op. cit.
4. Letter, Governor Harrison to Governor Young of the Federal Reserve Board, November 27, 1929. Harrison Papers.

Chapter Fifteen

For material on Hoover, and on the Federal Reserve Board meeting, see sources listed above. Discussion of the Supreme Court comes from the Court's *Proceedings,* Fall 1929 session; *The Supreme Court from Taft to Warren,* by A. T. Mason (Louisiana State University Press, 1958), *The Supreme Court in Crisis,* by R. J. Steamer (University of Massachusetts Press, 1971), and R. S. Allen and Drew Pearson, *Nine Old Men* (Doubleday, 1937). Additional material on Holmes is from Catherine Drinker Bowen's *Yankee from Olympus* (Little, Brown, 1944), *Mr. Justice Holmes* by Francis Biddle (Scribner's, 1942), and *In the Court of Public Opinion* by Alger Hiss (Knopf, 1957).

1. Robinson memoranda, from Hoover Library.
2. Ibid.
3. Ibid.
4. Quoted in *The New Republic,* June 12, 1929.
5. *Washington Merry-Go-Round,* op. cit.
6. Ibid.
7. *Sons of the Wild Jackass,* Fred R. Barkley and Ray Tucker, (L. C. Page & Co., 1932).

Chapter Sixteen

1. RCA Central Files, programs of October 24, 1929.

Chapter Seventeen

Discussion of the army is from John W. Killigrew's unpublished doctoral thesis (Indiana University), "The Impact of the Great Depression on the Army, 1929–1936." Discussion of Hitler is primarily from *Before the Deluge,* op. cit.

1. Whitney "Speech" op. cit.
2. Quoted in *The Rockefellers,* Peter Collier and David Horowitz, (Holt, Rinehart & Winston, 1976).
3. Quoted in *The Hoover Administration,* op. cit.
4. Ibid.
5. Ibid.
6. Ibid.
7. *State Papers,* vol. I, June 15, 1931.

Epilogue

1. *Middletown Revisited,* S. Lynd (Harper, 1936).
2. *Children of the Great Depression,* op. cit.
3. Ibid.
4. Ibid.

Acknowledgments and Sources

Most references on the previous pages are to materials as they are held in the New York Public Library. When contemporary sources are not cited individually, they are from *The New York Times,* the *Herald Tribune,* and other daily papers. The Public Library allowed me the use of the Wertheim Room for research and provided other valuable assistance.

The library and staff of the New York Stock Exchange provided figures, information, and assistance not available elsewhere. The Herbert Hoover Presidential Library in West Branch, Iowa, was extremely helpful, as were the Federal Reserve Board in Washington and the library of the United States Army War College in Carlisle, Pennsylvania. The Baker Library of the Harvard University Business School provided me access to the Thomas W. Lamont collection. The Columbia University Library provided the George Leslie Harrison Papers; the Columbia Oral History Project was the source for interviews with George Whitney and James Paul Warburg. Other assistance was rendered by the NBC-RCA library and central files, the library of the Harvard Club of New York, the Schomburg Center of the New York Public and other New York Public branches. O. Ernest Moore furnished me an early draft of his article about Benjamin Strong; Jack Simpson generously provided an extensive memoir; the Northwood Institute and the Iowa Bankers Association have given me their privately circulated publications for use in this book.

Stock Exchange members Elmer Bloch, Robert Rooke, and Henry Watts were helpful in providing background information about the Exchange, as was former member Robert F. Shelare. Other interviews which were especially helpful were with David Donnelly, Michael K., Matty and Gloria Harris, Irving Manney, Jim Reed, Jack Ronger, and Liz Sachs. They and other correspondents came to me initially through the courtesy of the National Association of Retired Federal Employees and the American Association of Retired People; these associations' journals assisted me in my quest for personal stories of the Crash. Over five hundred people from nearly every state took the time to answer my inquiries; all the letters were helpful, though only a fraction of the stories gathered were able to fit into this book. I wish to thank, once again, all those who wrote to me.

Research assistance and spiritual guidance were provided by Gail Pellett, Nancy Peckenham, Pat Anderson, and Maria de Luca; cogent suggestions were often tendered by Bernard Weissberger, Bill Wilt, Nancy Rambusch, my son Noah Shachtman, and daily by my wife Harriet Shelare. I alone, of course, am responsible for the book's shortcomings.

TOM SHACHTMAN
NEW YORK CITY, 1978

Index